They're Playing Our Song

A MEMOIR

CAROLE BAYER SAGER

Simon & Schuster

NEW YORK   LONDON   TORONTO   SYDNEY   NEW DELHI

Simon & Schuster
1230 Avenue of the Americas
New York, NY 10020

First Simon & Schuster hardcover edition October 2016

SIMON & SCHUSTER and colophon are registered trademarks of Simon & Schuster, Inc.

For information about special discounts for bulk purchases, please contact Simon & Schuster Special Sales at 1-866-506-1949 or business@simonandschuster.com.

The Simon & Schuster Speakers Bureau can bring authors to your live event. For more information or to book an event, contact the Simon & Schuster Speakers Bureau. at 1-866-248-3049 or visit our website at www.simonspeakers.com.

Interior design by Ruth Lee-Mui

Manufactured in the United States of America

1   3   5   7   9   10   8   6   4   2

Library of Congress Cataloging-in-Publication Data is available.

ISBN 978-1-5011-5326-6
ISBN 978-1-5011-5328-0 (ebook)

For Cris and Bob

This is my song
And for too long I sang to someone else's melody
It wasn't really me
Somehow I took myself for granted
In someone else's eyes
I saw reflections of the girl I was who caught me by surprise
Seeing a woman who's defined by you, I never realized
I can't love you, I can't love me
Through someone else's eyes

—"Someone Else's Eyes,"
Carole Bayer Sager, Burt
Bacharach, and Bruce
Roberts, 1991

They're Playing Our Song

One

MORE THAN ONCE IT'S crossed my mind that if my mother had been just the tiniest bit more nurturing, if she'd have looked at me a little less critically, maybe I would have felt like enough. But then I would never have had the intense need to be seen and heard, and I wouldn't have had the life I'm about to share with you.

My mother, Anita Bayer, was pretty much afraid of everything, from flying on an airplane to being raped in her apartment to the idea that my father might love me more than her. When I was two months old she was giving me a bath when I slid out of her hands like a bar of soap and slipped underwater. Instead of lifting me out, she panicked and raced *out* of the bathroom, leaving me alone and submerged.

"Help! The baby's drowning!" she screamed to her oldest friend, Sally Held, who, thank God, was visiting. She rushed in and pulled me out of the water. As Sally later told the story—and believe me, she told it often—it was she who calmed me down and laid me in my bassinet, at which point my mother put her face really, really close to mine, kissed me on my forehead, branding me with her bright red lipstick imprint, and said, "Never scare me like that again!"

•   •   •

MUSIC PLAYED ALL THE time in our Manhattan West Side apartment. My father, Eli Bayer, favored classical music and could pick out any song on our piano by ear—with one finger. My mother loved all the great divas. Her favorite, Judy Garland, blasted daily through our walls. We had records of all the top musicals, and I grew up knowing the lyrics and melodies from every show by heart.

Addie, who took care of me while my parents were at work, taught me to say my prayers every night. We would both get on our knees, clasp our hands in front of us, and, despite the fact that I was Jewish, recite the Christian child's prayer: "Now I lay me down to sleep, I pray the Lord my soul to keep. If I should die before I wake . . ."

If I should die before I wake? Who thought to put *that* idea into a kid's head? Now each night I had to worry about not waking up. The fear of death, so intuitively instilled in me in that bath, took an even stronger hold. Falling asleep was very high on my list of Things That Were Unsafe.

Oh, and my dad went to prison. Always the good guy, he helped his older brother by bribing an army officer friend to keep his nephew out of World War II. When I was two he spent six months in jail. Of course, I have no cognitive recollection of what his sudden disappearance from my life felt like, but I didn't have to remember the feeling. It remembered me. It especially remembered me at bedtime when the panic would engulf me.

People used to say I was the image of my father. When I was a baby they said, "Put a cigar in her mouth and she'll look just like Eli." All I saw was that I had his hazel eyes and we both tanned easily, unlike Mom, whose skin burned in the sun. And my dad always carried some extra weight, so that's another tendency I may have gotten from him.

Anita Nathan was five foot two and with a more than ample bosom. She happily passed to me her diminutive stature but withheld her big boobies. As an assistant dress buyer in the Garment District, she managed, with little money, to cut a fashionable figure. She loved when her more sophisticated friend Sally let her tag along to her uptown parties, where one night she met Eli Bayer, twenty-two years her senior. They began going out, and when he got her pregnant, he did "the right thing" and married her. Anita would have definitely been happier if I hadn't come along so fast, but then, without me the deal would never have been sealed. She was still a child herself who wanted my dad's complete attention, so I grew up feeling her resentment of his deep love for me. In truth, she would have preferred that I wasn't there.

AND THEN THERE WAS the real world outside of apartment 10-A, with all of *its* dangers. For one thing, there was polio. Millions of kids worried about catching it, but I was certain I already had it. I lay in bed at night imagining myself becoming paralyzed. In an attempt to allay my fears, my mother had bought me a walkie-talkie so I wouldn't feel so afraid.

I buzzed. "Mommy, are you there?"

The walkie-talkie crackled. "It depends who's calling."

I knew this was her being funny, but this was no laughing matter. "It's me. Carol. I'm scared."

"Polio again, I'm guessing?"

I heard my mother get up from her comfy bed and dutifully come into my bedroom. She took my plump leg and bent it backward and then forward. She did the same with the other one.

"See! They both bend. If you had polio, they would not bend. Now, get up and walk around." I walked once around my small room.

"If you were paralyzed you would not be able to walk. You're fine." She gave me a kiss on the cheek and left. Unfortunately, her reassurances only lasted until she was out of sight. I counted backward from a hundred, and then, still awake, I got up and hurried into their room.

"I'm still scared," I announced.

"Eli," my mother said, "tell me what's wrong with her. Why can't she just go to sleep like a normal child?" How could I tell them I didn't feel normal?

Some nights I got lucky and they let me sleep in between them. As I got a little older and it became less appropriate, I would tiptoe back into their room after Mom was asleep. I'd tap my father and he'd get out of bed, point for me to sleep on his side, and shuffle off to sleep in my room. I'd pull his blankets way over my head so if Mom woke up she'd think I was him. In the morning, he would wake me up and I'd quickly run back to my room, trying to shake off the humiliation from my bizarre nighttime ritual. I would go off to school showing no signs of the crazy drama each night held. I was one of the popular kids. I was happy by day, so none of my friends had any idea of the other Carol.

When Jonas Salk came up with the polio vaccine, I escalated seamlessly to fearing leukemia, which was not only incurable but harder to diagnose. I always had black and blue marks—what kid didn't?—but it *was* a symptom, and I thought I had lymph nodes sticking out in my neck. How many eight-year-olds knew the words *lymph nodes*? Yeah, I was a piece of work.

And then, of course, there was the bomb. Like millions of other pre–baby boomers, I spent most of my early school years worried about Russia wiping us out. This fear established itself in grade school, when air raid drills were a part of the fabric of the Fifties. On no notice, sirens would blare, and we were sent scrambling under our little wooden desks with their attached seats, the protective qualities of which I always questioned. Plus, with my extra pounds, it wasn't such an easy fit.

And the bombs didn't only have to come out of the sky. This was the era of the tabloid-dubbed "Mad Bomber," George Metesky, who for sixteen years cut holes in movie theater seats and left explosives in them, turning the normally pleasurable experience of moviegoing into, for me, yet another exercise in terror. Many a subplot was lost on me as my eyes scanned each row in search of crazies with paper bags.

MY WEIGHT WAS ONLY perfect once in my life, when I was six pounds seven ounces at the age of a minute. I was always either putting on pounds or on a diet. I loved food, but eating it—at least the foods I desired (carbs and more carbs)—had terrible consequences. While I was definitely plump, I was never obese, though if you believed my mother I was always just a doughnut away. On the other hand, my father would say, "Don't worry, Anita, she's beautiful. She'll lose the baby fat."

So shopping for clothes, as you can imagine, was a nightmare. One afternoon, walking down the street, completely out of nowhere, my mother said, "Walk behind me, fatty. You're embarrassing me." That hurt. It felt awful. It still does. I understood even then that my mother only saw me as a reflection of her own narcissism. I didn't know the word yet, but I knew how sad it made me feel. I was afraid to feel the anger so I stuffed it down with more food.

After failing to find a birthday dress to fit me at Macy's, off we went to the plus-size store. "Welcome to Lane Bryant," the slim hostess said, as she held out a silver tray of big freshly baked chocolate chip cookies. "Would you like one?" she asked. As my hand leapt to grab one, my mother just as swiftly pushed the woman and her tray away from me.

"They should be ashamed of themselves!" she said emphatically to no one in particular. "What a racket! God forbid they should lose their chubbies." We never went back there again, though we did buy one ugly pink party dress (think plus-size and that's a lot of pink coming at you) that I would wear at family occasions where my mother and her sister Lucille— whose daughter, my cousin Joan, was also a "fatty"—would commiserate, eyeing us and shaking their heads as if to say, "I can't believe this happened to both of us."

ONE NIGHT AFTER DINNER, my father began to have chest pain. Really bad pain.

"Dr. King is on the way," my mother announced, hanging up the phone. "I have to run down to the drugstore and get Daddy some medicine. You wait up here with him." Before I could suggest that maybe I should go down to the drugstore, she was out the door and I, a scared ten-year-old, was left to stay with my seriously ill father.

The pain was so great he could hardly breathe. I hoped that my interrupting his sleep every night hadn't caused him to take ill. "Please, Daddy, don't die," I prayed silently. It became a mantra. He was pretending to be calm, but I could see he was as scared as I was. I could barely breathe as I watched him turning blue. Please, Daddy, don't die. Please, Mommy, come back with the medicine. And, through it all, the most terrifying thought: *What if he dies before the doctor gets here?* But the doctor did come and an ambulance took my father away to Mount Sinai Hospital. He was having a heart attack.

I never slept in my parents' room again. And I began saying my prayers before trying to fall asleep. I would end them with "Please let my daddy live a long life," always repeating the word "long" exactly fifty times. If I lost track, I had to start again.

Thankfully, he did recover, and came home a week later. But now my fears had a solid foundation to build on.

Two

WHEN I HEARD A song I loved on the radio, it could easily get lodged inside my head. Some phrase of the chorus would repeat and repeat as if on a loop, sometimes for hours on end, displacing whatever fear had taken up residence there. I loved writing my own lyrics to pop tunes. When I was nine years old, I remember rewriting a song called "Wishing Ring." I was in love with the TV show *I Love Lucy*, and rewrote the lyric like this: "If I had a wishing ring / I'd only ask for just one thing / That Lucy—yes, Lucy—was my mom."

While away at summer camp, I began writing lyrics to our camp songs. Everyone liked them and sang them on campfire nights. It was then I knew I wanted to be a songwriter. I loved to pick out melodies on the piano like my dad did. My mom took this as a signal to sign me up for lessons. And it turned out that my piano teacher had recorded a hit song of his own, "Petticoats of Portugal." Becoming proficient at piano gave me the confidence to audition for—and get accepted to—the highly competitive High School of Music and Art.

MY DAD HAD A second heart attack when I was thirteen, and I worried about him a lot. We had our own dance. We'd walk up the hill from Sixth to Seventh Avenue on Fifty-Seventh Street, and when I'd notice him sneaking

a nitroglycerine tablet under his tongue for his chest pains, I would immediately stop and pretend to be looking in the window of whatever store we
were in front of. "Daddy, look at the new stereo Rabson's is selling. Let's go
in and hear how it sounds." This would give him enough time to catch his
breath and feel the relief from the nitro.

Along with constant drilling and horns beeping impatiently, fire engines
and ambulances made up the soundtrack of the city. Every time I was away
from home and heard a siren, I feared it was an ambulance on its way to my
father.

I WAS A SNEAK eater, as in candy bars at school and Nedick's hot dogs on
the way home, so my mother could never figure out why I wasn't losing any
weight from her broiled chicken and steamed string beans. When I was in
fifth grade, she decided I needed a medical intervention. Each week I got a
new set of colored pills. My cousin Joan got them, too. They made us thin,
until we went off the pills and got fat again.

I longed to be thin and wear fun, trendy clothes, but instead I wore things
that I imagined hid my shape. I lived one entire winter in a gray felt A-line
dress with cap sleeves, its hem falling just in the middle of my knees, which I
hated for being too wide. "That's from your father's side of the family," my
mother was quick to point out.

All through high school I wore these ugly flesh-colored girdles that were
so tight they squished my extra pounds, causing them to pop out in places they
had never dreamed of popping before. When I removed the girdle, indentation
marks showed angrily on my skin. I think the main reason I kept my virginity
till the end of high school was because I would have been humiliated for any
boy I liked to discover the complete second wardrobe I was wearing underneath my clothing. (A padded bra accompanied the aforementioned girdle.)

But, hey, maybe those guys did deserve something for the effort involved
in trying to get far enough under my armor without being wounded by the

metal stays poking out of the girdle. (One date, looking down at his red and swollen hand, asked me if I had any ice.) And when they would totally give up in exhaustion, I'd hear them unzip their fly and fumble for my hand to caress their jewels. I pretended to like how they guided my hand up and down, up and down, until they released with delight. I just wanted to go home and get undressed. That was enough release for me.

IN HIGH SCHOOL, I found my new best friend, Sherry Harway, who lived three long blocks away—especially long if, like me, you hated even as minor a form of exercise as walking. We bonded immediately over our love of pop music. And this is when my passion to write popular songs really overtook me.

After school we would come back to my apartment and rush through our homework so we could get to the piano and try to write songs like the ones we heard on the radio. Elvis Presley had long since replaced Perry Como as my true love. We were doing the twist with Chubby Checker, listening to the Drifters and Dion and the Belmonts, and wishing we could compose a song as good as the Shirelles' "Will You Love Me Tomorrow."

We tried to write all the time. Sherry and I both wrote music and lyrics. Our songs sounded the way songs might sound if fifteen-year-olds were writing them from their own experience. One of our first songs was called "Let Me Tell You 'Bout Ronny":

Well, he's got a cool car
And he wears cool clothes
Mention his name
And everybody knows
That's Ronny
Whoa, whoa, whoa, that's Ronny.
Yeah, I'm talkin' 'bout Ronny.

We were just learning how to write pop songs. I began to study every song I heard on the radio, dissecting each one to find out what was that special thing that made *it* a hit. What wasn't I doing yet? Was it in the melody? Was it in the lyrics? Or was it only when you found the perfect combination of the two? We kept writing, and we had the advantage of living in New York City, being ten blocks away from the famed Brill Building at 1619 Broadway, and having a piano teacher, Marvin Kahn, who knew a publisher in that same building.

Writing songs at sixteen years old was unusual back in the early Sixties, but Marvin was able to open the first door for us. He introduced us to the Mills Brothers, who had a music publishing company in that building. They listened to our songs and liked them. When I told my mom, she called our neighbor, who was an entertainment lawyer, and he happened to know Harold Orenstein, a music attorney who represented the legendary Broadway composer Frank Loesser (*Guys and Dolls*). Harold asked to hear a tape of my songs, and I guess he liked what I sent because I soon found myself sitting in saddle shoes and ankle socks in his wood-paneled office on Fifty-Seventh Street.

Harold had graying hair, and there was something warm and fatherly about him. He was the first person to teach me the all-important value of "a song," without which there was nothing to sing or produce or sell. "The whole music business rests on songwriters like you," he said, adding, "I'm the one who's going to protect you." There was no better sentence he could have uttered. So, at meeting's end, I had my first songwriting attorney, with whom I stayed for decades.

SHERRY AND I WOULD finish a song and rush back and forth between the two headquarters that housed the writers of all our favorite songs: the Brill Building had Burt Bacharach and Hal David, and Jerry Leiber and Mike Stoller, and 1650 Broadway had Aldon Music, with Carole King and Gerry Goffin, and Barry Mann and Cynthia Weil. Though we were met with a lot of encouragement, publishers were not ripping our songs out of our hands. Still, we persevered. My love for music was a deep and abiding one, so for me there was no other choice but to keep trying.

Finally, we got lucky. It was at United Artists Music Publishing, one block farther east on Seventh Avenue, that we signed our first contract with Murray Deutch, who agreed to pay us each twenty-five dollars a week to write exclusively for them and to own the publishing royalties to all our songs. We got to keep the writers' share. We were ecstatic. They showed our songs to producers or singers looking for material but we weren't getting them recorded. Still, this whole deal amounted to some really good money for us, since at the end of the three-year deal, we still hadn't written a hit song and I was now finishing my second year of college. I remember feeling disappointed but it only served to fan the fire within me that was determined to write hit songs.

We never wrote one in the three years we were there. These were, as it turned out, the last years before the British Invasion and the emergence of the singer-songwriters that would mark the end of the dominance of those buildings and their music.

TWO EVENTS SHAPED MY junior year at NYU: John F. Kennedy's assassination, which increased my disturbing feeling that danger lurked everywhere and, less than two months later, the arrival of the Beatles, which further solidified the place of music at the center of my life. I was in love with Paul, though John was a close second. I adored the Beatles. Each one had his own distinct sound, and their first album was, for me, perfection. After that, everything could be classified as either pre-Beatles or post-Beatles.

As much as I loved the Beatles, I did not respond in kind to the Stones. Their carnal aliveness was too threatening to ~~the~~ me who felt too self-conscious to embrace my sexuality. And much of the rock 'n' roll that followed was too hard-edged, too loud, and too angry. Blistering electric guitar solos and screaming lead vocalists assaulted me. I resented not being able to make out the lyrics buried in the deafening tracks. I needed melody, which the Beatles rarely failed to give me.

In the meantime, Sherry met a guy, fell in love, and was getting married. She wasn't going to write anymore; she was just going to "be with Kenny." I didn't get how she could just stop writing songs, but I was happy for her. Still, I had come to rely on, and to look forward to, the immediate feedback of someone sitting next to me, so I never even considered writing on my own. I immediately began a search for a new writing partner.

Three

MY MOTHER WAS A pragmatic woman. "Eli, how many people do *you* know who write hit songs? Let her at least get a degree to teach school so if it doesn't work out she has something to fall back on."

My father agreed emphatically. "Good idea!" he said. It was rare they were in agreement. I had hoped to teach the dramatic arts. When I learned this was not an option in New York high schools, I crammed as many speech courses into my senior year as possible so I could teach in the public school system.

With Sherry out of the picture and United Artists choosing not to renew my contract, I brought a tape of my songs to Emil La Viola, an A&R executive at Screen Gems Music. He liked what he heard and told me he wanted to introduce me to a young staff writer there, Toni Wine, as a possible new writing partner. A few years younger than me, she was attractive, effusive, and dressed with music business flair. Toni was already known for her background singing and was trying to write songs. We hit it off immediately, so much so that Screen Gems signed me to a new three-year contract. Still, I needed to uphold the promise I had made to my parents, so while writing songs with Toni, I got my degree and took a job teaching school.

AT THE END OF my first day at the all-girls Mabel Dean Bacon Vocational High School in Manhattan, I came home proudly clutching my new books, stood in the foyer, and said, "I'm a teacher." The smile on my parents' faces reflected not only their pride in me but also their satisfaction at my having taken their advice.

With a lesson plan in one hand and a pad and pencil in the other to write down lyric ideas as I thought of them, I began work as a teacher. Most of my students were reading at third- and fourth-grade levels and there was no point in teaching Shakespeare, so I encouraged them to bring in their favorite song lyrics. We would read them and listen to the records on a small turntable I schlepped to class with me, and that is how we would learn English.

Needless to say, I was the most popular English teacher in the school. The girls that bothered to attend loved my class. I stopped asking the absentees why they'd missed school on a particular day because I didn't know how to deal with answers like "'Cause my father beat up my mother," or even worse, "beat me up." These girls were struggling. They were not hoping to go to college. They would be happy if they could learn to be secretaries, hairstylists, or nurse's aides. It saddened me to know that at their young ages their fates were for the most part sealed, but what could I teach them that could do any good?

One day a girl brought in the Righteous Brothers' single of "You've Lost That Lovin' Feelin'," and, as I played it on my portable player, I witnessed the power of music and words to transform and connect, taking me and my entire class to a place where worries all but disappeared. At least I could do that much for the girls.

DONNIE KIRSHNER, THE SELF-NAMED "man with the golden ears," and then only around thirty, had just sold his company, the monumentally successful Aldon publishing firm, to Screen Gems, a subsidiary of Columbia Pictures. Along with buying his company, the Columbia board gave Donnie complete control of what was to be Screen Gems Publishing. Donnie convinced all of his Aldon writers, who were less than exuberant about working in a new place for new people, that a close association with a major studio would afford them great new opportunities, like writing songs for movies and television.

Donnie liked me and my songs and, though I was still teaching school, offered to pay me fifty dollars a week in exchange for the exclusive rights to 100 percent of my publishing for the next fifty-six years. In turn, I would receive my writer's income. At the time it seemed like an amazing gift. I felt like the luckiest girl in the world. Years later I'd realize how much I gave away.

Tall and a little overweight, Donnie was larger than life to me. He had under contract some of the best pop writers on the planet. Still, he was insecure. Though his instincts were serving him perfectly, he would ask whomever he crossed paths with that day: "You got a minute? Can you listen to something?"

And then he would play us something as surefire as "I'm a Believer" and ask anxiously, "Do you think it's a hit?" "How big do you think it'll be?" "Will it go to Number One?"

At Screen Gems, Toni and I were given the smallest cubicle to write our songs in. The proven hit makers occupied the bigger rooms, some even with windows. Toni immediately went to the piano, and I sat down next to her with a pad and pencil. When I liked something she was playing, I began to write words. At that time, I could have as easily gone to the piano and she could have picked up the pencil, but somehow I seemed to fall into the lyricist role. This established a pattern in collaborations to come, where the people I chose to write with were far more accomplished than I was on the keyboards, and so I gladly left the composing primarily to them.

Around this time, I changed the spelling of my name from "Carol" to "Carole." It was only a little *e*, but I thought it looked prettier, less truncated. It was the first step in what would become a lifetime of trying to enhance little Carol Bayer, who was always trying to be more than she was.

Often we wrote at my parents' apartment, only a few blocks away. It was more comfortable. The first song we wrote together was called "Ashes to Ashes."

Our second, "A Groovy Kind of Love," was recorded by the English group the Mindbenders (originally Wayne Fontana and the Mindbenders). Toni, it appears, had taken a chunk of her melody directly from Muzio Clementi's "Sonatina Opus 36, Number 5." I had no idea until one of my future collaborators told me, "Oh, I used to play that as a piano exercise." Fortunately, Clementi had passed more than a century earlier and so was unable to assert any rights.

I was in a taxicab the first time I heard our song on the radio, and I started screaming with delight. My students were beginning to hear it, too, and they were so excited for me. I would run down to the phone booth in the school lobby every Wednesday to call *Cashbox*, a music industry magazine, and find out where the song was going to chart the following week.

IN THE SUPERMARKET MY mother ran into an acquaintance and began bragging about my song, which was already a huge hit in England. The friend was Paul Simon's aunt. Together they decided he and I would be a perfect pair, so within a few days the fix-up was on.

When the evening was upon us, my mother was far more excited than I. "Eli, I have a very good feeling about this," she said, as she'd been saying for days. "He writes songs, she writes songs, it just feels right to me."

Our doorbell rang at exactly eight o'clock. I was going toward the door when my mother beat me to it. She looked out our peephole, said she didn't see anyone, and started to walk away.

The doorbell rang again. Again she looked out and saw no one, but this time she also looked down, and there was Paul. In a stage whisper that could be heard throughout the building I heard: "Forget it, Eli. Midgets! That's what they'll have. They'll have midgets." She walked away, leaving me to open the door.

"Hi, I'm Carole," I said.

"Paul," he answered. Maybe he saved his words for his songs.

Simon and Garfunkel had just exploded with their first Number One hit "Sounds of Silence."

"Ready?" he asked.

Feeling no spark between us, we quickly headed out to the street. I think the highlight of the evening was behind me, because all I remember of our "short" date was an argument about which of us first used the word *groovy* in a song. He claimed credit for "We've Got a Groovy Thing Goin'," the flip side of their hit. And I countered that "A Groovy Kind of Love" had already been number 2 on the British charts. We didn't go out again. We've seen each other in passing many times since, and neither of us ever acknowledges "the date."

MY FATHER, HAVING SUFFERED his third heart attack, was in the hospital again when "Groovy" started climbing the American charts. Lying in bed in his little puke-green shared room, he had a nurse paste up the *Cashbox* Top 100 page with a big red crayon mark circling number 80, where it had entered. He would show all the doctors and nurses when they came on their rounds. He was so proud of his baby.

"A Groovy Kind of Love" was the first song of mine that anyone recorded, and it hit Number One on the *Cashbox* chart in May 1966. My first record went to Number One! Oh my God!

As "Groovy" climbed the charts, Dad was losing weight and, because his kidneys and liver were shutting down, his now-hollow face had a green-yellow pallor. He had been in and out of the hospital so many times in the past ten years for his attacks and for numerous episodes of heart failure. I wanted to believe that, despite his deteriorating condition, he would yet again recover and come back home. He didn't.

My beloved father died of congestive heart failure several weeks before "Groovy" went to Number One. I was devastated, but there was no unfinished business between us. We both knew how much we loved each other.

My father left no money, and worse, he had borrowed against his life insurance and never told my mom.

Within what felt like seconds after my father died, my relationship with my mother changed. With Dad gone, I was no longer the daughter she competed with for his love. I became the beautiful, talented daughter she took enormous pride in, and would soon depend on to take care of her.

four

HAVING A HIT SONG *was so easy*, I thought. *You write it, it gets recorded, and goes to Number One.* As their follow-up, the Mindbenders released "Ashes to Ashes," and it went to number 55. The following week it went to 61. Huh? And then it basically disappeared, as did the Mindbenders.

MY HEART STARTED TO beat faster one day when I saw Carole King walking down the hallway at Screen Gems. She had very curly hair that fell in ringlets around her face, whereas I was always obsessively styling mine into anything but what it wanted to do naturally. Carole wore no makeup that I could see and dressed in jeans or mid-length flowered dresses. I admired how comfortable she seemed to be with who she was. I summoned up all my courage, introduced myself, and asked her if she would want to write a song with me. She was very polite and even congratulated me on "A Groovy Kind of Love," but she said she wrote only with her husband, Gerry Goffin. I knew she was telling me the truth so I didn't feel rejected.

Undaunted, I channeled my mother's chutzpah once more and asked Neil Sedaka, one of the most successful singer-songwriters of the early Sixties with great records like "Breaking Up Is Hard to Do" and "Calendar Girl," if he would consider writing a song with me. He was very sweet and answered, almost in a melody, "Oh, *yes!*"—his voice going up half an octave—"I would *love* to do that." Wow! A famous recording star just agreed to write with me!

Neil, too, came to apartment 10-A to write on our piano in the living room. He possessed a great joie de vivre and a childlike energy. His lovely wife, Leba, a few years older than Neil, also served as his manager and took care of everything he needed, down to the details of making sure he had enough money for the subway ride home.

My mother loved celebrities, so she was thrilled when Neil would come to her home and play on her piano, which she told him had once belonged to Dave Dreyer, who in 1927 wrote "Me and My Shadow" with Al Jolson. I'm not sure Neil was impressed but she went on to repeat our piano's history to every other collaborator who ever tinkled our ivories.

There was something incredibly innocent about Neil. Melodies just poured out of him with ease. Every time he'd go to the keyboards and begin to play, I would hear lyrics that fit in perfectly. I would sing them out loud, and he would get all excited and start clapping, saying, "Ooooh, I *loooove* that!!," which made me feel confident enough to spill out more words. When he'd sing back anything we were working on, it immediately sounded like a hit, just because Neil Sedaka was singing it and he was a pop idol. His voice was made for pop songs.

Demos are made for publishers to play for the artist or for the record companies who are always looking for new material. When we make these demos, to us they're Polaroids of what we feel the song should be. Our demos were so good they already sounded like hit records, but often they were not. I had to learn to separate the song from the singer, and to be sure that the song held up even if Neil wasn't singing it.

The first song we wrote together was called "Cellophane Disguise." It was about someone who, once you saw through them, was not who you thought they were.

The morning mist is clearing from my window
A shade of doubt has broke the spell you weaved so well
You had me hypnotized

But now at last I see before my eyes
Cellophane Disguise

Cellophane Disguise? I was trying to be poetic with that title, and I failed miserably. I have no idea where those words were coming from. They just sounded right to me when Neil sang them. And he was clapping his hands together. The man who'd sung "Happy Birthday, Sweet Sixteen" was jumping up and applauding again. How bad could it be?

Pleased with the ease of writing, we charged on to our second song, called "Teach Me How":

Teach me not to cry when you say good-bye
Teach me how
to let you go although I know
I'll always love you

A month later, Neil and I were at a session at Columbia Recording Studios in New York watching Steve Lawrence and Eydie Gormé—who I had only ever seen on *The Ed Sullivan Show*—stand together in the recording booth singing our songs in their beautiful rich voices. At that moment, all was right with the world. I was not overweight, Russia was not about to drop the bomb on us, and my "leukemia" was in complete remission.

DONNIE'S PROMISE TO HIS writers came true. Colpix, Columbia's TV division, had created a show and wanted Donnie to provide the music. The producers cast a group of young guys modeled after the Beatles, handpicking four young musicians and creating a TV show for them that would be accompanied by a record album of all the songs featured in the episodes. The risk was that auditioning individuals and then throwing the best four together in a band provided no guarantee that there would be charisma between them, but of course there was.

Donnie's instincts were solid. Davy Jones, Michael Nesmith, Peter Tork, and Micky Dolenz became the Monkees, and the show was an instant smash in 1966. Tommy Boyce and Bobby Hart wrote their first hit, "Last Train to Clarksville," and Neil Diamond wrote their second and even bigger one, "I'm a Believer." Every week Donnie made sure the show featured at least two songs by his writers.

The Monkees had been on the air for only a month or two when Donnie called me and Neil Sedaka into his office. "I'm going to give you a golden opportunity," he said. "I'm going to let you write a song for the Monkees. Give me a great song and I promise you they'll record it."

"Oh, wow," I said. "How fantastic."

Neil was on his feet applauding. "Yes, yes, we will write an unbelievable song!"

We were thrilled, though our excitement was tempered by our awareness that all of Donnie's writers had been offered the same chance, so now everybody was scrambling to write the best song in the shortest amount of time. Neil and I wrote quickly together. His enthusiasm was contagious. I knew our song would at least sound like a hit, because Neil would be doing the demo.

We went straight from Donnie's office into Neil's, and in less than an hour we wrote "When Love Comes Knockin' at Your Door." Neil's demo sounded like Sedaka meets the Beatles. I knew Donnie would love it, and he did.

Left to my own devices, I would always go for the sad ballad of unrequited love, but this was for the fun-loving Monkees and so I wrote:

> *When love comes knocking at your door*
> *Just open up and let it in*
> *It's gonna be a magic carpet ride*
> *So, little girl, now don't you run and hide*

Donnie put it on their second album, *More of the Monkees*, which spent eighteen weeks at Number One on the *Billboard* album chart. It was the first of three of my songs that the group recorded, all with Davy Jones singing lead vocals, which made me happy because he was the Monkee I had a crush on. I'd met them when they came to New York on a publicity tour and Davy asked me if I wanted to hang out with him. I was hardly the only girl who liked Davy. He was the Paul of the group, with that floppy-haired adorability and his wonderful Manchester accent.

I knew I wasn't "girlfriend material" for a star like Davy Jones. I knew he thought of me more as what we now call a "friend with benefits."

One day we walked hand in hand from his hotel to Screen Gems, with young girls lining the streets of Fifth Avenue five deep screaming "Da-a-a-v-e-e-e!" He was the first star I was ever involved with (not counting the Paul Simon date), and I felt the rush of being the one he was with, envied by hordes of screaming girls behind barricades.

After he returned to LA, I saw in a magazine that he was dating a really pretty actress out there. I felt a little sad, but he'd never said anything to make me expect more.

I was used to being the girl with the "pretty face," code for don't look past the neck. I hid in shapeless clothing as much as I could, all the while knowing I wasn't hiding a thing.

I CAME HOME FROM Mabel Dean Bacon one day to find a check in the mail for $34,000. Thirty-four thousand dollars! It was my share of the royalties for "A Groovy Kind of Love."

That I could do something I would have paid to do, something that felt effortless, and receive a check that size for it was unfathomable. I was teaching school five days a week for $5,100 a year. It was crazy. I completely saw the inequity. I knew how hard it was to reach and teach those girls. I saw that musical talent got rewarded in a hugely disproportionate way. As unjust as that seemed to me, I decided I had to pursue what I loved doing, and for the first time I could afford to focus full-time on my passion. With the money coming in, I was able to rent a studio apartment on Fifty-Ninth

Street, diagonally across from where I grew up. I moved out of my lifelong home, to the extent you can call relocating a block away "moving." I had never lived alone, and I quickly found that I didn't like it at bedtime, even with the love of Benjamin, my first little Yorkshire terrier. I didn't like sleeping in the apartment alone any more than I did in my bedroom as a kid.

I started seeing a psychologist, Marci Lakos, twice a week. Marci suggested that I begin going to her group therapy as well, and I did. My first evening there, I was told by someone in the group that I reminded him of a former group member, Toni Bayard, and a number of the group agreed. Toni had recently passed away. "Oh, how sad," I said. "What did she die of?"

"Multiple sclerosis," someone answered solemnly.

I don't know if it was an hour, an evening, or the next day, but there it was, the irrational leap: "Bayard? [*beat*] That sounds very close to Bayer." Immediately I was in such fear that I instantaneously found myself beginning to twitch in different parts of my body. I had found a new disease to terrorize myself with. This one had such a garbage pail collection of symptoms that it would remain with me for quite some time.

"You're not afraid of dying," Marci told me. "You're afraid of living." I knew instantly it was true, and yet it changed nothing. I just wasn't able to act on it.

I reacquainted myself with our family physician, Dr. King—yes, this was a time when middle-class people could afford a family doctor *who would even sometimes come to your house*. I told him my eye was twitching. He opened a thick doctor's manual and told me eye twitching was benign. In the ensuing years, I'd call with more frequency, reporting each new symptom and invariably being told I did not have multiple sclerosis. In time, he learned to dodge my phone calls whenever he could.

This non-disease, which was nonetheless completely real to me, led me to my long-standing relationship with sleeping pills. I knew if I could identify the nature of my true fears I might be able to confront them and be free of them, but they lay buried beneath a pile of unreal fears, which kept them hidden deep within me.

five

I HAD BEGUN SPENDING more and more time with a guy named Andrew
Sager. I'd known him socially since the early Sixties, but now we were kind
of becoming a couple. He was handsome, with brown hair, hazel eyes, tan
skin, and a great smile, and he dressed beautifully. Khaki pants or jeans with
a form-fitting white shirt, and honey-brown loafers with matching socks. He
wore clothes the way I would have liked to, with confidence and ease, and
had a tall, lean body that allowed him to feel that way.

Three years older than me, Andrew was soft-spoken with a certain class
about him. He came from a very affluent New York family whose fortune
was in real estate, but Andrew's manners made it seem like the money had
been in the family since they stubbed their toe on Plymouth Rock.

We spent a lot of time in discotheques—Andrew loved to dance, though
I wasn't all that comfortable doing more than my dumbed-down version of
whatever was in vogue. I didn't feel sexy. I just tried my best to blend in. I
looked like I was doing what everyone else was doing just enough that no
one would notice that my hips were not moving in the same sensual way. For
all my musicality, the music stayed in my head and never found my feet. I
was, at best, a barely average dancer.

On Saturday afternoons, Andrew and I would have lunch and shop. Six-
tieth Street between First and Third Avenues was a hot fashion street. The
style was to wear the tightest jeans possible, and no, Lycra did not yet exist to

make this less of a torture. I would have to lie on the floor of the store to zip them up. Andrew had a great sense of fashion, and he was helping me find my own style. I might not have felt completely comfortable in my body—or in some of those clothes—but I was learning how to look like I did.

At one point with Andrew I was weighing in at 105 pounds, my lowest adult weight ever, and looking great in tight jeans, cotton or silk man-tailored shirts tucked in with a belt and sometimes worn with little hand-knit vests. I dared to wear miniskirts and boots, even with the wide knee issue, and actually liked the way I looked.

And, with Andrew, I had finally found a replacement for sleeping at my mother's.

ONE DAY WHILE WALKING along Central Park South, I bumped into Phil Spector, who I'd known when Sherry and I were first starting to write, and told him I'd had a big hit with "A Groovy Kind of Love."

"When you've had as many hits as Goffin and King, or Mann and Weil, I'll congratulate you," he said. "One hit does not make you a songwriter."

How right he was.

A year after my Number One record, it was still easy to proudly boast that I wrote "A Groovy Kind of Love," but my pride steadily faded as more and more time passed without another hit. I was fearful that I could turn out to be one of those one-hit wonders who ten years from now would be muttering my by-then-passé single credit under my breath to whoever still asked.

Being on three of the Monkees' albums, plus a few others like the soundtrack to *To Sir, with Love*, I felt I was still in the game. I was still writing with Toni Wine and had also started working with George Fischoff, a songwriter who looked oddly old-fashioned to me and, with his bald head and high brown trousers, older than his thirty years. George had come to Screen Gems with only one dream: he wanted to write a Broadway musical. Just to remind them he was there, he wrote two pop hits during that time: Spanky and Our Gang's "Lazy Day" and Keith's "98.6."

One afternoon we were standing in the hallway when he asked me out of the blue if I'd like to write a musical with him based on the movie *Georgy Girl*.

"Sure," I answered. One word, with little to no thought, launched me on a two-year misadventure in the world of musical theater.

I loved Broadway musicals. For my birthday as a child my parents would take me to see the latest hit show. *The Pajama Game*, *Damn Yankees*, and *My Fair Lady* transported me to a magical place. When the cast would take their curtain calls, I got goose flesh all over. The excitement of a live performance thrilled me—the big emotions conveyed in song, the way each one told a story that all added up to a much bigger story—and now *I* was going to be writing one.

The film *Georgy Girl* had been a surprise hit, with its catchy title tune by the Seekers and its bittersweet love story of an awkward, overweight music teacher played by then-unknown Lynn Redgrave. I couldn't help but feel a connection to her.

But a musical is very different from a film, and making a musical from what many considered a "perfect" small film was even more challenging. In a musical you need to find the scenes where the character has a feeling so big that it deserves to be sung, or you need to replace what would be dialogue with song instead.

Attention was on us from the very beginning. At first this was fun. *Time* magazine wrote about how I raised the production money almost single-handedly by singing all the songs at the backers' auditions. My mother was walking on air—her Carole was writing a Broadway show. To celebrate, I bought her a little dog like mine, a Yorkshire terrier, and named her Georgy.

Fred Coe, whose credits included *The Miracle Worker*, *Two for the See-saw*, and *A Thousand Clowns*, was the producer, and Peter Hunt, fresh off of *1776*, was hired to direct. Tom Mankiewicz, son of Hollywood legend Joseph Mankiewicz, wrote the book. An unbeatable team! And then there was George and me. I wasn't sure if George's talent as a composer was equal to his passion to write for Broadway, and I was certainly no Alan Jay Lerner. I was young and naïve and had not learned to trust my instincts. But I didn't like who my unbeatable team cast as the lead. I had wanted them to audition a pop singer named Melanie, who later had a big hit with "Brand New Key." She was a little plump, with a sweet face. Instead they cast Dilys Watling, a British actress that no one in America had ever heard of. I don't know if anything would have made a real difference in the end, but with a star at least we might have had reasonable advance ticket sales.

When I saw a mock-up of the set, by the famed designer Jo Mielziner, my apprehension increased. "It looks so dark and unhappy," I said. "Isn't it supposed to be a children's playground?"

"Don't worry," Jo said. "Wait till you see it when it's mounted." Mounted, it looked exactly the same as the model, only now it was very big and very dark and very unlike any playground I ever played in.

On the road, everything that could go wrong did. Another writer, Peter Stone, was brought in to rewrite Tom's book, which was unrecognizable afterward. Somehow, our songs still fit, though I wish we'd had someone to help us think them through more carefully.

Andrew Sager showed up in New Haven, where we had opened for tryouts, and asked me to marry him. It seemed to come out of the blue—yes, we were going together, but I had been so focused on *Georgy* that his proposal took me by surprise. I told him I couldn't give him an answer in the middle of what was going on. "Let's wait till after the show opens."

The block-long marquee of the Winter Garden Theatre was already announcing the February 1970 arrival of this wonderful new musical whose tryouts in New Haven were promising but somehow, in Boston, got worse instead of better. So much worse that Fred Coe—who, to me, was shrinking in stature with each successive city and now seemed weak and in way over his head—told us after two weeks in Boston that he was going to close the show before bringing it into New York.

George immediately threatened to kill himself, convincingly enough that Fred, not wanting a suicide on his conscience, reluctantly agreed to bring it to Broadway. Still, he cautioned us that we'd be lucky if it ran five nights. At each evening's tryout, as Fred paced the back of the theater, there was a small figure pacing alongside him—my mother. She was at every preview, oblivious to any impending doom, and already saw herself as the proud mother of the writer of a hit show.

On opening night, my uncle Jack flew in from California to escort Mom and me to the theater. All dressed up, we walked out of our apartment and down the hallway. As we rang for the elevator, Uncle Jack looked at me wistfully and said in the Russian accent he never lost, "Oh, how I vish I vas here for your vedding. *That* vould make me so happy and proud." I had a show opening at the Winter Garden Theatre, I was the youngest lyricist ever to write a Broadway musical, but in my uncle Jack's eyes I was a failure. At twenty-five, I was already a spinster.

I remember the opening night audience applauding wildly, but then there were so many invited guests. Everything would ride on the reviews, and we went to Sardi's to wait for the late editions. It didn't matter that the *Daily News* loved it, or that the *New York Post* didn't. The only thing that mattered was Clive Barnes in the *New York Times*.

The theme song from the movie *Georgy Girl* had been a huge hit: I have no idea why we didn't use it in the show. This omission on our part allowed Barnes to end his unfavorable review with "I left the theater humming the title song. Unfortunately, it was from the movie and not the musical." Words that to this day are seared in my memory.

Fred Coe had overestimated the show's potential. It ran for three nights. And while *Georgy* was DOA, the marquee with our names prominently displayed remained up for almost a year, a big, block-long reminder of our disaster.

I thought I was totally responsible. It was as if there'd been no Fred Coe failing to notice that the set was awful, no Peter Hunt failing to realize our lead was completely miscast, and no George Fischoff, who was at least responsible for the music. All I did was write the lyrics. Still, I took it upon myself to feel that if they'd only been better the show might have been a smash.

I went into a depression, thinking I'd had neither the good sense to avoid attaching myself to this colossal failure nor the talent to know how to save it. Andrew, though disappointed himself, was being very kind to me. Three nights after it closed we were walking to P.J. Clarke's and I managed to walk straight into a glass door on East Fifty-Fourth Street. I was rushed to the hospital and stitched up in the emergency room. To this day I still wear bangs to cover the scar on my forehead, my secret mark of failure.

My mother, too, was devastated. She took *Georgy*'s failure as her own, and she winged off to Puerto Rico to recover in the sun with a piña colada in hand. When she returned home she threatened to change the name of her Yorkie. "Why should I be the only one left with this bomb Georgy? Couldn't you have named her Gypsy, or Fair Lady?"

It would be a long time, eight years in fact, before I thought about Broadway again.

Six

SEVEN DAYS AFTER THE final performance of *Georgy*, my publishers at Screen Gems called me in for a meeting.

By now, Donnie and the Monkees had come to an end. The boys, flush with success, wanted much more creative control, and when they got it, they managed to bury their show. Donnie, who had fought back, was unceremoniously let go as president of Screen Gems.

"Is there anything we can do for you, Carole?" Irwin Robinson, the new head of the company, began. "We know how bad you must be feeling. We feel terrible, too." Of course they did, I thought. After all, their parent company, Columbia Pictures, had lost close to seven hundred thousand dollars producing this flop, so I was grateful Irwin was being so kind to me.

"You know," Irwin continued, "we still think you are a wonderful talent." I sat there hopefully, waiting to hear their new plans for me. "But the guys upstairs," he went on, "well, they just don't want to have any reminders of such a big mistake, and unfortunately, Carole, you are a reminder. So . . . it pains me to say this, but we're going to have to let you go."

Wait a minute! First, they were asking how they could help me and now they were firing me. This was not going well at all.

Within a week, my show had closed, I had stitches in my forehead, and I was unceremoniously thrown out of Screen Gems. As if all this wasn't bad enough, Andrew's eagerness to get married seemed to have waned with the absence of klieg lights in my face, just as my shrinking self-esteem was making a wedding look like my only salvation. Fearing that I might have just seen my last music-related job, I put my creativity to work convincing Andrew to marry me. Finally, he said yes.

My mother booked a small room at the Regency Hotel and with about forty or so friends and family members around me, I was rescued from singledom in September 1970. My recollection of all of this is more than a little hazy because in times of great stress I tended to split off and be present in body only. I do remember asking my friend Carole Pincus if she had any smelling salts in case I fainted going down the aisle.

I was not really in love with Andrew. I wanted to be, but there was always something off. I would sometimes see a kind of vacancy behind his eyes, and I knew he was longing for a different life from the one he was living, but I didn't know what it was any more than he did.

Andrew had a lot of talent as an illustrative artist. His freehand sketching was better than much of the work coming out of Parsons School of Design, and yet he cut himself off from what could have fulfilled him. Instead of following his passion, he went to work for his uncle, Walter Reade, who owned a chain of movie theaters. But he would often sit in our living room with a pad and pencil sketching women who looked like they stepped off the pages of *Vogue*. We were pleasing our families—he by trying to be a "businessman" and me by getting married—but neither of us was happy.

After the wedding, when the full flush of desperation had faded, I took a good look at the man I'd married and realized I didn't really know who Andrew was. I wondered where he went when he left our apartment and stayed out until all hours after we had a fight. Or why he took such a curatorial interest in how I dressed. I had an inkling that he might be gay. I asked him, "Andrew, are you bisexual?" He looked me in the eye, then looked away and said, "No, of course not." Still, we certainly enjoyed sleeping together, and he had a more than healthy sex drive.

These lingering questions were less important than his escalating drug use. What had started out as a mild fondness for smoking grass, which I also enjoyed for the way it put me in a more open and creative space, had escalated to *Midnight Express* in my living room. Andrew and his friends would sit for hours with a strainer, a scale, and a brown paper bag filled with pot, measuring it and placing it in one-ounce Baggies. I was not amused. "Drug dealer" was not part of Andrew's résumé when we married.

The biggest trustbuster in my marriage came the day Andrew decided to take some mescaline and asked me if I'd like to join him.

"No, thank you," I said, having a strong feeling that hallucinogens might not be the best way for me to go.

Andrew and his brother Ricky wanted to see the movie *Patton*, which none of us had seen when it came out, despite President Richard Nixon's enthusiasm for it. We stopped on the way to get pizza and Cokes, then took a taxi to the theater. About an hour into the movie—which, not being a fan of the ravages of war, I can't say I was loving—I noticed the American flag was now waving in 3-D. The bomb blasts were deafening, the flames and explosions felt alarmingly close to my seat, and George C. Scott, in some uniform, was screaming at me. It was everything I never wanted in a movie.

With my eyes and my ears under assault, my single working brain cell wondered, *Am I having a normal experience with this film, or am I perhaps tripping?* I tapped Andrew on the shoulder. He seemed very caught up in the movie.

"Something's wrong," I whispered. "Did you give me that mescaline?"

He grinned. "I knew you'd like it once you took it."

"Like it? I feel like I'm going crazy. I have to get out of here."

I got up and walked out and Andrew followed me. I guess Ricky stayed.

Andrew said everything any person begging for forgiveness would come up with. I didn't want to be alone with him, so I told him I wanted to go to my friend's house. He insisted on coming with me.

I knew Carole Pincus from high school. She was fun to be with and loved my songwriting. I called and apprised her of the situation, and she urged me to come over. Carole was a single mom, and somehow Andrew and I found ourselves making love in her five-year-old son Craig's room, surrounded by lots of happy red-mouthed clowns all over his wallpaper. Right in the middle of what was feeling like unusually more-than-okay sex, I heard Carole calling.

"Caaa? Where are you, Caaa? Carole? Carole!" Now she was knocking on the door. "Your mother's on the phone."

News flash! Mescaline can really mess with your reality, because my mind immediately went to *My mother is here in the apartment with us. Right outside this bedroom door.* I couldn't get dressed fast enough. My mother! Oh my God. She caught me having sex. The wallpaper clowns all looked miserable now and were flying around me, and at that moment I felt like I was five years old and my mother was about to get angry at me. I felt myself beginning to cry.

"Carole! Pick up the phone!" Oh, right, she was only on the phone. I opened the door and took the phone, pissed off that Carole couldn't have saved me from this. Ever hear of "She's not here"?

My mother was a tracker. Within a few calls to whomever, she could find me. I imagined she knew everything by my voice, when in fact she knew nothing. And what *was* everything anyway? I was having sex with my husband?

I don't remember how I got off the phone but moments later I was in Carole's kitchen looking for the Ajax, Brillo, and rags. With all of them in hand, I locked myself in the bathroom, bent to my knees, and frantically cleaned the bathroom floor, compulsively scrubbing those small black and white tiles like Lady Macbeth trying to clean myself of my sins. And for the next hour I refused to come out of the bathroom. Four small walls were holding me together.

I took a Valium as soon as we got home. Andrew was still apologizing, but I wasn't feeling forgiving. My *husband* did this to me. He asked me if I wanted to trip with him, I responded with a polite sentence that prominently featured the word *no*, and then he spiked my Coke with mescaline.

I knew two things. One, I would never ever take that drug again, and two, I had to find a way out of this marriage. I didn't know how long it would take me, because it wasn't like I did Alone so well. In fact, I didn't do Alone at all. Not even in my own bedroom as a kid. All of my fears multiplied at bedtime and somehow leaving Andrew at that moment wasn't even an option. Being on my own seemed too frightening. But I did know I had made a mistake.

Seven

TOMMY VALANDO, WHO RAN Metromedia Music, believed in my talent and asked me if I wanted to sign with them. I was so relieved that anyone wanted me after *Georgy* that I happily signed a three-year contract to be a staff writer, almost immediately after being let go by Screen Gems. At Metromedia I met Frank Military, head of their publishing department, and instantly felt I was in good hands.

Frank suggested I try writing some songs with Peter Allen. I knew who he was. He'd been discovered by Judy Garland, who fixed him up with her daughter Liza Minnelli while she was working in London. They married and moved to New York. I had seen him perform on *The Tonight Show*, as one half of the Allen Brothers. They sang a song he had written and I remember thinking it was really good. It turned out they weren't actually brothers—it was just a gimmick to help break them as performers. As soon as Peter found his way to the epicenter of fabulous New York, he parted company with his fake sibling (who went on to become an airline pilot in Oregon).

Andrew and I were now living in a two-bedroom on East Sixty-Fourth Street. The first time Peter came over to write at my apartment, he glided in with a big olive-green satchel draped over his shoulder. Ignoring my piano, a Yamaha upright tucked modestly away on the right-hand wall, he modeled his bag with flair.

"A gift!" he said joyfully, feeling the soft leather of his newest accessory.

"From *Halston*! Can you believe that?" In his strong Australian accent, he recounted, "Saturday night we all went back to Halston's house after Studio 54, and we were talkin' all night with the help of a little you-know-what, and I admired his bag, and Halston said, 'Here, it's yours.' Isn't it just divine, Carole?" he said, taking what seemed like his first breath.

"It sure is. Bring me some of his signature dresses next time he's feeling so generous."

"I originally met him when I first got to New York with Liza, but we're still friends even though Liza and I are getting divorced. When we got married I forgot to tell her I was gay, so it didn't help my marriage when she walked in on me one afternoon in bed with this beautiful boy I'd happened to meet leaving Arthur the night before." He smiled wryly.

"I guess she should have called first," I said.

"Really? When it was her apartment?"

I was loving his cheekiness, his sweet but slightly wicked smile, and his limitless energy. He'd already been around the room twice while talking to me.

"Nice apartment. I'm downtown, in the Village." He spoke quickly. "Well, I'm stayin' with friends downtown, but now I'm thinking of getting my own place. Saw this fabulous little loft. All brick, wood-burning fireplace. I mean, I've been here four years, it's time, don't you think?" He was still moving. "Who's *that* a picture of?" he asked, picking up a silver frame from the piano and examining it.

"Oh, that's me and Andrew. Our wedding."

"Ohhh," he said playfully. "He's a handsome one, isn't he?" His accent made everything sound just a little more fun. "Do you share?" He looked at me, his eyes playfully flirtatious, and laughed. "You'll get used to me. I love to joke."

Cutting to the chase I said, "Should we try to write a song?"

"Darlin', that's why I'm here."

"Jennifer," the song we finished that afternoon, became a hit for Bobby Sherman. It was the first of so many songs Peter and I would go on to write.

After he left I called Frank Military to let him know how well I thought it had gone with Peter. "I had a feeling about the two of you," he said.

Peter was a complete original: sophisticated, witty, facile, and complicated at the same time. He moved dizzyingly in the fast lane, yet there was nothing he didn't catch. He had his own take on everything. Perhaps he moved so fast in order not to dwell too long on his own past, which was filled with some very dark memories, not the least being finding his father's body after he'd shot himself. He had a wisdom beyond his years, and that helped him see through façades to who people really were. Lean, muscular, and agile, he was so attractive—charming and instantly likeable.

Back at my apartment the next day, we were sitting at the piano—well, Peter was sitting at the piano, I was sitting in a chair next to him, with a yellow pad, fresh pencil, and my usual amount of fear about whether I would ever think of anything to fill that blank page looming on my lap—when Peter said, "You know what I'd really like to do?"

"No, what?"

"How about we try and write a song about all those early days, you know, all those early days at Arthur? You were there, right, when we were stayin' out all night and havin' those crazy great times—"

"Oh, yes!" I said. "I was there." We weren't close enough yet for me to feel free enough to tell him I was there but I *wasn't* there. Andrew enjoyed himself at Arthur, the Studio 54 of its time, but I never did. For me it required dancing in shoes that hurt my feet because I wanted to be taller, and one upbeat song was all I could manage before I wanted to sit down. The same part of me that made me a good collaborator was at work in my social life as well. I knew how to pretend I was like the others, to attempt to move like all the girls around me, but the truth was Arthur only reinforced what I already knew: I wasn't very good at having fun. And for being as completely musical as I was, I was not a good dancer.

Peter began to play some chords and sang the first line. "Once there was a time when this town was so high that we'd never come down." I liked it and offered back, "What about 'Rules did not apply.'"

"That's good," he said.

"We would drink fountains dry," I mumbled quietly, then louder, "How about, 'We would drink fountains dry'?"

He played it. "Love that, darlin'. I think this is gonna be a good one."

That's all it took. Now I was part of *his* song. Even though I had never really lived the life I was starting to write about, part of me was *becoming* Peter. In Woody Allen's movie *Zelig*, the character took on the identity of any strong personality around him. If he stood next to Freud, he became a psychoanalyst. If he stood next to Hitler, he became a Nazi. I seemed to have a similar ability. I mean, I kind of knew Peter's life. I would have liked to have been living it, actually. I loved how he traveled all over the world . . . At this point I began thinking more about Peter than the song we were writing. I broke our musical spell and asked him, "Where'd you say you were going next weekend?"

"Is that a lyric?" he asked, eyes twinkling mischievously Then, "Paris, darling. You know my friend Stefan."

"No, I don't believe I've met him."

"Honey, you know who he is. He owns that famous club in Paris that's all the rage now." He raised his arm dramatically with a dancer's flair as he dragged out the word *ra-a-a-a-age*. "So I'm goin'. All they had to do was ask me. Come on, let's get back to the song. I have to go see my friend who's holding five Hawaiian shirts for me . . . *vintage*." I was impressed.

Peter had his own style. A scarf around his waist instead of a belt.

He started playing again. I loved the way he played, and the way his Hawaiian shirt hung open on his willowy body. Sometimes I'd look at him relaxing on the couch and he'd look like a model. Not his face so much, it was way too unique, and he wasn't tall but he was long, and graceful, and everything about him told me he liked his body. He just moved that way.

I was not a mover. I barely moved, and when I did, I hoped no one was watching me. I was kind of a stealth mover.

Peter kept playing. I got up from my seat to join him on the piano bench. He slid over to make room for me. I pushed my fingers over his right hand

and asked him, "Don't you think the melody would be better if it went *here*?" I played a few notes. He might have been surprised, though he said, "Yeahhh, that is better." That was one of the things that would turn out to be so great about writing with Peter. We both did everything. Sometimes he'd give me a lyric, and sometimes he'd change a melody because he liked what I was hearing more.

We got to the chorus, and I suggested it start with "Nights would end at six a.m. / Sleep all day and then start dancin' again."

"Fa-a-a-abulous!" He started to sing it. Just like that, he created a melody that sounded like the words were written to *it*. I loved it when songwriting felt seamless.

It took a little while for us to finish the chorus. I had the line "We were much younger then," but it seemed like forever until Peter was able to come up with "We did the Continental American." I wasn't exactly sure what that meant, but I told him I loved it because I did love the way it sang, and my brain was starting to go on overload. And Peter, too, was getting antsy.

"You know, darlin', I keep thinkin' about those shirts, and how I'd like to just look at 'em and make sure I still love 'em."

That was another great thing about us. We had almost equally minimal attention spans. "I could come by tomorrow for an hour or so," he said, "and I bet we could finish this."

"What time? Two?"

He pulled out his green leather calendar. "'At'll work for me," he said, noting it down with an oversized pen someone or other had given him. He snatched up his satchel, threw it over his shoulder, and before leaving, gave me a hug and said, "We're very good together." I smiled. I was so glad he said that. I really loved writing with him.

Eight

I HEARD MELISSA MANCHESTER'S unmistakable voice for the first time in June of 1972. Andrew and I were mesmerized in our seats in Carnegie Hall, loving every minute of Bette Midler's first concert. I had seen her perform before in New York's gay Continental Baths and knew I was watching a star about to ignite.

Bette was one of a kind. She could tell the bawdiest jokes like Mae West, strut around the stage, her hands flapping like fins, her red hair bopping and her breasts bouncing in sequined dresses, and though she was all of five foot two, she was bigger than life. She would sing and dance to the Andrews Sisters' "Boogie Woogie Bugle Boy" with her three backup singers, the Harlettes, behind her, and then stand alone in a pin spot singing the John Prine song "Hello in There" and have you in tears. Johnny Carson had her on *The Tonight Show* a few times, and after those successes, she had rented out Carnegie Hall in a risky move that paid off in spades. She was a brilliant performer, and after that first night at Carnegie Hall everyone knew it.

Bette's conductor at the time was Barry Manilow. He was just beginning to have his own following, so before intermission, Bette gave Barry his own fifteen-minute segment to do a few of his songs. That was the first time I heard "I Am Your Child," which I still think is the best song he ever wrote.

Each Harlette sang alone with Barry, and when I heard the earthiness and honesty that poured out of Melissa—the Harlette in the middle—I fell in love with her voice. It had a great timbre to it, rich and full but not over-the-top sappy. It had a "pop" sound infused with soulfulness, and I wrote her name down when Barry introduced the girls.

I thought she would be perfect to sing on a demo I wanted recorded, so after the concert I called Barry for her number. He said she was out of town for two weeks but one of the other Harlettes would gladly do the demo. I said I'd wait until Melissa got back.

"HEY," I SAID TO the girl who looked nothing like she had on stage. Her hair was wild and curly, and I thought she must like it that way. A little over-weight, sort of shapeless, but she had a pretty face that she wore no makeup to enhance. "Hi, I'm Carole."

We were at the Dick Charles Recording Studios on Fifty-Fourth and Broadway. I had a studio band—some of the best session players in New York—and I was excited to see what we'd come up with for this song I'd written with Peter.

"Yeah, hi. I'm Melissa. Nice to meet you."

"I waited two weeks for you to come back from wherever you were so that you could do this demo for me," I said. "I totally fell in love with your voice when I saw you with Bette."

"Oh, thank you," she said, sincerely.

"You know, I ran into Barry last week on the street and I asked him if he would consider giving me piano lessons. He said, 'Carole, I've got a career here I'm trying to start. You want me to give you piano lessons?'" Melissa and I laughed together.

"Okay, let's do it," I said. I was eager to hear what she sounded like. You never know how someone's voice is going to translate on mike. Some sound great, and others that you thought would don't.

She went into the recording booth and her voice sounded spectacular coming through the studio's speakers. She made the song sound better than it was, and she was better than the song. I pushed the button so she could hear me in the booth. "Wow, I'm glad I waited."

Two takes and we were done. She nailed it. The band was happy they could get out early. Before doing a quick mix with the engineer, I went out to thank Melissa and to say good-bye.

"You're just so good," I said. "Really. You should record "

"Well, I would like that. I'm hoping to."

"You don't happen to write, do you?" I asked.

"I do," she said. "I'm signed to Chappell as a writer." Chappell Music was one of the best publishers in the business.

Jackpot, I thought. A songwriter who wants to and should record. If she can write melodies, this might be a very good thing.

"Well, let's try to write a song together," I said. "It could be fun."

She took out her date book and flipped through the pages. "I have a commercial to do on Tuesday, but are you free Wednesday?"

If I had something, I'd have canceled it. "Wednesday's great. Why don't you come to me?" I said. "I've got a good piano and if you want something to eat—"

"No, I'll be coming from a lunch meeting, but we can have some tea." A coffee drinker all my life, I instantly agreed.

SHE WAS RIGHT ON time. Two fifteen and she was at the door. "Hi," I said, "come on in."

"Hi-i-i-i." She looked around. "Well, this is a beautiful apartment. It's so . . . grown-up."

I laughed, wishing I had some idea what being an adult felt like. "I'm excited to try to write something," I said. I motioned for her to sit down at the piano, but instead she sat herself on the sofa. "Why don't we have that tea we talked about first?"

"Oh, sure," I said. "What kind do you like? I think I have Lipton or chamomile."

"Chamomile, please. I try and stay away from caffeine. It makes me feel exiled from myself."

I got up, hoping I knew where Andrew had put the tea bags in the kitchen cabinet. I wasn't sure if I ever drank tea in this apartment. Happily, I found them, right next to what was either loose green tea or some of Andrew's grass.

I called from the kitchen, "Do you want milk? Or sugar?"

"Do you have any agave?"

Agave? "No, I don't think I do."

"It's really the best one, especially for singers, because the nectar coats your throat and soothes the vocal cords."

"I'll get some tomorrow," I said. "Meanwhile, I do see some honey."

"Okay. Just no sugar."

I brought us each a cup of chamomile tea and sat down on the other end of the sofa so I could see her better. She looked like a flower child, pensive, with a semi-smile on her face. "Life is so mysterious," she said. "Don't you think?"

"Yeah, I guess. Of course it is."

"I mean, is it coincidence that we're here together, when a week ago we were strangers, dancing through the universe without the consciousness that we would even meet. That's what I mean by mysterious."

I noticed that she had an odd way of expressing herself. I tried to steer the conversation toward what we were both there for. "What kinds of things do you like to write about?"

"Well, love, of course," she said. "All sorts of love. Unrequited love, fated . . . The heavens, the struggle . . ."

"I can relate to that," I said with a sort of laugh. "You have no idea how hard I work on myself. I'm in therapy, learning a lot."

"So am I," she said. "Not in therapy—I don't think I need therapy—but I do go inward a lot on my own, searching for each invisible dot that connects me to myself."

Very different from Peter, I thought.

"I know what you mean about finding yourself," she said. "It's harder for a woman, don't you think?"

"Yes, I do. But I've never felt it on a personal level in music."

"I get a lot of answers through meditating. And a lot of visuals for songs. Close your eyes," she said. "Can't you feel the sadness and the loneliness, the subtleties of silence as a source of our wholeness?"

I now had no idea what she was talking about. "I'm not sure I'm following you," I said.

"You know, in silence we can feel the disappointment in our own hearts. It's always within the darkness that we can taste the loneliness. And then we emerge, acknowledging ourselves as women. I love when I feel the empowerment of becoming whole."

"Maybe we could write a song about that," I said. "You know, finding ourselves as women."

"Good idea," she agreed, then smiled. "This tea is just lovely."

I wondered if I should have put a little Dexedrine in it to get her moving. I was very goal oriented, while Melissa was now sinking deeper into the sofa, wallowing in getting to know each other. "Let's talk about marriage," she said. "Are you married? I am."

"Yes, I got married about a year ago. But I've known him for a long time. Do you think we should go to the piano now?"

Ignoring my suggestion, Melissa went on about her marriage and the challenges of being married to someone who was managing her. I imagined a giant crane swooping in and lifting her from the sofa and depositing her in her maroon skirt onto the piano bench where I wanted her. I walked over there by myself and sat down.

"Oh, I'm sorry," she said. "I just got so comfortable here talking with you. You're so easy to talk to. It's good." She came over and sat down beside me. She started to play chord progressions, and some little figures with her right hand, and then some more chords. She hummed a little, and I liked what I was hearing. She played something else.

"What did you just play before that? I liked that. Go back. Play that

again." Play that again! How many times in my life have I uttered that
phrase? She played it again. "That's great! I hear words! Maybe like, 'I wake
up and see / the light of the day shining on me.'"

She sang it. Finally, there it was: that voice. That voice I fell in love with
and waited for. That voice that made all of this foreplay worthwhile. I was in
heaven. I was floating right next to her. We finished the first verse together.

> *I wake up and see*
> *The light of the day*
> *Shining on me,*
> *Make my own time; it's mine to spend*
> *Think to myself, my own best friend,*
> *It's not so bad all alone,*
> *Coming home to myself again*

I was immediately in love with what we called "Home to Myself." I certainly
didn't feel the words I wrote at the time, but I hoped I was writing this lyric
to my future self who would actually feel this way.

I was learning something here. In order to be a good lyricist with certain personalities—particularly with singer-songwriters—I would have to
sublimate whoever I was. This was the easy part, since I was never certain
anyway. I often felt almost chameleonlike in my ability to fit myself into
Melissa's life, or anyone else's I was writing with—to morph into what they
needed me to be. Maybe not the healthiest quality for day-to-day living, but
in my collaborations, my adaptability turned out to be a real asset. I realized
I could bond with anyone, which allowed them to feel co-ownership of my
lyrics. You had to do that with someone like Melissa, who wanted to be Joni
Mitchell or Laura Nyro.

Home to Myself became the title of Melissa's first album. It meant a lot
to both of us. We had cowritten seven out of the ten songs together (that's
a whole lot of tea and agave). I was so invested in its success that it honestly felt like it was *our* album. We were thrilled when Larry Uttal decided to

release it on his label, Bell Records (soon to become Arista Records, helmed by Clive Davis). Though there was no hit off of that album, as for many singer-songwriters of the time who did not crack the Top 40, there was FM radio. And a music press that listeners really took seriously. The right review so mattered in those days in a way it would not today. Plus, record companies let artists have a few albums to "grow on."

Home to Myself established Melissa as a new artist to be very aware of. It was well reviewed and set her up for the records that would make her a star.

Nine

ONE NIGHT ANDREW TOLD me he wanted me to write under the name Carole Sager.

"I can't do that, Andrew. I'm already sort of known in the music business. It would be like starting over."

"Well, then add my name. Be Carole Bayer Sager. It's the least you can do. You wanted my name in marriage. Why wouldn't you want to use it when you write?" I was already having second thoughts about the viability of this marriage, but he was so adamant and I was so passive that I agreed. I find it just a little north of ironic that from the time we divorced in 1977 until today I have dragged around this "Sager" thing, which has had absolutely nothing to do with me for the past forty years and little enough back then. All it's done is make me, particularly after my subsequent marriages, "The Girl with Too Many Names." As Neil Simon pointed out while presenting me with an award one evening, "Carole Bayer Sager Bacharach Daly could have been one of the great law firms." How could I have known that by the addition of that one little *e* to the end of Carol, I was unleashing what would eventually become a torrent of names that would become the brunt of many a jest over the years?

Songwriting was the only truly right thing in my life. It was when I was my happiest. I loved my big new dual cassette player with slots for two tapes. I loved the sound of Melissa's piano—it made me hear lyrics I would never have heard. I loved hearing melodies begin to form and the raw power of Melissa's voice. I felt so good when I wrote, because all my fears were put on pause, the self-recriminations stopped, and the only sounds in my ear were music.

Music saved my life and gave me life. It was where I allowed myself to feel fully alive, where it was safe to feel passion. As long as I stayed in that lane, I was protected from the frightening stories I would otherwise tell myself. And some very strong part of me whispered at every step of my musical career, *Don't fuck this up! This is where you live.*

THE FOLLOWING YEAR, MELISSA and I wrote "Midnight Blue." My marriage was still in trouble, and I hoped Andrew would listen to it and make an effort to help us get whatever it was we had back on track. I guess, like my dummy in a ventriloquist act I had as a kid, I was letting my lyrics do the talking for me.

> *And I think we can make it*
> *One more time*
> *If we try*
> *One more time for all the old times*
> *Midnight Blue*

Richard Perry was one of the hottest young music producers of the day, with Carly Simon's "You're So Vain" as his biggest credit, and I pretty much stalked him to get him to listen to our song. Finally, after I cornered him at an industry party, he agreed to listen to our demo.

He summoned me to his suite at the Warwick Hotel on Fifty-Fourth Street. I was a nervous wreck as I knocked.

"Uuuhh, hello," Richard said with a slight stutter left over from his childhood, when it had been a true impediment for him.

"Thank you so much for seeing me," I said, starting to pull the demo out of the huge, soft, brown suede bag I carried at the time that opened like a hippo's mouth. (I always kept a half dozen demos with me, just in case.) "I really appreciate your taking the time to listen."

Richard had a very long face, and his mouth was large even in proportion to the rest of it, with very big teeth crammed into it. But the same could sort of be said for Mick Jagger and Carly Simon, both sexy and great-looking in their own ways. He was also tall, which is something a short person always notices. He motioned to me to leave the demo in my bag.

"Uuuhh," he said in the deepest baritone, "before I listen"—he spoke very slowly and deliberately—"could you just come with me for a few moments while I resolve a problem? I just need to check out a couple of other suites."

"Haven't you been here for a while?" I said. "I know I've been calling you for a week, which I apologize for, but I just so want you to hear—"

"That's all true," he interrupted me, "but I don't feel like I'm in the right room yet. I just want to have a few more choices."

Accompanied by a junior manager, we rode the elevator up and down and up again, looking at several suites, none very different from the one he was currently in. Finally, something about one of them inspired Richard to declare, "I think this one is perfect. Could someone have my things moved up here?"

"Certainly, Mr. Perry, just give us a few minutes," the manager said. "How much longer will you be staying with us?"

"I go back to LA tomorrow," he replied, then turned to me and said, "We'll go back down and listen to your demo while they pull all this together."

Back in his soon-to-be ex-living room, I pulled out my demo once again. "Melissa Manchester, the girl I wrote the song with, is singing here," I said, "and she wants to record it. She's had two albums on Bell Records but hasn't had a hit yet. And I was hoping if you liked it maybe you'd produce it."

"Let me listen." He had almost a whole studio set up in his living room, which was a lot of stuff to move for just one more day. He took my tape but instead of putting it in his cassette player, he went into his bedroom and returned with a joint. He found the hotel matches, lit it, and took a really big toke. A quarter of the joint was missing by the time he exhaled and offered it to me. "Would you like some?"

"No, thank you," I said. I didn't know what his rejection might feel like, and I preferred not to find out stoned.

Once again, he picked up the demo and this time actually put it into his player, which was attached to two big speakers, on either end of the sofa, that he'd rented for his stay in New York. *Wow*, I thought, *it sounds better than I ever heard it at home*.

When Richard finally listened, he really listened. It finished, he said, "Uuuhh," and then started it again. I was a nervous wreck but thought the fact that he was playing it twice was encouraging. I was staring mesmerized at the little white cogs of the cassette as it played when he suddenly stopped it in the middle. Slowly and deliberately, with the slight stutter that was good-naturedly imitated throughout the industry, he said, "I . . . I . . like it," adding, "This song could be a big hit."

I was ecstatic.

"I have a young producer who works for me, Vini Poncia, and I think he could make a really good record with Melissa as the artist. I'd executive produce it."

Basically all Vini and Melissa did was make a better-produced version of our original demo, but listing Richard Perry as executive producer gave the record much more credibility. He played it himself for Clive Davis, the head of Arista Records, who released it as a single.

Clive, formerly the head of Columbia Records, was responsible for signing a breathtaking roster of talent: Laura Nyro, Bruce Springsteen, Billy Joel, Santana, Chicago, and Earth, Wind and Fire. Despite his huge success, he was asked to leave Columbia after being accused of using the company to bankroll his son's bar mitzvah.

After taking some time off to write his first autobiography, he then dissolved Bell Records and started Arista Records. Clive cleaned house of almost all of the Bell artists but decided to keep Melissa and Barry Manilow, and then went on to sign acts such as Dionne Warwick, Aretha Franklin, Eric Carmen, Air Supply, and Alicia Keys.

It was the 1975 record simply titled *Melissa* that contained our first hit together and established Melissa as a real artist. "Midnight Blue" went to number 6 on the *Billboard* Hot 100 and topped its Easy Listening chart for weeks. We were both in heaven. I heard it on the radio all the time. It had been nine years since "A Groovy Kind of Love." I had never considered quitting songwriting, but now I felt vindicated in my belief that I could write more than one hit.

There was another song on the record, much lesser known, that meant just as much to me and contained one of my favorite lyrics written with Melissa. "This Lady's Not Home Today" captured how trapped I felt by the demands of catering to Andrew's large family and the odd assortment of friends he smoked and dealt grass with.

> *Got a house on the hill*
> *And it's constantly filled*
> *With a number of passing acquaintances*
> *But I'm tired and spent*
> *From all the friendships well meant*
> *And the rent's getting high on my maintenance*

Now, *that* was a lyric I could connect with.

IN 1976 MY DEAL with Metromedia was up, and my áttorney Harold Orenstein made my first major publishing deal with Chappell Music, where Melissa was signed. This allowed me to own 50 percent of the proceeds from my own songs, with the other half reverting back to me after ten years. Finally, after eleven years in the business, I was going to start receiving publishing income. Chappell paid me an advance for the right to publish all songs I wrote under the agreement, and I was thrilled to have half ownership of my own copyrights and to know eventually I would own them completely.

Many of them could be found on Melissa's fourth album, *Better Days and Happy Endings*, which included what I believe is the best song she and I wrote together, "Come In from the Rain." We had developed a real flow in our working process. While we still had our obligatory warm-up conversations, either I'd become very used to them or Melissa simplified her language enough for me to have enjoyed them. I just accepted that this was the way we found the subjects for each of our songs. And while "Come In from the Rain" is written as though it is being sung to a close friend, I felt I could have been writing it to part of myself. Though never a huge hit, it was to become one of my most recorded songs: Liza Minnelli, Shirley Bassey, Barbara Cook, the Captain & Tennille, Rosemary Clooney, Diana Ross, and others all found something in it.

Well, hello there, good old friend of mine
You've been reaching for yourself for such a long time
There's so much to say, no need to explain
Just an open door for you to come in from the rain

Melissa was enjoying being a recording star, and I was enjoying being a key part of that success. She was booked at Carnegie Hall in December 1975 to do her first really big venue.

I remember being there, excited, proud, and happy: her own concert, her own fans, in the exact place I'd first noticed her singing. It was what we'd worked so hard for. The legendary hall was packed, she sang beautifully, and she received a number of standing ovations, all on the songs we'd written together.

Before her closing number, she introduced and thanked her band members, then went on to acknowledge all of the people who'd helped her achieve her success: her producers, her manager, her label head, her mother, her voice teacher . . . She was practically up to thanking the janitor when I realized she was not going to mention my name. I was shocked—more hurt than angry. I couldn't believe that after all the time and the songs and my having championed her to anyone who would listen, and finally connecting her with Richard Perry, she never uttered a syllable of my name.

I didn't say anything to Melissa at the time. I was never very good at confrontation.

By now we were well into the era of the singer-songwriter: Bob Dylan, James Taylor, Carole King, Phoebe Snow, Paul Simon, and so many others. I know Melissa wanted to be a part of that group, and I tried to rationalize it by thinking that was why she couldn't afford to acknowledge needing a writing partner.

Neither Melissa nor I could have written the songs we wrote together with anyone else. The two of us tapped into issues women were facing, and because of that our songs touched many women going through their own struggles. It's obviously gratifying when someone tells you, "Your songs helped me through the most difficult time of my life," and I heard that more often about the songs Melissa and I wrote than about those that came from any other of my many collaborations. Those songs are part of my really becoming a songwriter and will always remain special to me. And while I still continued to write with Melissa, that night changed the course of my career. I decided that I was never going to be so dependent on any one collaborator again.

I did eventually ask her why she hadn't included me among the cast of thousands she'd thanked that night. "I'm so sorry, Carole," she said earnestly. "I just forgot."

Ten

I STARTED WRITING WITH Peter again. I was always happy sitting next to him at a piano. He was so clever, so edgy, and he made me feel that way, too. I imagined that if we lived in the Twenties we might have been guests at the Algonquin Round Table, listening to Dorothy Parker holding court. Looking back, one of the best songs I ever wrote with him was called "You and Me (We Wanted It All)."

> *You and me we wanted it all*
> *Passion without pain*
> *Sunshine without rainy days*
> *We wanted it all ways*
> *You and me*
> *We reached for the sky*
> *The limit was high*
> *Never giving in*
> *Certain we could win that prize*
> *I should have seen it in your eyes*

Frank Military, then at Chappell Music, played the song for Frank Sinatra (they had a friendship that went far back), and he said he would hold it for his next album.

Frank Sinatra wanted to record our song! To a songwriter, Sinatra was one rung under God. He was a legend. (I can hear Peter saying, "Thank you, Carole, for pointing that out to us.") I'm sure every writer has their own list of who, in a perfect world, would record their songs. Mine had Sinatra right at the top, along with Barbra Streisand, Aretha Franklin, Stevie Wonder, Elton John, Michael Jackson, Steve Perry, Michael McDonald, Phil Collins, and Ray Charles, to name some of the greatest talents.

I remember the day—many years later—when I realized every one of the top ten names on my list had actually recorded at least one of my songs. That was a really good day.

But back to Frank. One year passed. Two years, and still no album. How do you take back a song from Frank Sinatra? It sounds like a very bad idea. We waited. And waited. Since he cowrote it, Peter felt entitled to do a version on his own record, but we continued to wait for Frank before offering it to anyone else. Finally, Frank kept his word and recorded it. The crazy thing is, as proud as I was that Frank Sinatra had recorded a song of mine, I liked Peter's version better. It felt more honest.

One day he told me he had played our song "More Than I Like You" for Liza. She liked it and wanted us to be there while she recorded it. I met Peter a few days later at the Columbia Records studio, where Liza, who was already in the booth, came out to say hi to both of us. She was so friendly to me I had to remind myself that we hadn't met before.

She spoke in her breathy broken sentences. "Petey, I'm so glad you and Carole are here. You can both help me make this a big hit." *Did Liza Minnelli have hits, like on the charts?* I wondered. Well, she did make standards, but with great songs like "New York, New York" and "Cabaret." I might point out even I knew "More Than I Like You" wasn't close to a great song.

Standing in the rain
Waiting for a train
There's got to be someplace it's going to

I really don't like trains
But I think I like them
More than I like you

At this point in the writing process, I started laughing. Funny song, yes. Hit song, no. But here we were. Liza went back into the booth to do another take. I watched and listened and was thoroughly enjoying myself. Liza was emoting in typical Liza style—big gestures, hands flying. I couldn't imagine what she could do on stage that she wasn't doing in that booth. When she finished her take, I applauded. "Great," I said. I was a fan.

"Should I do another, or was that it?"

Before I could say anything, Peter said, "I'd do another if I were you. Watch your pitch." And to me he said, "Close your eyes on this one. Performing is her genius. Don't look at her, just listen."

Obediently I kept my eyes closed like I was playing hide-and-seek. She began to sing. Uh-oh. *Oh my*, I thought. Peter had a point.

"I better get in that booth," he said. Eventually he pieced together a performance.

PETER AND I WERE writing a lot together. I knew that if the songs were good, he would record them and they would serve as excellent demos for other artists who would mine his albums for material.

Without making any particular effort to target her, we wrote Melissa's second big hit, "Don't Cry Out Loud."

Don't cry out loud
Just keep it inside
Learn how to hide your feelings
Fly high and proud
And if you should fall
Remember you almost had it all

A note about this song. It was Peter who had the title, and I, who had the ability to shift into whatever the song required, wrote the lyric around his title. For years after, when I would hear it, I would question if that was how I really felt. I mean, didn't I really believe in sharing my feelings? Letting people know how I really feel? Why else would I be writing this book? The lyric is the antithesis of a memoir, and yet I wrote it. With Peter.

I was told that Melissa was reluctant to record it. Maybe she thought as I did, or maybe it was because she didn't write it with me. I know she didn't like that Clive Davis was adamant about having her sing it. Clive was an executive who was passionate about his artists, and he thought he knew exactly how their careers should progress and what songs they should record. (His greatest pride while at Arista would come a number of years later when he discovered and signed Whitney Houston as a teenager and helped mold her stratospheric career.)

Meanwhile, I wasn't fully grasping what a performer Peter was becoming. He honed his craft at Reno Sweeney, a small Village club in the Seventies that had a cool and eclectic following. His outfits were becoming more and more outrageous: red sequined jumpsuits replaced jeans and a tee. His gestures were getting bigger—he jumped up and draped his body across the piano while he sang—and so were his venues. He could never come on stage on a camel (and later an elephant) at Reno Sweeney, but he could and did, flamboyantly, at Radio City Music Hall, where he also did high kicks with the Rockettes (he was a really wonderful dancer, very smooth), and he bantered with the audience as though they were old friends dishing the dirt.

But watching his bigger-than-life performance, I still saw him as the intimate songwriter who, with only a piano, would let us in on his deepest secrets, reminding us what a really good storyteller he was.

I lived *through* his stories, but I didn't *live* his stories. Unlike Patti Smith and Robert Mapplethorpe, we never shared the same experiences. I was the one he told his experiences to. He would regale me with his dangerous nights at Studio 54, so high on Quaaludes yet still dancing till dawn with the gorgeous guy he found that night, the guy who was gone in the bright morning sun.

I soaked in these stories, but I had none of my own to share in turn. Except for loving taking a Quaalude, not to dance on but before bedtime to fall asleep. I was probably the only person in New York City in the Seventies using this pill as prescribed by my doctor, to induce sleep.

Peter loved champagne. I could only toast him with a Tab because I was too frightened to drink alcohol knowing my bedtime sleeping pill awaited me each night. He was trying to inhale every sensual, sexual moment of the decadent Seventies, and I watched lovingly from a ringside table at the intimate club, glad to hear our songs sung by him night after night. He never failed to introduce me, and while remaining seated, I took in the applause of the packed room. And that, for me—especially if I'd taken a Valium—was as close to being part of the Swinging Seventies as I got.

One night after Reno's, Peter and I went uptown to grab a burger at P.J. Clarke's. Leaning over their famous red-checkered tablecloths, we got a chance to talk.

"Honey, I've met someone. I can't believe it!" he said. "I'm *crazy* about him. I can't wait for you to meet him. You'll love him. He's gorgeous, and he's so sweet, with such a good heart. Not at all the kind I'm used to. I think I might actually be in love."

"Oh, Peter, I'm so happy for you," I said, sounding a bit like Wendy in *Peter Pan*.

"So how's your love life going?"

"Oh, Peter," I said, sounding now so much less like Wendy. "I think we hit a wall. This is not what I want. When I'm not writing I'm bored. I can't talk to him and feel like we're having a real conversation."

"Well, I told you he was handsome. I never told you he was the brightest bulb in the box. Honey, you're smart. You need to be with people who get you."

"And he gets angry. And he hit me. Only once, and not hard, but still . . ."

"That's crossing a line," Peter said. "Honey, why are you still in this marriage?"

"'Cause unlike you, I hate to be alone. I mean, I like to be alone sometimes, but that's when I'm with somebody. And I need to be with somebody."

My close friendship with Peter was one of the mainstays that got me through some difficult years. I was spending time in therapy trying to find the strength within me to leave my marriage but I would continue treading water until I could.

MY MOTHER WAS NOT a big fan of Andrew's, I think she thought him immature, but she loved Peter. She too went downtown to watch him perform. She was of the belief that whomever she loved felt the same way about her. My mom's drinking, which could once have been described as social, had escalated into full-blown alcoholism. She spent many a day writing apology notes for her inexcusable behavior the night before, where she would hurl insults and fire cruel jokes at her diminishing number of friends.

She decided to move to Florida for the winter. She called and invited Peter and me to come over while she was packing because she had a few items she thought he might like. Peter said, "Let's go see what she has for me." On entering her apartment, Peter saw my mother in her full alcoholic state for the first time.

"Here," she said to Peter, while carrying three purses out of her bedroom. "You want any of these?" They were three big satchel-like bags. He dismissed two of them but liked the Gucci one she was offering. "Oh, thank you, Anita, this one is lovely."

"Don't try and return it," she said. "It's fake. But no one's ever guessed it." She was now flying through the apartment, singing off-key to *Judy at Carnegie Hall*, and reentered with a bunch of scarves.

"Oh, those are beautiful, Anita. Why would you want to give them away?"

"I'm not, and don't put your hands on them. They're coming with me."

She launched into an alcoholic rant about how I never had time for her and so she was getting the hell out of New York. She was completely out of control, slurring her insults as she was forcing more and more things into her already overstuffed suitcase. Months later, Peter told me he wrote in his journal that night, "The miracle is not that Carole Bayer Sager is a really good song-writer. The miracle is she can put one foot in front of the other."

It would be another year before my mother returned from Florida and found her way to an AA meeting in New York. I am proud to say that through her many illnesses that were to follow, she never picked up another drink for the rest of her life. I still have her thirty-five-year sobriety chip in my drawer.

Eleven

DURING THIS TIME I got a call from Albert Hammond, a young English-man from Gibraltar who'd had a huge hit a few years earlier with his song "It Never Rains in Southern California." He had a melody that he needed a lyric for, but the guy he usually worked with was nowhere to be found and he needed the song immediately for a record he was making. Chappell had sent him my way.

"Why don't you come over and play it for me?" I told him. "If I feel I can do something with it, I'll write it with you." Within a few hours Albert was standing at my door. He was a nice-looking, curly-haired young man who spoke with a Spanish accent, and he cut right to the chase. He took out his guitar and, with the enthusiasm of a child, began singing nonsense syllables to his untitled melody.

I had to admit it was very catchy. I had never written with anyone who played the guitar before, and I felt it brought out a whole different kind of lyric in me. There was something about a guitar that suggested "country" to my ear rather than "pop." I always associated country songs with stories, so without trying to, I immediately began to hear words that told a story rather than concentrated on feelings. It wasn't *my* story, but it felt kind of right.

I wrote the lyric so quickly that I dismissed it as unimportant. Less than two hours after arriving, Albert packed up his guitar and left with this song:

When I need you
I just close my eyes and I'm with you
And all that I so want to give you
Is only a heartbeat away

That was it. Thanks, let's do it again. Great, see you around. Done.

"When I Need You" was the title track of Albert's 1976 album, but it wasn't released as a single. Richard Perry loved the song and produced it with Leo Sayer, a new, clear-voiced artist out of England who had just had a big hit with "You Make Me Feel Like Dancing." His version of "When I Need You" went to Number One on the UK singles chart in February 1977, after three of his earlier singles had stalled at number 2. It shot to Number One on the *Billboard* Hot 100 in May 1977 and became a worldwide hit, topping the charts all over Europe and in Australia. It was my second Number One record and my biggest copyright to date, despite my dismissiveness of it when we wrote it.

Unfortunately, a piece of that melody Albert had come to me needing lyrics for was very similar to a melody written by Leonard Cohen, for his song "Famous Blue Raincoat," and he sued us. When the song was published, instead of "music by Albert Hammond, lyrics by Carole Bayer Sager," the credit attributed music and lyrics to the both of us, so we were both legally party to the claim.

I wasn't going to get into a thing with Albert. Maybe he wrote a line here or there in the lyric and maybe I sang a little phrase in the melody, so I just asked Harold to settle it and split with Albert whatever percentage he worked out with Leonard Cohen. I was too embarrassed to admit that not only had I never heard his record but I had no idea who Leonard Cohen was. I was not, as you might have surmised by now, an "underground" type.

BY 1976 PETER ALLEN was spending more and more time in LA, getting ready to record his first album for A&M Records. He asked me to come out and do some writing with him. The New York music scene had turned very punk, and a number of New York writers were migrating to Los Angeles, where there seemed to be more opportunities, and I wanted to be part of it all. The question was, how was I going to get there?

If you're a generally fearful person, being afraid of flying is pretty much a given. Whatever plane I was on was surely the one that wasn't going to make it.

This fear began, as did so many others, when I was quite young. When I was eleven, my family flew to California for my cousin Trina's wedding. Back in the Fifties, nonstop cross-country flights were rare, and the trip could take as long as ten hours, instead of today's five or six. I was seated next to my mother when the plane hit turbulence. I looked to her for reassurance, maybe even for a comforting touch. Instead I detected a distinct look of terror in her eyes as she gave me a little push away, said loudly, "Okay, everybody's on their own now," and proceeded to sink deeper into her own fear. The next moment the turbulence stopped and my mother was laughing with the stewardess (yes, that's what they were called back then) about something or other, but she'd left her terror safely with me. I would hold it close for a long time to come.

I had once driven to California with Toni Wine, and it took forever. There's a point where you just want to be there, and you're not, and here's the news flash: you won't be there tomorrow, either. Or the next day. But no, don't take a five-hour flight.

So driving was out of the question. The railroad! There's an idea. Not in the sky but faster than a car. When I told my mother I was thinking of taking the train, she said, "I'd rather die in a plane crash than with a hot piece of steel up my ass." I couldn't agree. Even if there was, God forbid, a train wreck, there *is* a chance you *could* walk, or more likely limp, away, even with that hot piece of steel. Falling 38,000 feet, not a prayer. The train it would be!

You could get from New York to California, as long as you didn't mind changing trains in Chicago with a six-hour stopover. I certainly didn't want to spend three and a half days alone. What would I do with just me? I knew my old friend Carole Pincus (now Carole Childs) was desperate to be in the music business. She did have a very good ear for what was a hit, and she was much more passionate about a possible job in pop music than remaining in her uninspiring job in New York's Garment District. I called her.

"I have to go out to California for a week," I said. "Do you want to come with me and see Richard again?" Carole was hoping to get a job with Richard Perry, who I had introduced her to in New York. We even spent a few evenings at Studio 54 together.

"Leave my job? Well, I guess I could take a little time off."

"Good. We're going to take the train."

"The train?" she said, laughing. "You're kidding."

"No, I think it'll be really relaxing. And I don't have to have any fear, and—"

"Caaa, that's a week of just travel. I can't be away that long. My boss'll kill me."

"Oh, Carole, you know you want to come to California."

"Okay, I'll go."

It was quite a ride. (I didn't tell her until we left Grand Central Station about the six hours in Chicago.) The accommodations were not deluxe: two seats by day, bunk beds by night, a toilet wedged in next to a tiny shower that drizzled on you, though not strongly enough to be sure that your hair was soap-free.

I looked forward to the starch-filled meals and sugary desserts in the dining car. I'd like to say I enjoyed the ever-changing scenery, but for the most part railroad tracks are rarely placed in the most beautiful areas of town. But Carole was fun and certainly made the trip go faster, though not fast enough, but you can't have everything.

When it came to travel, I was a mess. And yet, at the end of the ride, my songwriting was alive and well and waiting for me in California.

Twelve

NOW THAT I WAS starting to have more hits, I too wanted to join the growing list of singer-songwriter artists. One of my first meetings in LA was with Joe Smith, who was the chairman of Elektra/Asylum Records. This was my favorite record label, primarily because David Geffen had built Asylum Records by signing the most talented singer-songwriters on the West Coast. It had become a "Tiffany" label with only the finest artists on its roster. But by 1976 David had left to become a vice president of Warner Bros. Pictures, and Asylum was now part of the larger Warner/Elektra/Atlantic family.

I walked into Joe Smith's very large office and was duly impressed with the number of gold records he had, clustered as close as bathroom tiles on his walls. He was a pleasant-looking man, not tall, maybe in his late forties, and I felt very comfortable with him. After some music business chat, he asked, "What can I do for you, Carole?"

"Well," I said, "I've been writing a lot with Melissa Manchester and Peter Allen, but I feel I'd like to record my own songs as well."

I was waiting for him to ask me to make some demos for him to evaluate the way I sang, but instead he said, "Have your lawyer call me and we've got a deal. Go make a great album for us."

I was shocked and exhilarated. I couldn't believe it. He never asked to hear me sing. Just like that I was given the green light to go make a record.

It's amazing, I thought, *what a few hits can do.* Soon my excitement gave way to panic. What if he hated the way I sang? I had a funny kind of voice. It was not the voice of a real singer. I didn't have great range or power to hold long notes. My voice would never have been a vehicle to sing someone else's songs, but when I sang my own, though it was breathy and occasionally gravelly, it had a vulnerability that was in keeping with the lyrics and a soulfulness that came from somewhere within me that was true. Which is sort of a dichotomy because where was that frailty when I walked in cold to Joe's office and announced I wanted to make an album?

Once again I was willing to put myself out there. Along with my fears, there was this fierce ambition to be heard and seen and to interpret my songs, my own way.

Brooks Arthur had produced Janis Ian's "At Seventeen," a classic song about teen angst and not fitting in. I liked him very much and thought he would be the perfect producer for me.

BETTE MIDLER AND HER boyfriend-manager Aaron Russo were renting a house in Bel Air in the summer of 1976. Aaron, a future failed candidate for the Republican nomination for governor of Nevada, was at the time focused on finding the right movie for Bette to make her debut in.

My good friend and sometimes collaborator Bruce Roberts was in Los Angeles staying in their guest room. Bruce was younger than me by about ten years. We'd met in New York City and had written some songs together. Always upbeat, he was on the short side, about twenty pounds overweight, and openly gay (after Peter Allen gave him permission by example to be himself). He was warm, funny, and impossible not to like. He was also wonderfully musical, had something magical in his voice, and would go on to record his own songs in the late Seventies and write "No More Tears/Enough Is Enough" for Barbra Streisand and Donna Summer.

I've always liked to share my friends so I introduced Bruce to Bette Midler in the early Seventies. My friendship with Bette evolved out of our sharing the same group of friends, mainly Melissa, Peter, and Barry Manilow. She and I have always kept in touch no matter who was living on which coast. For me that Bicentennial summer was our most enjoyable—and certainly craziest—time together.

At Bette's request, Bruce and I decided to take a stab at writing some songs with her while we were all in LA. Bette was like no one I've ever written with, before or since. Her brain rarely stopped, and when it did, you were never sure where it would be rushing off to next.

"Why do you always use the same words when you write your songs?" she asked me as we began. "I mean, why don't you ever bother to find new words? You're lazy."

At that moment, I'd enjoyed a number of hit songs as a writer. As a writer, she'd had none. And yet that accusative, brash, know-it-all manner made me feel ever so slightly intimidated, though not enough to keep me from laughing at how inadvertently funny she was. Like the Wicked Witch in *The Wizard of Oz*, she pointed her finger and said, "You'd have even more hits if you used more unusual words."

"Well, that's your feeling. I have spent years and years trying to condense the words in my songs to be honest, almost conversational, and deceptively simple. I believe that lyrics should make a direct connection in the shortest amount of time to the listener's heart. So you're basically asking me to go against my nature and my entire philosophy of songwriting."

"I still think the same words get boring," she said, getting in the last word.

One afternoon Bruce sat down at the keyboard. I took my place in a cushioned chair, yellow pad and pencil in hand as always. Bette, instead of sitting, began to pace the room, pulling books off the shelves that lined her living room wall.

"Look at these words," she said, randomly opening a book. "'Curious'! You've never used the word 'curious' in a song. That's a good word." She opened another book. "'Iconic.' 'Misfit.' 'Drunk.' Where are these words in your songs? Everything's 'home,' and 'rain,' and 'light.'" She was impassioned now, glasses on the tip of her nose, shouting random words at me while throwing down one book and picking up another. "'Dangling'! 'Branches'! 'Forbidden'! Those are good words! Have you ever used any of them?"

"Come on, Bette," I said, "let's write a song. You asked me to come here and write songs."

"Yes, but we're here to write *better* songs. *Fresher* songs."

Bruce started to play something so she'd be intrigued enough to move toward the piano.

"Let's write a song about someone who's breaking up with her boyfriend," I said.

"No-o-o-o!" Bette said, making sure the *O*s resonated in the room. "You didn't hear anything I said. We're not here to write some sad breakup song like you always write. Let's throw the moron out of the house."

"That's funny," I said, something I often say instead of actually laughing. I threw out two lines:

I stayed out late one night and you moved in
I didn't mind 'cause of the state you were in

Bruce was already playing a riff that had this great sense of fun to it, like a metronome in a heavy four feel. Bette came up with the next line:

May I remind you that it's been a year since then

This set the tone for the insanity of the rest of the song. We decided to laundry-list what the guy had accumulated while he was mooching off of her. The whole song that followed reeked of Bette's sensibility. She was pulling out rhymes, taking enormous pleasure in herself when she came up with something that amused her, like "your mangy cat away," and when I said, "your baby fat away," she cackled her approval. Without Bette, there's no way Bruce and I would ever have thought to write this song.

So pack your toys away
Your pretty boys away
Your 45s away
Your alibis away
Your Spanish flies away
Your one-more-tries away
Your old tie-dyes away
You're moving out today

Now Bette, on a high from having finished a song, was up for immediately starting another. Bruce started to play some chords, a little on the melancholy side, and we started a ballad called "Amelia," which I believe began, though surely didn't end, as an homage to the aviatrix. Bette and I were both contributing lyrics, and I think, certainly in looking back, that neither of us had any idea what the other was writing about.

Amelia,
A thousand miles from home
Bound for Corsica
She left the radio playing
Amelia knew all the saints by heart

At this point I felt the song making a sharp turn toward some other Amelia.

The neighbors quietly agreed
She'd go a long, long way

Now came our chorus: "And ohhhhhhhh," Bette sang so seriously,

I will remember you
Light up a candle
And I will say a prayer or two

"A prayer or two"? How could that line have gotten past me? How did I not change it to "a prayer for you"? But the next two lines confirmed the futility of trying to edit the song.

> *The doctor came today*
> *but she'd already gone*

What doctor? Who was this woman and where did she go? This could maybe, just maybe, have worked if it were a *Sgt. Pepper* song and we were the Beatles. And they'd know who the doctor was.

> *Amelia*
> *Hair of gold*
> *Eyes of blue*
> *Carry on*

There was more.

> *Monday, the day they brought her home*
> *I wore my Sunday best*
> *and heard the radio playing*
> *Amelia*
> *Your secret's safe with me*
> *It doesn't matter now*
> *that they would never leave us both alone . . .*

In a ten-day *They Shoot Horses, Don't They?*–like marathon, we wrote five or six songs. One of them became a Top Twenty R&B hit by the Moments called "Oh I Could Have Loved You." Which, by the way, was exactly the kind of song Bette announced to us that she did not want to write.

Occasionally, Bruce and I would be witness to one of Aaron and Bette's brutal rows. They always started the same way. Aaron, overweight with long black hair, would enter the living room and announce, "Bette, my love, I have found you the perfect script. The perfect movie to make you the star you are."

"Let me see!" she'd say suspiciously, ripping the script out of his hand. A few beats and then a very loud "*Whaaaat?* This is a fuckin' part for Julie Christie. You don't even know who I am! I can't play that part. You gotta find a part for *me*."

Aaron screamed back, "Believe me, I know you're not Julie Christie."

Then she'd shut him down with "Get the hell out of here. Can't you see we're writing?"

Out of all the songs we wrote, the only one Bette recorded was "You're Moving Out Today." She liked it so much that she added it as the only studio track on the live album she was about to release. Bruce played keyboard on it and did all the wacky voices meant to evoke the evictee.

Atlantic Records released Bette's version as a single in the United States in early 1977. It got up to number 42. Bruce, ever the diplomat, provided those very same services for me when I recorded it for my first album.

Thirteen

BACK IN NEW YORK and still unhappily with Andrew, I got a call from someone at A&M Records asking me if I would consider writing a lyric with Marvin Hamlisch for some long-forgotten TV pilot.

Marvin Hamlisch had won three Oscars in one night: Best Original Score for *The Way We Were*, Best Adapted Score for *The Sting*, and Best Song, "The Way We Were." He had won a Tony Award and the Pulitzer Prize for *A Chorus Line*, one of the greatest musicals ever. Marvin Hamlisch was every Jewish mother's wish for her unmarried daughter

"Sure," I said coolly. "I'd like to meet him."

When he called, he was very matter of fact. We set a time to meet at his apartment, and he immediately got off the phone.

A week later I rang the bell. He answered the door with a phone to his ear.

"Come in, come in," he said, motioning for me to sit down on the chair he had placed next to the piano. "Hold on a second, I'm just wrapping up this call."

"Listen, Suzanne," he said into the phone, "I rewrote the string section for Liza and she pushed the session back and now it's tomorrow afternoon. Why don't you come over and I'll show you where to make those changes on your scores? Thanks."

He was off the phone as abruptly as he had ushered me in.

"Hi, I'm Marvin. I didn't think you'd be so cute."

He was tall and thin. He had dark curly hair, cut close to his head so you couldn't really tell it was curly, but I could. (Having wavy hair myself, it was one of those things I paid attention to.) Behind his horn-rimmed glasses I could see dark, intense eyes. He had a prominent nose and a largish mouth. He was wearing a dark suit, with a vest and tie. I thought he'd either come from or was going somewhere important, though it turned out this was just his casual look. When he got really loose he'd lose the jacket and put on a wool patterned sweater vest with a pair of tan trousers.

"Thanks," I said. "I didn't think you'd be so tall."

"Would you like me to be shorter? I can sit down."

"No, no. I'd just like to be taller."

"Well, I can't help you there. I'm a composer, not a magician." He walked into his kitchen. "Want something to drink? Water? Tea?"

"Water would be good. No ice, please."

"No ice? Who drinks water without ice?"

"It's much better for you without ice," I said. "Easier on your stomach. A nutritionist told me that."

"Oh, a nutritionist," he teased. "Don't tell me you're one of them."

"Who's 'them'?"

"You know, those airy-fairy vegetarians who haven't had a good meal since they were breast-fed. I had a doctor once who told me to stop eating all the foods I love. Corned beef, pastrami, ice cream. I asked him, 'Tell me, doctor, if I eat that way, will I live longer or will it just seem like that?'"

I laughed. "No, I eat. Believe me, I can eat."

This whole conversation was taking place in double time. Marvin talked at the speed of light, and I easily matched his pace because, remember, I am a chameleon, and also a New Yorker. I thought he was funny.

"All right, I'm getting distracted," he said. "Let's write the song they want, though I think the show is going to bomb."

"Oh," I said, a little deflatedly. "I'd hate to think that the one song we write together is going to be a bomb before we even write it."

THEY'RE PLAYING OUR SONG

I don't know if he heard me. He was playing his piano and suddenly I realized he was playing "Don't Cry Out Loud."

"Great song," he said. "I love a good pop song." He stopped playing. "Well," he said, "if we don't get something today, I'll be back in a couple of weeks. I have to go to London." He said he was going over to write the score for the next James Bond movie, *The Spy Who Loved Me*, and that he'd also be writing the theme song.

"I just thought of a great title," I said. " 'Nobody Does It Better.' "

I don't know how I came up with it. I just thought about James Bond and that's what popped out of my mouth. Marvin instantly loved it and within seconds we'd both forgotten about the song we'd gotten together to write and he was playing the melody of the chorus of "Nobody Does It Better." I remember marveling at how he changed keys in a second.

We sang it and I added the words

Makes me feel sad for the rest
Nobody does it half as good as you
Baby, you're the best

I knew, having taught English, that "half as good as you" was not proper grammar, but writing "Nobody does it half as *well* as you," which is correct, sounded terrible to my ear. Many times in writing songs, I made grammatically incorrect choices because certain words just sang better and sounded better to me than others. And besides, Marvin loved it immediately.

We were such an improbable pair, kooky little me in the tee shirt and jeans that I wore every day, and him looking like he was on his way to a business meeting. Total opposites, but right from the beginning when we created music we were absolutely in sync. He played it again and added most of the verse melody in what seemed like seconds.

And I loved it.

He wanted to sell it, and me, to Cubby Broccoli, who produced all the Bond movies. He needed to convince Mr. Broccoli that even though I wasn't a seasoned film collaborator, I was absolutely the right lyricist for this job.

I felt a spark between us. He was fun. And while he wasn't handsome to my eyes, he was so attractive when he was connected to his music. Marvin and I met one more time in New York, when he put the melody to "Nobody Does It Better" on tape for me to work on while he was gone, and when we said good-bye, he kissed me. That was surprising. What was more surprising was I liked it.

I wasn't sure what our bond would turn out to be, but having this new person in my life gave me the courage to finally pull the plug on my marriage. I dreamed of a bigger life than Andrew did. I don't even know if he dreamed, and if he did, I had no idea what his dreams were. I told Andrew I wanted a divorce. He was surprised, which just served to prove how disconnected we'd become. He said we should work on it more with Marci. I told him we'd been working on it for years. I was done. The divorce consisted of Andrew relinquishing any claim to ownership of my copyrights, and me leaving our apartment with only my clothes and my *Tapestry* and *Sweet Baby James* albums.

fourteen

I HAD BEEN SPENDING more time in LA because both Melissa and Peter had moved there, and I decided to see if it would work for me.

I knew I couldn't do the train thing again, so I discovered Captain Cummings's series of tapes on overcoming your fear of flying. He was a pilot for American Airlines and his tapes came highly recommended by Neil Diamond's wife, Marcia, who suffered as I did. I booked my flight (on American, of course) to LA.

I boarded the plane, carry-on in hand. It contained my headphones, my tape player, my tapes that I'd been listening to for two weeks now, and my Valium. I was shown to my seat by a stewardess whose face I studied intently, trying to determine if she was meant to have a long life or if this was going to be her last flight.

Okay, Carole, listen to Captain Cummings now. As the engines geared up for takeoff, I put on my headphones because I knew that for the entire flight my thumbs were going to have to remain upright, as if the plane needed two extra thumbs to keep it in the air, to remind it to stay UP

Oh! It's a little bumpy. I hate when it gets bumpy. But Captain Cummings did say it's just like a car driving down a road. The road has a few bumps, it means nothing. I looked for the stewardess. She was busy with babies and old ladies, but she saw me craning my neck to make eye contact and eventually came over. I whispered to her, "How long do you think this turbulence is going to last?"

"Turbulence?" she said, surprised. "I don't feel any real turbulence."

"You don't?" I said, stunned. "What do you call this? It's very bumpy, isn't it?"

"I just call this light chop."

"Oh. I call it turbulence."

"I've had a lot bumpier flights, believe me. You should see it when the plates fly around."

I took a deep breath. Captain Cummings had never mentioned flying plates. She began to walk away. "Wait! Wait," I said. "But how long will *this* . . . whatever *this* is, last? When does the pilot say it will be smooth again? Can you ask him?"

"I'll try and find out," she said, walking away while making a mental note to avoid my aisle. We finally hit a smooth patch and I got a little cocky. I was feeling numbness in my thumbs, and was overwhelmed with the urge to shake my hands out, but I couldn't. I'd made a deal.

Who was it I made this deal with? God? "Hello, this is God talking. If you keep your thumbs erect for five and a half hours, you will have a safe flight to Los Angeles." But could God really need me and my thumbs to keep the plane up? Isn't that His job? No, it couldn't be God.

Well, who was it? Was it the Devil? "I'll get you to California," he'd say, "but you'll have to give me five hours of unrelenting fear. Deal?" And I guess I said "Deal."

I RENTED A HOME on Kings Road, just above the Sunset Strip. Looking out at the expansive view of the city twinkling brightly from almost every room, I was thrilled to be away from the physical and emotional claustrophobia of New York. The house was comfortable and homey, with three bedrooms.

Bruce Roberts moved into one of them, because being alone was still not my strong suit. When I was alone, all of my fears would come up. I would lose pieces of the adult woman who was becoming so competent and get dragged back into old familiar worries that I had as a girl about dying.

Meanwhile, producer Cubby Broccoli agreed to let me write the lyric to "Nobody Does It Better," but I had to finish it alone in LA while Marvin remained in London scoring *The Spy Who Loved Me*. This was my least favorite way of writing because you don't have the instant feedback from your partner of "I *love* that line" or "You can do better."

I prefer being in the same room with the composer. He or she plays a couple of chords and I start to hear words and one line triggers a melody or a melody line triggers a lyric. We become one, inspiring each other to write the best song we can, and if something sounds untrue or mundane or tired, we're both there to try for something better together. Maybe he or she has a better lyric line, or I have an improvement on the melody, and if so, we both know it. There is constant honesty. I have given a complete lyric to a composer and he or she has put a melody to it, and vice versa. But writing together will always be my favorite way to craft a song.

Marvin would call from London, and I would sing him the new lines. He would write them down and then sing them back to me at the piano. "Good," he'd say in his abrupt way. "Try to finish it soon. I can't hold them up on this." When Marvin was in the midst of taking care of business, he was all business. But with that part out of the way I was finding he could be very romantic and tender, even on the telephone.

Bruce acted as my sounding board, and I finally did it. I loved the finished song, but I had yet to hear it sung by anyone other than Marvin or me, and neither of us could be considered "singers" in the real sense of the word. And while I wasn't required to get the title in, every Bond song thus far was the name of the movie it was in, so I was proud of myself for getting it into the song's first verse:

But like heaven above me,
The spy who loved me
Is keeping all my secrets safe tonight

Now we needed to find someone to record it.

We both loved Carly Simon, so Marvin flew to New York City and played the song for her in her living room. She loved it as soon as she heard it, and they laid it down immediately on a tape recorder in her home. Marvin flew out to Los Angeles before returning to London to finish the scoring, and we both played the demo for Richard Perry, who proclaimed it a hit. Knowing the added plus that it was going to be the new Bond theme, he agreed on the spot to produce it.

Richard recorded the basic track in LA and put Carly on it. Then he and I traveled from LA to London for Marvin to record his orchestra on the song.

We had to fly. Over an ocean. And I did it. And the song sounded great. Carly's voice and Richard's production made the song very sexy, and my feeling that it was going to be a big hit was quickly borne out. The record went to number 2 in America and in England and it stayed there for weeks.

Fifteen

WE STARTED WORKING ON my album. I had seven songs I wanted to record, and in the course of making the record, I cowrote three more. I liked working with Brooks Arthur, even though I did play each track for Richard Perry to get a second opinion. Brooks made me feel secure and nicknamed me Lark, and with each take I would hear, through the studio speakers, "Beautiful, Lark! Uno mas!" I actually felt happy in the recording studio, and Brooks's encouragement and enthusiasm for my voice helped me feel less insecure.

I had California's best session players (Nicky Hopkins, Russ Kunkel, Lee Ritenour, Jim Keltner), Paul Buckmaster (a brilliant arranger who had worked with Elton John on his first five albums) did all of the string arrangements, plus famous friends (Melissa, Peter, Bette, Tony Orlando, Brenda Russell) sang backup for me. It never ceased to surprise me that in the midst of all of this, there was me, the nonsinger singer making her own album.

WHEN MARVIN FINISHED HIS work in London, he came to LA and we quickly became a couple.

It's easy to think you're in love when you have no idea what love feels like.

Together we were like two Jewish jumping beans, I with my fears and rituals, and him with his monumental mood swings. Still, he acted and looked like the grown-up while I was still a needy child-woman, and that seemed to work for us. We were best together when we were writing, and we spent a tremendous amount of time doing exactly that.

One day when I was going to the recording studio, Marvin said, "I'd like to write a song with you for your record." I was so flattered. That was a big compliment coming from him, because he was so successful in my eyes and had worked with only great singers. It validated me.

That night we sat down and wrote a really tender ballad called "Sweet Alibis." Marvin was brilliant at knowing how to write for the artist who would be singing his song. He kept the melody small in range, staying where he knew my voice would sound its best. When I recorded it, he played the piano and basically coproduced the song with Brooks Arthur. And with that song my album was complete.

It stunned me that Marvin didn't seem to appreciate how musically dazzling he was. He knew how to put an act together better than most directors who did that for a living, and he proved a savior many times over to three huge, first-named stars: Barbra, Liza, and Ann-Margret. They all depended on him to diagnose the weak spots of their acts. If Marvin was there, you felt safe. He was as kind as he was talented.

On the cover of my album I stood shyly against an all-white background, wearing a tee shirt and a pair of white painter's pants, head down with a sprig of violets coming out of the pants pocket. I felt it represented the vulnerable side of me, which matched my singing voice. Today, for more and more people, album art is a two-inch square image at the iTunes store, and before that we had a quarter-century of five-inch CDs, but before that people really looked at album covers because they were large. You often studied the back cover while you were listening to the record, each song in its carefully considered order, with credits of the musicians and writers. And liner notes that someone actually thought about and wrote, and listeners enjoyed reading.

• • •

THE RECORD, SIMPLY TITLED *Carole Bayer Sager*, was released near the end of 1977. My version of "You're Moving Out Today" was released as a single in America and it enjoyed even less success than Bette's had. So imagine my surprise when I got a call from Steve Wax from Elektra Records telling me that my single was in the Top Ten in England and moving up the charts in Australia, where it soon spent a month at Number One.

Bette's label and my label were under the same umbrella outside of the United States. To this day I have no idea why they decided to release my version internationally.

Bette was furious, and I could understand why. She was the star. This song was her inspiration. She accused me of planning the entire maneuver, sabotaging her record just to elevate mine to platinum status in a country half a world away.

"Bette, I swear to you, I had nothing to do with this," I said. "I didn't even know they were putting it out. No one told me a thing."

Her eyes narrowed until they were almost crossing themselves. "Falsehoods! Untruths! Fiction! I don't believe a word!" And she stormed off in a huff, and we didn't speak for over two years.

When we made up, which was inevitable given that she knew in her heart she had no bigger fan than me, the incident was never really mentioned. She just let it go. But then, we carry each other's history, and how many people can you say that about?

And as another friend once told me, "If you get eighty percent in a friend, or a husband, consider yourself lucky. If you want more, you'll spend your life alone."

NOT LONG AFTER IT came out, Andrew called to tell me how painful it was to hear my name or see it in print, and asked me to change it back.

"Are you fucking insane?" I said, perhaps insensitively. "You insisted I use the name when I didn't want to. Now I've really had hits. How can I go back to Carole Bayer? I'm known now as the girl with three names."

The album didn't sell a huge number of copies, but there was a lot of industry buzz. I was surprised and delighted by how many important publications and reviewers liked it. Robert Hilburn, the music critic for the *Los Angeles Times*, included it in his year-end Top Ten and wrote, "This debut is the most appealing adult mainstream collection since Janis Ian's *Between the Lines* . . . Sager's lyrics carry a quiet wisdom that is both contemporary and relevant: Her singing may be a bit mannered and ragged on first listening, but it eventually asserts a character and conviction that gives the songs added bite." Wow. In my own way I *could* sing.

Like Peter's albums, mine proved to be a great platform for other artists to hear a song they liked and figure, "I can sing it better than she did." And they did. Dusty Springfield, Diana Ross, Ann Peebles, Rita Coolidge, Rosemary Clooney, and Barbara Cook, among others, all recorded songs from the album.

Joe Smith wanted me to play a few clubs to support the record, so Marvin helped me put a small act together, and I performed it in New York, Philadelphia, Chicago, and finally LA at the Roxy. I had not gotten on a stage and performed in quite that way since my days at New York University.

I had this need to take chances and push myself into uncomfortable situations like performing. My stage fright was unbearable. My eyes would always go to the one person in the room who seemed not to be having a good time, and I would continue to check in with that one unhappy face. Still, somehow I got through all four cities. Marvin would tell me how magical I was when I captured the audience. I sang with conviction, believing my words to be true. I also found that when I relaxed I could ad-lib and sometimes be funny, which the audience loved. Once I felt that connection, I would actually enjoy the rest of the set, but I didn't know how to hold on to those feelings from one city to the next. I felt like one of those vending machines where the coins get stuck on the way down and are never truly deposited.

Sixteen

ONE NIGHT MARVIN CAME over and handed me a small box that I recognized instantly from its iconic color. I couldn't imagine what he might have given me from Tiffany, but I certainly was not expecting a sparkling diamond heart on a thin platinum chain. He put it around my neck.

"Oh my God, Marvin. It's so beautiful. I'm stunned that you would buy me something so beautiful."

"I want you to wear this so you know how I feel about you," he said. It was a little more than a carat, and no one had ever given me a diamond before. He made me very happy.

JUST AS THE FIRST song of mine that was recorded went to Number One, the first song I'd ever written for a motion picture was nominated for an Academy Award.

Nobody does it better
Makes me feel sad for the rest

For most people, this line evokes sultry Bond vixens drifting across the screen and the throaty, velvet voice of Carly Simon. For me, on the night of

April 3, 1978, it meant a wardrobe crisis and the worst bout of stage fright in my thirty-four years on the planet.

Marvin and I entered the enormous Dorothy Chandler Pavilion with our mothers in tow and began to move to our seats on the aisle in the fifth row. My mother walked in regally, or at least as regally as you can manage at five foot two, with her head held high and her ample chest puffed up and out. She was dressed as though she were about to open as a headliner in Las Vegas: all in gold, like the trophy she was hoping we'd go home with. As she walked, I could hear the *cling-clang* of her one too many bracelets.

"These are *great* seats," she said. "I think I'll sit right here in the 'Carole Bayer Sager' seat. After all, you wouldn't be here without me."

I was about to keep moving down past the place where my name was taped but Marvin, in his black Armani tuxedo—the outfit he looked and felt most comfortable in—intervened.

"Come on, Anita, move two seats over," he said. "That's Carole's seat and then there's mine. Move down next to my mother. See how nicely she's behaving?" Lilly Hamlisch, portly in the same black dress she wore when cleaning her house, was seated somberly, looking like she could just as easily have been at a funeral. My mother, Anita, who was happy talking to anyone, even—and often, preferably—herself, launched into a jittery monologue.

"Exciting, huh, Lilly? Who ever thought we'd see this. Your son, my daughter—I only wish Eli was alive to see this." Lilly, who was rummaging through her bag, didn't respond. Anita, lacking all boundaries, reached over into Lilly's bag. "Is that a tissue? You better give me one, too, Lilly," she said. "I don't know if I'll be crying tears of joy or sorrow."

"Mahvin," Lilly said in her thick German accent, "make her stop. I only have two tissues, one for me and one for you." Anita, paying no attention, continued. "Well, this certainly makes up for the debacle of *Georgy*. What a night this is. What a thrill!"

"Mom," I finally said. "Please, leave Mrs. Hamlisch alone. Can't you see she's not a talker?"

"These people have no idea how to have fun," Anita mumbled to herself, then laughed. "Ha! No one's going to spoil *my* night."

She was having the time of her life, oblivious to the fact that I was paralyzed with fright. I guess anybody would be nervous on a night like this—until now I'd only seen the Oscars on television. Even when I was really young, they let me stay up and watch. But I wasn't just nervous. I was convinced that there was no way I was going to be able to get out of my seat if we won.

Looking around the star-studded auditorium, I was sure I didn't belong there. My dress wasn't glamorous; my hair was not just ordinary but brown. I was too short, I had no breasts, and my weight was not where it should have been. There was no way I could enjoy myself. I had taken a Valium but it hadn't kicked in yet, and I was wondering if I should maybe take another half of the one probably crushed by now in my overstuffed purse.

"I am so scared," I said, trying to take a breath. "You have no idea."

"You're scared?" my mother said. "You should be excited. Look where we are!"

"Don't be silly, honey," Marvin said. "It's the greatest thrill in the world to win an Oscar. Trust me. I ought to know. And if we win, I'll hold your hand and lead my little princess to the greatest moment of her career."

"Okay," I said, barely there. "That sounds good."

So I sat there waiting to be led to the greatest moment of my life as Michael Caine and Maggie Smith came out to present the Best Song award. My heart started to pound in my chest, with its occasional skipped beats—something I'd already consulted my doctor about, and had been as reassured as someone like me could be that these were simply "benign extra systoles" usually triggered by stress. It also occurred to me that I might be having a heart attack, and that would be a great way out of here. I could imagine someone in the audience saying, "They took her out on a stretcher. I don't know who she was."

As the nominees were announced, I felt like I was outside of my body, watching myself judging myself mercilessly, with only a small part of me wanting to win. When I heard, "And the winner is . . . 'You Light Up My Life,'" my disappointment was overshadowed by my relief at not having to walk on stage and make a speech in front of the whole world. I just wasn't ready yet.

"Agghh!" I heard from the familiar voice on my left. "I never liked that song. Or that girl. Or her father. Carole, don't you *ever* write *anything* for Debby Boone. You were robbed. Marvin, sweetheart, *you* were robbed. Lilly, my friend, don't you think they were both robbed?"

Lilly, who after the tissue incident had tuned my mother out, did not answer. If she was thinking anything at that moment, it was most likely how she might get away from Anita, and probably me, too, if she could. She would have been happiest just to have gone home with her Marvin, who looked downtrodden.

Twenty-six years later, the American Film Institute honored "Nobody Does It Better" as number 67 of the 100 greatest movie songs ever, and some online list named it the number 2 best Bond song, behind "Goldfinger." And Thom Yorke, the lead singer of Radiohead, performed it in concert and called it "the sexiest song ever written." Sometimes losing is winning.

BEFORE OUR NOMINATION FOR "Nobody Does It Better" was announced, Marvin had been hired to score the motion picture *Ice Castles*, and he asked me to write the title song with him (which Melissa Manchester wound up singing). The film was about a young figure skater who loses her sight in an accident but begs her coach not to reveal she is blind so she can enter a big ice-skating competition. Thus my title, "Looking Through the Eyes of Love."

When we sat down to write it, he played a series of chords until I said, "Wait, I like that."

"This?" he said, playing it again.

"Yeah," I said, "that's so pretty. What if we start, *'Please don't let this feeling end,'* as though she is in the middle of skating."

Marvin sang those words to his melody and went on to play the rest of the phrase. I offered up: *"It's everything I am, everything I want to be."*

He sang my new words, writing the whole melody so quickly that I was suddenly playing catch-up with my lyrics.

"Listen, I can hear the string line coming in here, and listen to this figure that would be great to start the record off with." He was talking very quickly.

"Hold on! I've only written the first line of the lyric. You're already arranging the finished record!"

"Just listen to this line for the intro," he said, as excited as if he'd just found the cure for any of those diseases I lived in dread of.

"Can you just play the beginning of the melody one more time, please? I think I have another line there."

We were practically talking over each other. Creating with Marvin was like being on three cups of espresso. We kept building on each other. Everything came together so quickly it was like a whirlwind—like if you blinked you could miss the whole collaboration. Before I knew it, we were done.

The song had a very positive lyric. Most of my "positive" love songs, it seems, have been written for motion pictures. As the lyricist writing for a film, your responsibility is to serve the film first—the lyric has to reflect what we are seeing in the movie. I liked this new discipline. I didn't have to write entirely out of my imagination. It gave me a map to help craft my lyric.

I can see what's mine now
Finding out what's true,
Since I've found you
Looking through the eyes of love.

The song earned me my second Oscar nomination in as many years. I felt somewhat more ready to get up on stage and accept an award this time, but we lost to the song from *Norma Rae*, "It Goes Like It Goes." That song is virtually unknown today, while the "Theme from *Ice Castles*," a very pretty song that was easy to sing, went on to be a favorite among Miss America contestants—a dubious achievement, I understand—and found an instant place in elevator music all over the country.

•   •   •

WE WERE ON A nice roll. Next we wrote "Break It to Me Gently" for
Aretha Franklin. Marvin played me a melody one day and said he could hear
Aretha singing it. I was less sure, but I trusted his feeling.

Marvin's melody in the chorus was so beautiful that we wrote that first,
which is unusual. I came up with

> *Break it to me gently*
> *Be careful what you say*
> *And save it, save it till tomorrow*
> *Maybe then you'll stay, one more day*

Then he wrote a melody that was his idea of how an R&B verse would
sound. I thought it was a little over the top. "It's so rhythmic," I said. "It
doesn't match the smooth chorus and it doesn't sound black."

"Trust me!" he said. "It's perfect. Give me some words and you'll see how
good it is." I still thought it was a little cheesy, but I wrote it anyway. We put
it down on tape. He played it back. I said, "Maybe it's better than I thought."

Marvin loved when I admitted he was right. He played it back again,
singing the verse and dancing, pretending he was one of Aretha's background singers, doing some kind of choreographed dance moves with his
hands and feet as he sang. He was hilarious.

Aretha was living in Encino at the time, so when the song was finished,
he thought nothing of driving us out to play it for her in person. Marvin
didn't make demos like the rest of us. He would just call an artist and ask if
he could come and play him or her a song, and because he was Marvin Hamlisch they'd say, "Are you kidding? Of course." I don't think he realized this
wasn't the way it worked for the rest of us.

Aretha immediately loved the song, and it went to Number One on the
Rhythm & Blues charts. So much for my doubts about Marvin's aptitude for
R&B.

Next came Alan Pakula's film of Jim Brooks's first movie script, *Starting Over*. Candice Bergen played a not-very-good singer-songwriter, so the challenge was to write her three very good not-very-good songs. The fun part of that was being in her apartment and teaching her the three songs. Candice herself was not a very good singer, so she sang them convincingly enough to earn a Best Supporting Actress Oscar nomination.

Meanwhile, Elektra was happy enough with the response to my first album that they wanted more, so I started working on my second, . . . *Too*.

With more money and more choices, I moved into a house on Schuyler Road in Beverly Hills. Marvin was becoming more bicoastal, taking more films to score than he might have if he weren't seeing me. When he was in LA we lived together in my new house.

My mother was still living in New York, and I was now covering her rent and helping to support her lifestyle. The truth is, it was worth it to have the physical distance from her required for me to have my own life. She was happy to stay where her life essentially was, and happy to dine out on the fact that I was dating Marvin Hamlisch.

If you look at the three years Marvin and I were together, you would see how heavily weighted the working and creating were. We wrote dozens of songs, many of them successful. Marvin and I were pouring out music constantly, and it felt pretty effortless. People were calling us to write for films, and Marvin loved having some hits in my world of pop that he had felt so distant from.

Everything was about music, and we spent very little time being social. We were both driven, we both wanted more hits, and I don't remember us ever turning down an opportunity because we wanted to spend time alone with each other. The truth was, I had more passion for the music and creating it than I did for us as lovers.

Seventeen

FOR THE FIRST TIME in my life I was living with the man I was writing with. But there was a price to pay for his kind of staggering creativity and output. Marvin suffered from horrible migraines. They were so bad he sometimes needed to lie in a darkened room for days, leaving him depressed and me feeling helpless.

Once, my friend Sandy Gallin (the manager of, among others, Dolly Parton, Michael Jackson, and Neil Diamond) was hanging out with me in the living room while Marvin was upstairs, presumably sleeping. Sandy said something funny that made us both laugh aloud. Marvin got out of bed and came downstairs, furious that I could find anything funny when he was feeling so horrible.

When Marvin got his headaches, he felt that the only person who truly knew how to take care of him was his mother. She had recognized his talent when he was practically a baby and nurtured it, and him, with complete devotion. He loved her deeply. Whenever we were in the same city, Lilly seemed to make his tea with warm milk better than I could, so I'd move aside and let her take care of him, though I wasn't clear on how I could fuck up a cup of Lipton's. It made me feel sad that he didn't think I could take care of him.

I suspected that Marvin might be bipolar, because his highs were off the charts and his lows were so devastatingly low and lasted longer than any headache I'd ever known anyone to have.

There were a few other red flags popping up.

When he was with me, Marvin, who was so brilliant, thought he was just an "old-fashioned composer" and I was some pop princess with the same kind of fame as Linda Ronstadt or Carly Simon. I was so not in their league. They sold millions of records; I sold a hundred thousand. Still, when I had success with a song that I didn't write with him, he was either jealous if he thought it was good or angry when it was a hit that he thought was undeserving.

But the biggest flag was about my performing.

It should never have been an issue, because I never loved performing, but Marvin feared my little four-city tour to support my record would widen to bigger venues and bigger audiences.

"I would definitely think about our getting married," he once told me, "if I knew you would never perform for more than, tops, about five hundred people." I found his comment to be weirdly specific, and though I was never pushing for marriage, I would tell him over and over again I had no intention of ever playing big venues. But I did have difficulty with someone telling me they loved me and then putting a limitation on what I could do or be. Love shouldn't diminish you; it should enhance you. Lord knows where I got this idea when my mother, who adored me, was also so relentlessly critical. But I believed it, despite the absence of proof, and I still do.

We also had two very different sets of friends, and neither of us was excited about the other's choices. His friends seemed to me too straight, too old-fashioned, too professional (as in doctors and lawyers) and mine seemed to him too "out there," too showbizzy, and too druggy. Though we were the same age, Marvin gravitated to older friends, and I guess I spent time with what he saw as a "faster" crowd: Sandy Gallin, David Geffen, Bruce Roberts, and Bette Midler.

I have been close to Sandy Gallin and David Geffen, the wunderkinds of the music business, for almost four decades. Sandy and I were fixed up on a blind date while I was still living in my parents' apartment in the early Sixties, when he was still bothering to go on dates with women. Obviously, that didn't work out. But when we re-met in the Seventies he quickly became my sorely needed closest friend in LA. Around the same time, I met David Geffen and learned that Sandy and David were best friends from their early days as agents, Sandy at GAC and David at the William Morris Agency.

Sandy, always full of fun, was about friends, parties, and spectacle. He was the perfect manager because he loved celebrity and had a very keen eye for talent. I remember him dragging me down to some hole in the Village to see Whoopi Goldberg at a time when no one knew her name. Sandy knew she would be a star and knew how to court her, sign her, and eventually deliver that stardom. Through Sandy I widened my social circle in LA. Over the years Sandy has become family to me, the one who by example reminds me how important it is to laugh and take things lightly. His homes, so many of which he's bought only to enhance and then sell, are places I feel instantly comfortable in. Sandy is like my brother.

David, meanwhile, was uncanny in his choice of artists, signing icons like Joni Mitchell, the Eagles, Jackson Browne, and Linda Ronstadt, and was brilliantly incisive, cutting right through the bullshit to the truth of any situation. When I was briefly dating Nicky Chinn, co-owner of Dreamland Records—a short-lived label with a roster of B-list talent—David said to him, "Ultimately, Nicky, your career is not only defined by which artists you sign, but also by who you don't sign." I've applied this bit of wisdom to all areas of my life, from things I've created to things I've acquired.

Between the energy of the two of them I couldn't help but feel "covered." There was alchemy in the combination of the three of us. I'm not sure quite how it worked, but I am clear that I loved them and still do. Although David can sometimes come down a little hard in sharing certain truths with me that I might prefer not to hear, they are almost always correct and I'm better for having heard them.

WHEN I RENTED THE house on Schuyler Road in Beverly Hills I hired a Sikh housekeeper, Dhanwant Kaur. The Sikh religion forbids cutting hair on any part of the body, so she wore a white turban over her long, voluminous, curly hair. Her unibrow (think Frida Kahlo) was in desperate need of trimming, but she wasn't looking to me for beauty advice. Or fashion advice. She was happy in a full-length white leotard swathed in layer over layer of crisscrossing cloth. If you had to describe her quickly, you might say she most resembled a giant gauze bandage with a face peeking out ten inches below the top.

But I liked that she was spiritual, did yoga, meditated, and ate healthfully. Marvin hated the tasteless, mostly vegetarian food at the house. "If you love animals so much," he used to tease me, "why are you eating all their food?" He longed for corned beef and pastrami and all the other treats that could not be found in our home.

Bruce Roberts, my songwriting friend from New York, was once again living with me, and the three of us sat at the piano one day to work on a song for Barbra Streisand's next album, *Wet*. (Yes, every song had to have a water theme.) We were writing what I thought was a beautiful song, "Niagara." Marvin was replaying the chorus when he stopped suddenly and started to wave his hand back and forth over his forehead, and then his ear.

"What are you doing?" I asked.

"Something's not right," he said, his face looking anything but okay.

"Oh. Now my heart is beating fast." Now his hand was patting his heart, fast.

"Calm down, honey," I said. "Maybe you're having a panic attack."

"I'm worried it's a heart attack," he said.

"Do you have any pain down your left arm?"

"No," he said, moving to the sofa and sitting down. He hung his head as if he was sitting shiva for someone he loved. His nose looked very long to me.

"But my heart's still beating fast."

"Take deep breaths. I'll get you some water, but take deep breaths."

He drank the water. "Better?"

"Yeah, sort of. I just felt weird. I wonder if that brownie I ate was bad."

"The brownie in the freezer?" I asked.

"Yeah. With milk. Of course there's no real milk here, just that one per-cent kind."

"Why would you eat a brownie that said, 'Do Not Eat'? Richard Perry left that. For me."

Bruce now started laughing hysterically. Marvin glared at him. "Come on, Marvin, it's funny. You're stoned."

"There is nothing funny about this," he declared. Then, "Carole, are there any real cookies in this house?"

I walked over to him and gave him a big hug. "Honey," I said, "this is the first time you've ever gotten high."

"Let's just write this song," he said, going back to the piano. His mind was so strong he could just decide not to be high anymore. And we finished the song, though he did send Dhanwant Kaur out for a run to Stan's Donuts in Westwood.

The result was one of my favorite of our songs. Now all we had to do was get Barbra to want to sing it.

We drove out to her lavender home in Malibu to play it for her. Sue Mengers, the infamous Hollywood agent, always ample in size, was on the deck soaking in a bubbling hot tub, oblivious to the fact that three newcom-ers were now viewing her large breasts as they alternately bounced up and down to the rhythm of the water jets. It was a sight that made you want to turn away even as you continued to stare, transfixed. And it was a sight that Bruce, to this day, remembers vividly, as he does her response: "What's the matter? You never saw a pair of tits before?"

"Not if I could help it," he stage-whispered to me.

Finally, Barbra came out and asked to hear the song.

We went inside and Marvin sat down at the piano. "What's it called?" she asked.

"'Niagara,'" I said proudly.

She scrunched her face, thought to herself for several seconds, then turned and seriously asked, "Is that wet enough?" Blanching, I said, "It's very wet, Barbra. It's Niagara Falls. What's wetter?"

"Oh, okay. Let me hear it."

Marvin played and Bruce sang it beautifully, with just enough Barbraesque touches to turn her on but not offend her, as I tried to read her reaction. Marvin played it in her key in case she was humming along in her head. Slowly she responded, "I like it." And she did, because she recorded it for the *Wet* album. It should have been the single, but I guess all songwriters say that about their songs.

Eighteen

I CONTINUED TO WRITE pop songs, and Marvin began working with Neil Simon to turn one of his plays, *The Gingerbread Lady*, into a musical.

While they were collaborating, Marvin would talk to Neil about what it was like living and working with the same person: how we once dashed off a song in our evening clothes, how we were always comparing our BMI and ASCAP statements to figure out which organization gave you more money, or how he never heard of tofu until he met me.

One day Marvin told me Neil had something he wanted to talk to me about, and that he was going to call me to take me to lunch. In the course of three hours at the Bistro Garden in Beverly Hills, Neil told me that he found himself more intrigued by the idea of a musical about two songwriters living and working together than by reworking *The Gingerbread Lady*. He wondered if I would mind if he took a pass at writing a book for a musical loosely based on Marvin and me!

Neil Simon had written some of America's funniest and most romantic Broadway shows (among them *The Odd Couple* and *Barefoot in the Park*) and the musicals *Sweet Charity* and *Promises, Promises*. He was America's premier comedy playwright, revered by theatergoers everywhere, and he found my life with Marvin interesting enough to base a play on. Was I going to say no to Neil Simon?

Marvin and I decided to put our major seemingly unsolvable issue—

that we were not in love but merely in like—on hold and to view writing the show as an opportunity to do some really good work together. The irony was that our relationship was waning just as we were starting to write songs about it. But we'd begun as friends, so I thought we could be that again.

Neil finished the first act as quickly as Marvin and I might have finished a few songs. We read it and liked it and act two soon followed. Now we were writing a musical.

The three of us were creating at warp speed. It felt almost bulletproof, having Neil Simon and Marvin Hamlisch as my collaborators. Our meetings were always quick and to the point, whether we were playing Neil a new song we'd just written or figuring out where the book needed a song.

"We need a song in the discotheque," Neil said. "They're out on their first date, what would they dance to?"

"Well, I'm not much of a dancer," I said apologetically. "I mean, I wish I were, but . . . maybe a slow song, I could dance to that."

"It's a discotheque, Carole," Marvin said to me. "Pay attention."

"Well, you're not a dancer either," I said defensively. "What would you dance to?"

"Carole, we're not Vernon and Sonia," he said. "This is fiction based on us. It's not our biography."

Neil laughed. "You're both so crazy," he said. "They're going to have to dance in this scene, so figure out what kind of song you'd dance to."

Marvin said, "Well, the only thing that would get me on a dance floor would be if they started to play one of my songs."

"That's funny," I said, almost stepping on his line. "Me too. I'd get up if they were playing my song. I'd feel excited."

At which point Marvin leapt up and raced to the piano. "That's it!" he said. "Listen! Can't you hear what they're playing?" He launched into the first two lines of the music and lyrics of "Oh-ho, they're playing my song, oh yeah, they're playing my song." I excitedly added, "And when they're playing my song . . ."

Neil was smiling from ear to ear. "This is so perfect," he said. "In fact, I think it's the title of our show. *They're Playing Our Song.*"

In two more minutes, if even, we completed the chorus of "They're Playing Our Song." And that's how easy the whole experience of writing a musical with Neil and Marvin was. Not that there weren't rewrites. We would all rewrite. One night in previews a joke wasn't working. Neil went home, gave it some thought, and the next night he put in another joke. This one got huge applause. "He goes home and writes the equivalent of a Number One song," I said to Marvin, "but it's a joke. What an amazing talent."

They're Playing Our Song opened at the Ahmanson Theatre for its out-of-town tryouts—you've got to have a lot of confidence to open your show in LA—in December 1978. Given my theater track record, I was nervous but by the time we went to New York, it had already made its investment back. (It was a two-character show with three backup singers for each character, so expenses were minimal.) It opened on Broadway at the Imperial in February 1979—less than a year after Neil dashed off that first act—where it would run for 1,087 performances over three years.

Robert Klein and Lucie Arnaz were simply amazing as "us." Robert, who by profession was a stand-up comic, had the ability to slip into the character of Vernon Gersch with ease, and Lucie brought a wonderful voice and great comedic timing to the role of Sonia Walsk. The show was nominated for four Tonys, and critics called our score "lively," "hummable," and "exhilarating."

Marvin often said that his favorite of all the hundreds of songs he'd written was "If He Really Knew Me." I think the lyric was very real for him personally. I felt the same way.

If there were no music
If my melodies stopped playing
Would I be the kind of man
You'd want to see tonight . . .
Does the man make the music?

Or does the music make this man?
And am I everything I thought I'd be?

Marvin went on to sing it in all of his concerts.

I loved the charm and humor of the title song, and the other song that I liked was "Fallin'," the opening song of the show, which is the first time Vernon Gersch (who was based on Marvin Hamlisch) sings alone at the piano.

I'm afraid to fly
And I don't know why
I'm jealous of the people who
Are not afraid to die
It's just that I recall
Back when I was small
Someone promised that they'd catch me
And then they let me fall

That lyric was pretty true to my life. I think the image of falling might have come from much earlier, with my mom and the bath all those years ago. It worked much better as the opener than a big showstopper would have done.

MARVIN HAD BOUGHT A beautiful apartment in New York, because that's where his heart told him he really wanted to be, and he wanted me to try living there with him. He asked Angelo Donghia, a famed interior designer at the time, to decorate it, and to design a study for me. It was feminine, which I liked. The walls were a pale gray silk and the furniture was done in shades of pale pinks and grays. It was sweet of him, but truthfully, I never felt at home in it. I still favored Los Angeles, not just because there were more songwriting opportunities there, but because it gave me the space to have my own life and create a new me. New York was too close to Anita. Though she had stopped drinking, for which I was grateful, when I would enter apartment

10-A, where her cigarette smoke stained the walls of the rooms I'd grown up in, I would lose my adult self and revert back to little Carol Bayer.

Marvin came out to LA one more time and tried to live with me, but I knew that wasn't working when I overheard him whispering sweet nothings into our bathroom phone, where he was clearly flirting with a young actress named Emma Samms. The worst part about it was it didn't hurt me and it didn't make me cry. In truth, it was a kind of relief because were it not for Neil, we would have parted company much earlier.

With the show a hit, many people wanted to interview Marvin and me about how close our characters in the play came to who we were in real life. My standard answer was, "If our lives were really the way Neil portrayed them on stage, we would still be together. These were our lives filtered through Neil Simon's brilliant wit." There was not a lot of me in my character, Sonia Walsk. She was the way Neil imagined me to be. I was not all that sunny and quirky. Well, maybe a little quirky, but I did not dress in costumes from different Broadway plays and Neil never touched on my often crippling anxieties. If Edward Albee had written it, it might have been a bit closer to the truth.

Nineteen

WHAT *THEY'RE PLAYING OUR SONG* gave me, other than a bit of fame for being that girl who wrote the lyrics for the musical about her life with Marvin Hamlisch, was a steady influx of cash for the next three years. Never one to let the money accrue, I decided the time was right to buy my first home.

I found my dream house on Donhill Drive in Beverly Hills, and Waldo Fernandez, a relatively new interior designer and friend at the time, created the most wonderful space for me. It was very open, modern, and had light coming in from all directions.

Single again, I began to date and spend more time with friends. I felt like I had gotten the Get Out of Jail Free card in Monopoly. Marvin had wanted me to conform to a life I didn't belong in. We were always mismatched, which is why Neil Simon saw the comedy of us as a couple.

Soon after Marvin moved back to New York, I attended a party in honor of Burt Bacharach. He was one of the most famous songwriters in the world, but this was the first time I had ever met him.

Burt was holding court in the back room and talking about his past accomplishments, and as staggering as they were, I saw him as a songwriter looking back, not forward. But then he asked me if he could drop a cassette off for me to listen to, and maybe write some lyrics to. I said sure, I'd be happy to listen.

The next day the tape arrived in my mailbox, with a note from Burt that simply said "New Melodies." I remembered Marvin having once made a dismissive remark about Burt's melodies being nowhere near what they used to be, and after listening to his tape I had to agree. I felt that his new melodies were like stops and starts that didn't land. Never having been good at saying, "Sorry, I don't think it's for me," I put it in a stack of cassette tapes and forgot to get back to Burt. (I did the same thing once with three melodies Andrew Lloyd Webber sent me, and although I lost the tape, I was almost sure I heard a variation on one of the melodies years later when I saw the megahit *Phantom of the Opera*.)

I next saw Burt a few months later when I was a guest on *The Mike Douglas Show* and he was the guest cohost for the week. I sang a song from my second album, . . . *Too*. Afterward, Burt asked me two questions: Did I want to have dinner? And would I like to write a song with him? I've often thought that if I remembered which he asked me first I would know a lot more about our relationship. The truth is I suspect I know very well. It's funny, because in some ways I think my "heat" at that time in the world of pop music brought the same excitement to Burt that Marvin had found so appealing.

Before Burt the men I'd been with had been life rafts. Now I was afloat without a man, which was pretty rare for me, but this wouldn't last long. Burt needed a muse—someone who could bring him back to that part of himself that could still write hit songs.

I got the job.

ON OUR FIRST DATE, he picked me up in a 1976 green Lincoln. It looked like a tanker that had drifted from its moorings. *That must be a loaner*, I thought to myself. *His real car must be in the shop.*

He took me to dinner at a little now-long-gone Chinese restaurant above the street on Rodeo Drive. (It only had about five people in it, so I'm not surprised it closed.) He was very attractive, and it was clear that he liked me a lot. Suddenly I began to see him in a different light. Isn't that weird: that moment, that split second when the "switch" happens. No charge! Then, *bam!* Charge! How does that happen?

There was something so boyish about him. He dressed like a kid. I remember exactly what he wore that night. Faded jeans, blue blazer, white shirt, crewneck sweater. His silver hair and blue eyes picked up the blue of the sweater. Suddenly he was no longer the Burt whose gaze was on the past. Now he was the *brilliant* songwriter who wasn't *so* old, was so crazy handsome, and whose speaking voice was beyond sexy. He spoke in the rhythms that he wrote his songs in: with stops and starts. To me it sounded like "Hey! [*count 1, 2, 3, 4*] Do you wanna, uh, [*count 1, 2*] uh, come down to Del Mar sometime, and uh [*count 2, 3, 4*] it would be fun. You know, I've got a piano . . . and it's uh, [*count 2, 3*] beautiful, just beautiful. Great tone. [*count 1, 2*] Great down there." He said the words like triplets—three notes tied together. "Greatdownthere." "The beach, [*count 2, 3, 4*] the ocean . . ." It took him a long time to finish a sentence, but he was so handsome, who cared?

We went through all the beginning stuff. He'd been married twice, most recently to actress Angie Dickinson. I felt a moment of insecurity. She was famously beautiful, with legs so legendary they'd been insured for a million dollars.

"So how long have you been divorced now?" I asked.

"Well . . . um . . . I'm not really divorced." [*count 2, 3, 4*] The rhythm of his speech, with its stops and starts and half-stops and stutters, all lulled me into not caring what he was saying, just liking the sound of his voice. I think he liked it, too, which is probably why he took as long as he did. "I'm . . . uh . . . separated."

"For the last three years?" I asked, surprised.

"Well, uh, there's never been any reason to . . . I mean . . . the marriage was over even before we separated, and I uh . . . just stayed that long because of Nikki . . . Nikki's my daughter. She's thirteen now and . . . she's . . . she's had a lot of problems. I wanted to be there to help her."

Knowing Burt as I do now, I'm sure he kept the tiniest little balloon of false hope hanging over Angie's head in case he changed his mind and decided to go back to his family.

"I worry so about Nikki," he said, looking very sad. I wished there was something I could do to make him feel better. He refilled our wineglasses. There was something so shy about him.

We talked about his work.

"I don't think I have it anymore," he said. "Not like I did."

"Of course you do," I answered reassuringly. "Talent doesn't go away. Where can it go? You just have to find new ways of accessing it. New inspiration."

"I don't know . . . It's really not all that important to me anymore."

His first lie.

We talked a lot more about his work, and a little bit about mine; he was very complimentary about the hits I had been having and said he loved "Don't Cry Out Loud" and "Nobody Does It Better." He poured more wine. He started to tell me some story about his love of horses, and he got to the part about loving the backstretch, but it was a long and boring story, and I left my body somewhere when he began to explain that "a jockey's athleticism was greater pound for pound than any other athlete." All I noticed was how incredibly great the streaks of gray and white in his hair were. And he was pouring more wine, and I was lost in how handsome he was. Since reaching adulthood I hadn't been this physically attracted to any man.

"That's really fascinating," I said, thinking that maybe it was and I had just missed the fascinating part.

My first lie.

"You know, I'm not used to drinking," I half-apologized. "I take Dalmane to help me sleep at night, and I don't like to mix the two."

"That's amazing," he said. "I, uh, take Dalmane every night, too."

Amazing! I felt this warm glow in my heart. We were bonding.

"Where do you work now?" I asked.

"Well, I've got a piano at the apartment, and I still keep my little studio at my old house. When Angie is out of town, I stay there sometimes. You know, to be with Nikki."

"Oh," I said, not understanding. "You mean, you and Angie are friendly?"

"No, not exactly . . . in fact, uh . . . I don't think she likes me very much. But I try to be there for Nikki. I just want to be able to help her." He looked sad again. I already knew that I wanted to be able to help him help his daughter.

"Why don't we try to write a song this week?" I offered. "It would be a shame for you to waste all your great talent."

Burt modestly shrugged. "I don't know. Hey," he said softly, "do you know you're really, uh, [1, 2, 3] pretty?" Then, as I leaned in, he added, "Boy, am I tired. I've kept you up much too late. I better, I . . . I better, uh, let you get some sleep." We left the restaurant and he drove me home. He walked me to my door.

"I'll call you this week," he said, smiling. "We can have another dinner and maybe try to write that song." He leaned forward and kissed me. I liked it fine. Not the greatest first kiss ever, a little stingy, but good . . . sort of.

Closing the door behind me, I knew that on this night, with many options to choose from, against my better judgment, I had already selected Mr. Green Lincoln, with his little-boy tee shirts, his sad look, and his dependence on sleeping pills, to be the great fake love of my life.

BURT CALLED THE NEXT day to see if I wanted to try and write a song.

"Yeah, let's try," I said. "If you come around noon, Digby could make us lunch." Digby was my everything guy. He took care of the house, kept it clean, and cooked. I had no way of knowing if he really was a very good cook. He was paid to go grocery shopping and buy unsalted almonds, low-calorie bread, all sorts of lettuce, a few fruits, a few cans of tuna fish, and an assortment of healthy grains like quinoa and brown rice, and an occasional sweet potato.

Burt arrived about forty-five minutes late. He apologized. It didn't matter. He was there.

He looked around and, with two comfy overstuffed sofas on one side of him and an equally welcoming large dark brown leather banquette on the other, he sat right down on the baby grand piano bench.

"Hey, babe," he said as he was trying out the keyboard that, thank God, had been recently tuned. "Nice piano. Come sit over here," he said in his breathy, gravelly voice. He tapped the piano bench and motioned for me to sit down. In the light of day his eyes were a deep sky blue. God, he was handsome.

"Do you know who Marty Kroft is?" I asked him.

"Yeah, I know Marty and his brother, Sid. They do those children's shows with those big wild-looking puppets."

"Yes. Well, Marty wants me to write something for his movie *Middle Age Crazy*, starring Ann-Margret. He needs a song about a marriage growing stale for a husband turning forty, in the throes of a midlife crisis. Do you want to try?"

"Sure, let's try."

Burt started to play piano with his signature odd rhythms, and I struggled to understand his unusual musical phrasing. He played something he liked. I couldn't quite keep hold of it in my head. "Could you play that again?" I said. "I need to hear it a few more times to find some words that fit."

He played it again. As he liked his melody more and more, he played it louder and seemed to get lost in it. He was playing it for about ten minutes while I sat with my yellow legal pad and pencil trying different words—just writing them down, not saying any of them out loud yet. Burt's melodies were more complicated than I was used to. I felt like they gave me very little room to fit enough words in to say something.

I think he might have been startled when I finally said, "What about . . ."

Hey you, Where did the time go?
Never saw it passing by me
You knew how to occupy me.

It was like doing a *New York Times* crossword puzzle, and not just any one but the Saturday one, the hardest of the week. My words had to fit exactly into the melody Burt kept playing.

I shyly put my few sentences on the music rack so he could see them. He read them, and then tried singing my words to his melody.

"Hey, uh . . . This is great. Wow," he said, nodding his head up and down like he'd just made a discovery. "You are really good . . . really good. I like that. Very good!" He was smiling at me, and I was glad I was pleasing him, and so very relieved that I had found a way to squeeze my lyrics into the small windows of his staccato beats. It was like playing jump rope as a kid. The beat of the rope does not change as it hits the pavement; you just have to find a way in. Burt's melodies were locked. Unchangeable. My lyrics had to adapt themselves to unusual rhythmic phrasings.

After working for two hours straight, Burt said, "Hey, I'm, uh, kind of hungry. Do you think your guy could make us some lunch?"

"Oh, sure," I said, calling Digby into the room. "What would you like to eat?"

"Oh, I like hummus, do you have, um, hummus, and a few carrots you could cut up with it?" Digby wasn't going to write it down, but when he saw Burt was still talking, he pulled out his little pad. "And, uh, do you have any fresh turkey?" That sexy voice could make ordering food sound exciting.

"Yes, I do, Mr. Bacharach."

"Um, and do you have any multigrained bread that you could lightly toast for me?" Digby nodded.

"And . . . and if you could put a little mustard, and a little mayo on the toast and some nice lettuce and tomato, I could have a sandwich. [*Beat*] And do you have any almonds?"

Digby nodded again.

"Can I get twelve of those, please, Digby?"

He looked at me. "A dozen almonds every day," he said. "Very important, very good for you . . ."

He trailed off without ever explaining the benefits of daily almond intake.

Wondering about their caloric content and having no idea what good they might do me, but feeling the need to catch up to Burt's level of health, I told Digby, "Okay, I'll take six with my rice cake. And you can put a little tuna on it. Without mayonnaise. And a Diet Coke." I noticed Digby put away his pad before I ordered. This same boring lunch order was now on its third month. Occasionally, if I was feeling crazy, it switched to lean turkey with tomato. But Burt hadn't quite finished yet.

"And some bottled water, Digby. Room temperature, please." And to me, "Have to hydrate. You don't want to surprise it that way. And you should get rid of those Diet Cokes. Nothing fake."

I was starting to feel like Marvin and I, or Peter and I, or even Melissa and I once she finished her tea, could have written a whole song in the time that it took Burt to order his lunch. And that was just the beginning. Next came the eating. He sat down and very slowly savored his late-afternoon meal. I would come to learn this was a quickie compared to his complex breakfasts. Not one to linger over crumbs from a tasteless rice cake, my lunch was finished in six minutes and that was stretching it.

By the time we finished "Where Did the Time Go" two days later, I felt like I had run a marathon. I had a renewed respect for Hal David, Burt's lyricist for many years, for his remarkable ability to find words that fit Burt's syncopated melodies and make them seem so effortless when in fact they were anything but. I barely knew him, but I so enjoyed studying his face and listening to his sexy voice that I didn't care that this song took about fifteen times longer to complete than any song I'd ever written. Marty Kroft was happy with it, so I called Richard Perry. He was producing the Pointer Sisters and told us to come down and play it for him.

Burt's name, even in his hit-free period, still commanded extraordinary respect, even awe. This was a man who'd had more than fifty Top Forty hits in the Sixties. He was an iconic songwriter. "Raindrops Keep Fallin' on My Head," "What the World Needs Now Is Love," "(They Long to Be) Close to You," "This Guy's in Love with You," and for Dionne Warwick, "Always Something There to Remind Me," "The Look of Love," "Alfie," "A House

Is Not a Home," "Do You Know the Way to San Jose," "Walk On By," and so many others had made Burt a household name. So much so that CBS gave him his own television specials in the early Seventies. Burt was movie-star handsome in a laid-back California way, with a lazy, ready smile, and audiences loved seeing him on their TV screens.

Richard listened to the song and said he would produce it with the Pointers and put it on their record and in the movie. Professionally, at least, we were off to a very good start.

Burt and I continued to see each other. One Friday night I was invited to dinner at my friends Joyce and Neil Bogart's home. Neil had founded Casablanca Records and his roster included Donna Summer and the Village People. Burt joined me, and at the party, we sat down and sang a few songs together. Neil loved what he heard and was excited by the picture of the two of us together.

Polygram had just bought up Casablanca Records, and Neil got the idea that Burt and I should make a record together for the new label he was forming, Boardwalk Records. We would write all the songs, I would sing, and Burt would do all the orchestrations and the production. Neil had the concept of one song flowing into the next without ever stopping musically. He fell in love with his own idea and believed we would have a huge hit if we could deliver the romantically themed, intimate record that he envisioned. At his urging, we agreed to try.

Twenty

I THINK ONE OF the reasons Burt stopped having hits was because he was spending so much of his time performing instead of writing. He called me from the Diplomat Hotel in Miami Beach, where he was wrapping up a weeklong stand, to ask if I wanted to come down to his beach house in Del Mar for the weekend. By Friday I was a bag of nerves. We hadn't yet slept together and we'd be together all weekend long. What would I wear to sleep in? Would I take off all of my makeup at bedtime or just some? How would I fare compared to Angie? The answer was, I wouldn't. When he chose me, he was definitely going another way.

I drove down to Del Mar, and Burt greeted me warmly. Showing me around his small, simply furnished home and the wide sandy beach outside its door, he seemed genuinely happy to see me. He said, "Come here, babe," embraced me and deftly guided me to his piano bench. *Oh*, I thought, *maybe he likes to make love at the piano. That could be really sexy.*

He sat down and pulled me down next to him.

"Sit right here." He kissed me. "I've been waiting for this all day."

"Oh," I cooed, "that makes me so happy."

"I've been waiting *all day*," he said again, "to play you this." He turned to his piano and dove into a melody.

I felt a pang of disappointment. I listened and wasn't impressed, but clearly he was. He was radiant when he turned toward me, put his arm around me, and whispered in my ear, "What do you think, baby?"

At this moment pleasing him meant more to me than making the song better. "I think it's good," I said, "but I need to hear it again."

I could feel his excitement. Maybe not about me but about this melody he thought was so great. The closer he sat next to me on the bench and the more I could smell his aftershave, the more the melody was growing on me.

"I do like this, Burt. It's actually . . . really good."

"So now let's put some great Carole Bayer Sager lyrics on this great melody."

"Now, Burt? You want me to do this now? I haven't even unpacked yet."

"Oh, that can wait. We're on a roll."

Three hours later, with the sun having gone down unobserved behind us, I had finished three-quarters of the lyrics to "I Won't Break," though I was still struggling for the verse. I had a few false starts because he refused to alter his melody to accommodate a few extra words. He was very clear. His way was better.

Finally, I said, "Please turn the radio up loud / Make it feel like there's a crowd."

"Good," he said. "Get rid of the 'please.' Just: Turn the radio up loud / Make it feel like there's a crowd . . ."

"Sure, fine."

He played it again, and again. Then he stopped. "What did you just say?" he asked.

"Nothing," I said apologetically. "That was just my stomach growling."

"Oh, babe, are you hungry?"

"Yeah. I think I am. I forgot to eat lunch."

"Well, I've got to get you something to eat."

How considerate he was, I thought. He got up and came back from the kitchen with a shiny red apple.

"Here," he said. "This'll hold you. Let's just spend another twenty

minutes here. Then I'll work out, uh, take a shower, and then I'll take you to
my favorite restaurant in Del Mar. You're going to love it. Great fish. How's
that sound?"

"Will it still be open?" I asked.

"You're funny," he said. He leaned over and kissed me softly on my lips,
then said, "I want to go back and get that verse melody right. It's still not
sounding the way I want."

Between the apple and the kiss, I was good for three more hours until he
finally made good on his promise for dinner. It was nine when we left for the
Fish House. Burt drank a bottle of wine that he thought he shared with me.
(Not being a drinker, I nursed my one glass as he went through the rest of the
bottle.) Starving as I was, I picked at a salad, trying to not gain one additional
ounce before our first sexual encounter.

"Great food here, huh?" Was he making a joke? He must have noticed
that real food was absent from my plate. We ate our dinner slo-o-w-wly—at
least Burt did, because he was also telling me a detailed story about the time
he conducted for Marlene Dietrich and she got hit on the head with a ball from
a juggler who was her opening act. I didn't follow the next part of his story
because I was starting to feel a little "gassy" from the afternoon apple and now
the raw salad, and I was getting anxious that the night could turn out to be a
total disaster.

Back at Burt's house, though he had worked out before dinner, he
wanted to go for an after-dinner walk to burn off some of those calories because he was told it's healthy to take a walk after dinner. When we finally
came in for the night, I was feeling tired and bloated as he grabbed me in his
arms the way I'd longed for him to when I arrived twelve hours earlier, and
finally deposited me on his bed.

"Listen to those ocean waves, baby. I'm uh, just gonna get myself ready."

"Ready? Should I get myself ready, too?" I asked, not knowing exactly
what that meant.

"Uh. Sure, babe."

While he was in the bathroom I quickly unpacked my things and put on a pretty cotton nightgown (so it wouldn't look like I was trying too hard to be someone I wasn't) and got in bed and waited. And waited. I had no idea what was keeping him in the bathroom so long and felt it would be too invasive for me to ask. All I know is I had more than ample time to position and reposition my body in what I hoped was an alluring pose as I listened to the waves, which were making me a little seasick.

Finally, he came out of the bathroom in his boxer shorts—showing off muscular legs that matched his former wife's in beauty—and some much-worn, torn tee shirt covering a chest that might have stored three or four extra pounds.

He got into bed.

"Come here," he said, pulling me close.

I loved the sound of his voice and the way he smelled as he made love to me. It didn't last as long as dinner, and not even close to our writing session, but he was kind and affectionate and I felt desired, and grateful that the first time was over and the lights weren't on.

He had taken his Dalmane before he even got into bed, so clearly it was not to be a long night of lovemaking. Before I knew it, he was fast asleep and I was left listening to the ocean outside competing with his sleep machine, which emitted a kind of white ambient noise that made its own steady counterpoint to his light snoring. Everything about this man was musical: the syncopated rhythm of the waves against his snores, over the white noise, sounded like a contemporary symphony that he'd written. I looked at him sleeping and admired the beauty of him and the more I did this, the more the illusion of Burt became real.

At breakfast, which I happily served him after he walked me through the composition of his morning meal, I watched him eat his yogurt, his toast, his mixed fruit, his cereal, his three almonds, and coffee. After finishing my protein drink, I picked up my camera and began taking pictures of him.

"You are so handsome," I said, looking at him through my viewfinder.

"Hey, baby, you should have seen me ten years ago." He smiled that lazy smile and I clicked the shutter.

•   •   •

I WANTED TO MEET Burt's daughter because I knew he wanted me to. Angie agreed that Nikki could spend Saturday at my home on Donhill Drive.

Thirteen years old when I met her in late 1980, Nikki had been born more than three months premature and as a result, her eyes had not developed properly. She had strabismus, a condition where the eyes turn inward, and she could only use one eye at a time. She had to endure three surgeries on them and spent the first three months of her life in an incubator, back when parents and nurses weren't even allowed to hold their preemies in their arms. Burt told me she was "never normal—how could she be with a start like that?" She was so attached to Angie that when Burt would return home after even a short concert tour, Nikki would scream and cry because she didn't want to be kicked out of her mother's bed.

On our first afternoon together, Nikki immediately asked where she could put on her full-length black wetsuit to swim in our pool. I told her my heated pool was very warm and just a bathing suit would do, but she refused to get in the water without her wetsuit. I knew the moment I met her something was off. Angie had insisted that I sit at the pool and watch her swim. I didn't fully understand her demand, since Nikki was taller and larger than me. Not knowing nearly enough, I felt as Burt did: Angie was enabling her to the point of keeping her infantile.

Nikki was pretty in a boyish way. She had beautiful blondish hair, blue eyes, and a lovely smile. I felt sad when I noticed her eyes struggling to focus. When we had lunch, she dominated the meal with one subject: Steve Perry, the lead singer of the group Journey, and his "extraordinarily beautiful" voice. Just as Burt's every utterance was musical, Nikki's was flat, lacking affect. She told me that Angie was going to take her to Tahiti so she could sit on the beach, watch the waves with her Walkman on, and listen all day to Perry's magnificent voice coming into her headphones as the waves danced. This was not conversation, even as a teenager would define it. It was more like a soliloquy from someone who needed to shut out the world that wanted to come in.

I was exhausted by her monomania, and after she went home Burt asked me how we could help her become more socialized. I said I thought we could start by meeting her doctor in LA and possibly increasing her therapy sessions to three times a week. After less than a month, the doctor told us she needed more help than he could provide.

Nikki loved her pet rat, and she brought it with her on a visit to the beach house. In the morning we found the rat dead, having been thrown against the living room wall. I was shocked and bewildered. There was no explanation for it, just as there was none for Nikki. It has been said that parents are as happy as their least happy child, and I felt the sadness that lay beneath the surface when Burt, whose mother had burdened him at a young age with the nickname "Happy," thought of Nikki.

BURT AND I WERE spending almost all of our time together, enjoying each other more with every week that went by. The next few months were a whirlwind of good work, good food (for him), and good wine (also for him). I was falling more and more in love with the fantasy I was creating of him.

So I was thrilled when he suggested he move in with me. I didn't mind that he wanted to keep his one-bedroom apartment at the Wilshire Comstock because both of us needed to see how this was going to work. A few days later, we were having lunch in Malibu and on the way back home Burt asked if I minded if we stopped at his apartment to pick up some sheet music. I was happy for the opportunity to see where he had been living.

The first thing I saw on walking in was his upright piano against the wall, with lots of sheet music sprawled on the floor and a small, ugly gold sofa against the other wall. That was it. It looked like a space used to store some stuff by someone who didn't live there. Burt went into the bedroom to pack a few things. I peeked in and saw a bed and a small dresser that looked like it had been assembled upon its arrival from a mail-order catalog. Could this really be his apartment? It had to be temporary, I thought, although at three years, it was giving off a disquieting aura of permanence.

While I was browsing through his sheet music, I was surprised to find a series of slides scattered around and beneath the piano. I held a few up to the light and was surprised by the sight of various alluring poses of a naked, full-breasted woman, with a phone number on the slides. *Oh, no*, I thought, *there's someone else.*

"Hey, Burt," I called.

He came out of the bedroom.

"What's up with these?" I asked. "Is there something I should know?"

"Oh," he laughed. "No. I, uh, get these all the time, from crazy fans."

"But look," I said, "this one left her phone number."

"Yeah," he answered, "but I would never call her."

Marvin never got anything like this, I thought, *or if he did he had the good sense to put it away.*

Back in the car, the whole thing started to replay in my mind. I could understand him getting sexy fan mail, and I could understand women wanting him, because I wanted him, too. But why hadn't these things been thrown in the trash? Why did he keep them? I started to worry and I asked the question I didn't want the answer to. "So, Burt, do you have a thing for big-breasted women?"

"What guy wouldn't?" he said enthusiastically.

"Well, I saw those photos and I was thinking . . . I'm not that. You know . . . chesty."

"Funny you should say that. When I took Nikki home last week I was talking to Angie and she was saying how beautiful she thought you were, and I told her, 'I must really be in love with her because she doesn't even have big breasts.'"

"Oh." I wasn't sure if that was a compliment or not, or how that might have sounded to his ex-wife, but I chose to focus on the "I must really be in love with her" part.

He loved me. He even told Angie. And he moved in with me.

Twenty-One

MICHAEL MASSER, ONCE AN attorney and now a hit songwriter ("The Greatest Love of All" for Whitney Houston, among dozens of others), tracked me down to write a lyric to his prewritten melody for the movie *It's My Turn*. Next to the still-new excitement of Burt, it seemed more like work I didn't feel like doing. Michael tried on more than one occasion to drop by and play it for me, but my head was just not there. I told him I was going to be in Del Mar for the week, and if he really wanted to, he could drive down and we could see what happened.

Within days he was standing in the living room of Burt's small home. After Burt said hello to him, and Michael sang his praises for the appropriate amount of time, Burt excused himself and told me he'd be out on the beach. Michael immediately situated himself on Burt's piano bench.

"Do you want something to drink?" I asked.

"Yes, please. I'd love an iced tea."

I looked at him. He was sort of cute, in an unorthodox kind of way. He had beautiful blue eyes and very blond hair that looked sun-bleached to me, and it fell on his face in a Little Lord Fauntleroy fashion, sort of like someone put a bowl over his head and cut around it. He wore a blue and green horizontally striped tee shirt and a pair of jeans. Eyeballing him, I guessed he was about twelve pounds overweight, and vertical lines might have been a better wardrobe choice.

"And could I also get a glass of water with that? . . . And, if you really wouldn't mind, a cup of coffee."

Okay, I thought. *This one's a crazy one*. I set off to bring him his three drinks.

Back at the piano he began to play the melody for me. I listened. "Michael," I interrupted, "is there any way you could play it a little less loud for me? It's kind of hurting my ear."

"Oh, sure. Let me start again."

He played it exactly the same, though I did make out what I thought to be a very pretty melody inside the piano that was being hammered so hard I wondered if a metal string inside could pop off like it might on a guitar.

"That's pretty," I said, meaning it.

"So are you," he said, smiling an almost too-big smile. "I know this is a hit. I even hear where the title goes." He began to play, and when he got to the chorus, he began to sing, if you want to call it that: "It's my turn, da-da da-da da-da," and he kept da-da-ing until he got to sing the title line again: "It's my turn, it's my turn." He was now singing so loud he almost drowned out his already deafening piano playing. However, I couldn't deny his talent. This ex-lawyer churned out hit after hit for Diana Ross, including "Touch Me in the Morning" and "Theme from *Mahogany*," and this could wind up being a single for her as well.

"Let me hear it from the beginning, Michael. Maybe I can start to write it." I quickly wrote words that were actually meaningful to me, and to my life as I felt it at that time:

It's my turn
To see what I can see
I hope you'll understand
This time's just for me
Because it's my turn
With no apologies
I've given up the truth
To those I've tried to please

They were simple but they fit his melody perfectly and as soon as I began to sing it, even with my limited voice, I really started to like it. Michael was so thrilled that he was finally getting a lyric on this melody that he'd already labeled a masterpiece that he was drinking his coffee and tea almost simultaneously and washing it down with his water.

"This is going to be a big hit," he said, smiling at me. What I admired was the confidence that poured out of him. How was he so sure? I'd not yet worked with anyone who was so certain of a song that was still unfinished.

"Okay, let's keep going," I said. And maybe because I did like it, or maybe because I just wanted to get back to Burt, I finished the lyric that afternoon. When Michael left, he gave me a kiss on the cheek and said, "I'm going to play this for Diana. You'll see. You'll be glad I came down here. We just wrote a hit." And indeed we had.

BURT'S PUBLICIST TOLD HIM that Michael Jackson wanted to have dinner with us.

I had met Michael in 1979 when he was not yet twenty-one years old. He was a few years away from becoming the King of Pop, but he was already a genius. *Off the Wall*, the first album of the brilliant trilogy produced by music legend Quincy Jones, spawned four huge hits. I was thrilled to have a song on that record. Quincy had heard "It's the Falling in Love," which I wrote with David Foster on my second album, and suggested that Michael record it.

The four of us went to Dominick's, an industry steak house.

Michael spoke in a high breathy voice, soft and gentle and melodic. There was something very childlike about him, but he had, even at his age, an encyclopedic knowledge about the songs, writers, and artists that had come before him, including all of Burt's.

"What are you up to these days?" he asked me. "Are you writing?"

"I'm making a record with Burt. He's producing, I'm singing, and he's doing all the orchestrations," I answered proudly.

"That sounds so nice," he said, smiling. His voice always went up at the end of sentences. "I would love to come by and hear what you guys are doing."

"You're welcome anytime, Michael," I said. "We're in the studio every afternoon. The Record Plant."

When he came by, I was recording a song called "Just Friends." He listened for a while, then asked, "Do you mind if I play around with something?" We didn't mind at all—Burt admired him as much as I did, which was saying something. Michael took Paul Jackson, a wonderful guitarist who was playing guitar on the session, into the bathroom with him to work on another concept of the track and came back with a totally different arrangement with a whole new feel that even Burt said was better than what he had done. Somehow I got up the courage to ask him if he would sing with me on the record.

"Sure," he said, "let's do it. Let's work it out. Let me hear you sing it." We started to trade lines, and he built some background parts where he was doubling his own voice to give it more thickness and texture in the musical track. I was thrilled. Michael Jackson and I were singing together. It was mind-blowing to me.

WE'D BEEN DATING FOR four months when Burt gave me his first gift, and I use the word *gift* very loosely: a pair of framed photographs for my thirty-fifth birthday. One was a photo of a racehorse. He admired their beauty and owned a number of thoroughbreds that he would race from time to time.

"Look at those legs, baby," he almost whispered to me as I looked, puzzled, at the photo. "Beautiful, huh? Look at those fragile legs holding up the weight of this big fuckin' horse."

The second photo was of a sexy woman's legs crossed in a provocative manner.

All I saw was his worship of the long-legged beauties that, at five foot one, I could never be. He didn't mean to be hurtful. He was just oblivious to the effect of his actions.

One night we were going out to dinner and I came downstairs in a little skirt and a pretty white shirt. Burt kind of stared at me and said, "Hey, you know, I think, uh . . . I think . . . you look better in pants." I stood there semi-stunned, my fragile-at-best self-image melting as he went on, "You know, longer. More . . . lengthy. Taller."

That was it. It only took one remark, from someone I wanted to love me, for me to cover a body part for the rest of my life. I went back up and changed into my jeans, and every skirt and every dress I ever owned hung in my closet, some with price tags still on them, from that night on.

He did like my eyes. He would often tell me how striking they were, especially when the sunlight was shining in them. When I would go on a talk show of any kind with him, he would tell the cameraman to make sure the light caught my eyes.

I was learning something here. It should have been to get the hell out of this relationship as fast as my short little legs could possibly carry me, but instead my lesson was to accentuate the positive and change whatever else I could.

First on my list: height.

My friend Dolly Parton, also vertically challenged, told me about a man named Pasquale Di Fabrizio, "shoemaker to the stars," whose shop made custom shoes for celebrities.

Inside his foot palace, shoeboxes were piled high against three walls, with famous names on every box: Sylvester Stallone, Judy Garland, Richard Gere, Liza Minnelli, Burt Reynolds, etc. Mr. Di Fabrizio gave stars a lift—literally. He once bragged to me in his Italian accent, "I am-a Burt Reynolds! I gave him two extra inches plus a third secretly built inside the shoe. You see nothing. He is a sex symbol, and it is all me. I even put the lifts in his bedroom slippers."

I was happy to have Pasquale solve my height challenge, though I realized that any of his future clients might be told how short I actually was. He measured my feet on tracing paper, made a mold, and then made the shoe. He gave me four and a half inches, and I happily joined his wall of stars with my name on a shoebox next to Debbie Reynolds.

Next: curves, in the form of breast implants. I never minded that I was basically flat-chested. I thought it had a kind of androgynous sexiness to it, but Burt was a breast man. Dr. Harry Glassman made them perfectly for me, small but very attractive. Suddenly my tee shirts were looking perky and alluring.

Finally, my eyes. He liked them? Well, let him like them even more. Let's get rid of those puffy bags underneath them. My second surgery was as effective as the first.

Burt never disagreed with anything I ever considered doing. He never said, "Why would you do a thing like that? You're beautiful as you are!" but rather "Hey, baby, that might be great." It was always only a little "fix," but that's what I was discovering it was all about. Little fixes. Nothing big, nothing obvious, just a tiny baby tweak to alter just a bit of the way I was born—a shot of collagen here, a bit of Botox there.

I never had to own that it was also about my own vanity. I was just trying to look like I belonged with Burt. He was my Hubbell, my Robert Redford in *The Way We Were*.

Twenty-Two

SO, WE WERE WRITING together, and now we were living together. My friend Arnold Stiefel, who was then at ICM (and has managed Rod Stewart since the mid-Eighties), thought that getting Burt a movie to score would be the best way to kick-start his comeback, and he hit a home run in his first at bat. He came up with *Arthur*, starring Dudley Moore, Liza Minnelli (Peter Allen's ex), and John Gielgud.

The director wanted a song to play over the opening scene, which is a songwriter's dream, because when it plays over the end credits, half the audience is already walking out. Burt and I watched the scene over and over on a small monitor in our living room. He was trying out lots of melody ideas as I was trying to think of words that felt right for the scene. In my mind I kept hearing the words to a not very good song that I had written years earlier with Peter Allen called "The Moon and New York City."

The title came from one night when Peter was flying to New York from LA, and his plane got stuck in a holding pattern, circling around and around. He pulled out his notebook and wrote, "When you get caught between the moon and New York City, you might as well fall in love." We wrote the song and, not long after, filed it under "things that will never get recorded because they really weren't good enough." The lyric was better than the melody, which had no hook at all, and we never put in the time to rework the song.

I said to Burt, "There's an unpublished song I wrote with Peter Allen that I keep hearing a part of whenever I watch Arthur drive around the city in his limousine." I told him the line, and it inspired him to write a melody for it. "When you get caught between the moon and New York City . . ." I added another line from the original—"I know it's crazy but it's true"—which led Burt to another musical line, and very soon—for him, certainly—he had the whole chorus melody finished. All I did was add "The best that you can do, the best that you can do, is fall in love."

"You know, Burt," I said, "I'm going to have to call Peter and ask him if it's okay with him to use this lyric."

"Why?" he asked. "It was from an unpublished song, and it's your lyric."

I explained that it was actually Peter's line and related the story.

"Well, call him," he said, "but, uh, I'm sure he's going to say just use it. He's not going to want credit for one line."

"Of course I want credit," Peter said when I called him. "For a song that could win an Oscar?" His position seemed fair to me. I mean, it was going to be the beginning of the chorus, heard more than any other line in the song. I'd have wanted credit, too. I suggested he come and help write the rest of the song with us. He agreed but said he couldn't come for another week. Within two days, Burt had found his way to the verse melody, and I'd written the first verse. All I needed to do was find an original way to serve the film— without, in this case, ever getting ahead of the story, since the song would play over the opening credits.

Meanwhile, Christopher Cross had just won five Grammy awards for his debut album and Warner Bros. wanted him to sing our song. He came over and we played it for him. He loved it but wanted to hear the second verse. Since we didn't have those lyrics yet, he and I wrote them in what seemed like a minute, and the whole song was finished in that same afternoon.

Well, of course, he deserved a writing credit, too. Burt could understand Christopher's claim, but he was still resentful of Peter, who never had a chance to come up and collaborate. I pointed out that his was far more than an incidental line. Even though we called the song "Arthur's Theme (Best

That You Can Do)," I told Burt, "To many, it will be known as 'The Moon and New York City.' "

So when Bette Midler, reading off the nominees at the 1982 Academy Awards, got to our song, she announced, " 'Arthur's Theme,' also known as 'The Best That You Can Do,' or that song about the Moon and New York City, or, as I call it, 'four on a song.' " It was unusual to have four writers collaborating on one song. Moments later, she opened the envelope, read off our four names, and we all stormed the stage.

Of course I would have preferred it if Burt and I were up there alone, but it was still a thrilling night. The unfortunate outcome was that Burt's resentment put a temporary wedge in my relationship with Peter.

WHEN I ASKED BURT if we were ever going to get married he said, "If we win the Oscar, we'll get married."

This was not exactly getting down on one knee with a ring! What was I pretending not to know here? The question of whether Burt was with me because he was wildly in love with me or because I was his muse was answered that night. But I was not looking to hear or know that then.

Burt told his mother that he was thinking of marrying me, and her response was "But she's Jewish." An odd thing for a Jewish lady to say, but then her son was surprised himself that he was with me. Burt didn't identify as Jewish.

We had finished our record for Neil Bogart, but before it was released he was diagnosed with cancer. He was not going to recover. Frail as he was, he and his wife, Joyce, still wanted to give us the wedding in their home. Burt didn't want a big wedding, and I was just so happy we were getting married after being together for more than a year that I didn't mind. Nor did I object, I'm ashamed to say, when he excluded my mother from the ceremony even though she was in town for the Oscars.

"Let's just keep it very small," he said, meaning just us, the Bogarts, and Neil and Marcia Diamond. I was so determined to not have anything spoil this night or our chances together that I agreed to keep my mother off the intimate guest list. "We can go by her hotel afterward," he said, "and have a drink with her in the Polo Lounge." Burt even acknowledges in *his* memoir that "It was not a nice thing to do for someone who is basically a nice guy. But it was like, if I'm marrying you, I don't have to have your mother there, do I?"

The judge who was marrying us asked Burt, "Do you take this woman to be your lawful wedded wife, in sickness and in health, till death do you part?"

Burt said, "I'll try."

Neil Diamond, in complete shock, blurted out, "Holy shit!" He often said that Burt became his hero at that moment. Me, I never even heard it. I just knew we were getting married, so I didn't react at all to his curious way of saying "I do." True to form, Burt was keeping that one foot out, even when he was in.

A wonderful photorealist, Jack Mendenhall, painted a portrait of us a few years after the wedding in which I'm looking straight ahead and Burt is positioned with one foot out the door to our veranda, looking away. Prophetic, no? After our divorce I immediately donated the painting to the Songwriters Hall of Fame while Hal David was still president. Why was I not surprised years later to hear that no one at the SHOF could even find it? Hal probably trashed it. He hardly got enough recognition for all of *his* great lyrics with Burt, so why would he want a big painting of his ex and me staring him in the face?

When our album *Sometimes Late at Night* was finally released, a few of my friends teased me because they said it sounded like Michael Jackson was trying to sound like me on our duet, "Just Friends." Just what I wanted: Michael sounding like me. From that day on, as Michael's popularity continued to grow until he was the biggest artist of his time, whenever I saw him, I would say, "You'd better be very nice to me, Michael, or I might just put our duet out as my next single," and he'd always laugh.

Neil Bogart wanted Burt and me to go around the country on what he called "The Living Room Tour." He wanted us to re-create for an audience the intimacy he felt when we first sang for him in his living room, and he didn't seem to care about the expense. He had his vision. So we flew from city to city with three background singers and a first-rate LA band, losing money in small clubs while touring as though we were playing large theaters. But then, the record we were promoting hardly sounded intimate. On most of it, I am drowning in Burt Bacharach orchestrations that were suitable for Dionne Warwick, not for me and my small voice.

You haven't truly traveled until you've traveled with a narcissist. Enjoy the thrill of catching planes one minute before takeoff—he liked the rush of it, and being a star, he hoped they might hold the flight for him. I just wanted to know I had my makeup and enough sleeping meds for the trip.

Pretty soon I no longer had any me time, there was just Burt time. And I, like he, was now late for everything.

MANY NIGHTS BURT AND I would talk about Nikki and what we might be doing to help her more. I so wanted to have a loving relationship with her, but it was more difficult than I thought it would be.

After months of therapy that seemed to be accomplishing nothing, we tried a clinic in the city of Brea. I knew in a matter of weeks that it was the wrong place for her. The children there were out of control with behavioral issues that bore no resemblance to Nikki's. A doctor in Los Angeles told us about the Wilson Center in Minnesota. They were fully accredited and had psychiatrists on staff to work with the emotional problems of adolescents.

Nikki was now sixteen. Burt and I were hopeful that these professionals would help her to grow out of some of the obsessions and phobias that dogged her and made it so difficult for her to have friends or an abiding relationship with anyone but her mother. It must have been so challenging for Angie to have her at home all the time, but she was against sending her to the Wilson Center. I think she intuitively—and, as it turned out, correctly—felt that Nikki belonged with her and there was no "curing" her.

Reluctantly, though, she acquiesced to Burt's plan after he threatened to have Nikki's therapists testify that she needed more intensive treatment than she could receive at home. Angie thought Burt didn't love Nikki because she wasn't perfect. I think Burt loved Nikki as much as he was capable of loving anyone.

Though the doctors in Minnesota sent us reports that she was doing better, when we would visit her, it seemed like nothing was changing at all. The only thing that was growing was her anger at us for keeping her away from her mom. The directors promised us that Nikki was beginning to make positive changes, and that we would be the last ones to see them because parents always are, and in any event it would take more time.

Nobody there ever said to us, "Hey, here's the truth. We can do therapy with her every day of the year, twice a day, and she's not going to get any better." They were earnestly trying to make Nikki capable of taking care of herself so, despite her pleading to get out of there, we agreed to give them more time with her.

ONE EVENING I WENT to a screening of Steven Spielberg's *E.T.* That strange creature, so alone, so ugly, transforms as the story progresses into a wise, big-hearted little being that everyone—in the movie itself as well as in the audience—falls in love with. When I returned home that night, I couldn't stop talking about *E.T.* I told Burt I would love to write a song called "Heartlight." Though the script never used that word to describe the little red heart beating in E.T.'s chest, I thought it would be a great title for a song about him.

Burt never ever asked me to write only with him. He said he totally expected me to continue to write with Peter or Bruce or anyone I had been working with. But having been so shell-shocked by Marvin's jealousy when I wrote with others while we were together, I assumed that Burt would respond the same way. Still, I would on occasion ask a third writer if he wanted to try a song with us, because Burt would tend to move along faster in the presence of a third person, and it was easier for me when someone else urged him to move on or even suggested a melodic change.

I had written a few songs with Neil Diamond for two of his prior albums, so I invited him to work with us on this song. We wrote most of it in Burt's New York apartment on East Fifty-Seventh Street. Once Burt got the verse melody, Neil swiftly came up with the chorus melody, and I had no trouble writing the lyrics because I was so emotionally invested in this little creature that inspired our song. We spent July 4, 1982, celebrating the completion of our song on a boat Neil chartered on the Hudson River.

"Heartlight" went to number 5 on the Hot 100, and stayed at Number One on the Adult Contemporary chart for weeks. It was Neil's biggest hit in years.

BURT WOULD SPEND HOURS searching for the perfect chord, trying it this way and that way, asking me which chord I liked better, until out of sheer self-defense or boredom I would say, "Okay, I like it that way." But it didn't really matter because he never truly cared what my opinion was. He just needed me there. I never understood why he had to have me in the room with him, but I think he just liked having a witness to his struggle as he created his melodies.

I had found, several songs back, that these marathon writing sessions were better endured with the help of a little marijuana. So, eventually grass became sort of a third writing partner, a regular occurrence in our creative process. Not a lot, just a hit or two, but enough to keep me content to sit in my chair listening to Burt's partial melodies over and over.

I felt compassion for what he needed to put himself through to birth his compositions, but I increasingly resented having to suffer with him for hours before he was even ready for me to work on a lyric. And when I would write words to the melody he'd finally settle on, we would have differences about that, too.

It wasn't easy being together all day every day. I didn't know another collaborator who was as territorial about his music as Burt: *This is mine, and that's yours, and don't cross over.* Maybe the truly great composers don't want their melodies tampered with by lyricists. Or maybe Burt was just very strict and controlling.

This was radically different from the way Marvin and I wrote. "That's it, done!" he would say in the same tempo as he said everything, prestissimo (very, very fast). "If you think it needs something else, I'm back in town next week and we'll look at it then." Marvin was so quick, it made *me* seem like Burt.

Nobody I ever worked with had a pace as slow as Burt's, and somehow, for me, that pace placed his work beyond criticism.

"What do you think of this?" he asked me one day, playing me something he'd been working on for several hours.

"What else have you got?" I asked insensitively.

He looked at me like I had just wounded him to his core. I would go on to hear about that moment more times than I'd like to remember.

"I'm sorry," I apologized. "I'm sorry. I should have realized how long this took you. I should have. I'm sorry. But it still wasn't that good, or I would have liked it and tried to write it."

"I probably would have had way less hits," he shot back, "if I was writing with you back then instead of Hal."

Twenty-Three

IN 1982, BURT AND I were chosen to write four songs for *Night Shift*, one of Ron Howard's earliest films. One of them was "That's What Friends Are For."

We began by working on the verse. Burt played, "Da, *dah*, da da da, da da da *dah*." I sang to that line, "I never thought I'd feel this *way*," and he said, "That's not what I played. I played, 'Da *dah*, da da da da da da *dah*.' Not just 'dah.' 'Da dah.' Nine notes, not eight. They're eighth notes, except for the triplet."

"Well, why can't you just drop the pickup note?" I asked.

"Because it's not as good." He was adamant. He played it again. "I want 'Da *dah*.' Can't you hear this?" He was getting annoyed. "Again. I want 'Da *dah*.'"

So finally I said, with a little built-up anger on my end as well at how dogmatic he could be, "Okay. All right!" I felt beaten down, and I said, with a little attitude, "Just sing 'And' first. '*And* I.'"

And he did. And he was happy. And the song now started, "And *I* never thought I'd feel this *way*." And I was wrong. When I first heard it playing on the radio I thought, *Shit! He was absolutely right. It* is *better with the pickup, that itty-bitty but crucial sixteenth note.* And I believe it's in those tiny details that his greatness lies.

I loved writing this song. I thought it was a perfect marriage of Burt's music and my lyrics, and in relation to whatever else we wrote, it took the least amount of time. I could never have foreseen that this song would one day become the anthem for a generation of young men, women, and children struck down by AIDS.

Rod Stewart recorded it as the closing theme in the film, but Warner Bros. thought the record was too soft to pull it off the soundtrack as a single for Rod, so it lay dormant for the next few years.

DIONNE WARWICK CAME BACK into Burt's life in 1984 after Aaron Spelling asked if Burt and I would consider writing a song for a new television series he had coming on the air called *Finder of Lost Love*—not exactly a title that screams "Hit!" for either a song or a TV show. And yet we said yes.

When we played it for Aaron, he loved it and asked Burt, "How do you feel about working with Dionne again? I think she's the one to record it." Burt said he needed to think about that because it had been years since they'd spoken to each other. They'd had a falling-out when Burt and Hal broke up their songwriting team after their highly publicized musical *Lost Horizon* failed miserably. Burt had begun to calculate how much time it took him to write and orchestrate each complicated piece of the score and decided this fifty-fifty thing with Hal was a crazy split. He was doing the lion's share of the work. I will make the assumption that Hal balked at the seventy-five/ twenty-five split that Burt offered to honor going forward.

Dionne—their very own diva—said, "But you guys have a deal to produce my records. I don't care that you can't work together. You have to, for me." When they failed to comply, Dionne sued Burt and Hal separately for their lack of services. The lawsuit was settled out of court. There was no way you could force two creative people to work together. That team was out of business.

It was funny that I was the one who urged Burt to call Dionne. The only experience I ever had with her—aside from enjoying her music—was when Burt and I played the Roxy in 1981 to promote *Sometimes Late at Night*. I opened the show with some of my own songs. I was stunned to see Dionne placed at a small table directly in front of the stage, and every time I looked in her direction her eyes were throwing daggers of hate at me. I could feel her rage spewing forth without even looking at her. Yet I did keep looking at her, like I was going to change her mind about me and she would suddenly love me.

Dionne didn't like me because she believed she and Burt always belonged together. Not necessarily romantically, but she definitely wanted to be the only woman in Burt's musical life. The fact that he had written an album with me for my less than perfect voice made her furious. Who was this interloper singing songs that should've been written for her?

She disliked me before she ever said hello. Still I pushed him to call her, and ultimately she did sing the song.

> *Finder of lost love, it's never too late to find love*
> *Put the past behind you, keep your heart open*

In the studio, I treated Dionne with all the respect that someone of her talent deserved. But I didn't really like her. She was haughty. There was an air of entitlement about her that said, "Back up, the only one I care about in this room is Burt."

And to add insult to injury, I had unintentionally pushed myself out of a job, setting up what would be years of their touring together after they "put the past behind them." The agents who had been booking Burt and me much preferred the package of a reunited Burt and Dionne—now, *there* was something they could sell—so I inadvertently ended the short performing career of Carole and Burt.

WITH PERFORMING BEHIND ME, I told Burt I would like us to have a baby. At thirty-eight years old I felt like if I missed this opportunity I would regret it when it would be too late, and I had this picture of us loving our baby together and becoming a family, something more than just the two of us.

I was trying to get pregnant but not succeeding, and so we also registered with an adoption agency in Beverly Hills. I know Burt was hesitant about having a baby, even though he wanted to, particularly for me, because I had yet to have one, but he was ambivalent because Nikki still had so many problems. He didn't know how she would react to having a sister or brother.

The months went by until one morning I got a call from our lady in Los Angeles who had completed her screening of us.

"Carole, this is Mrs. Mintz. We have a beautiful baby boy for you if you and Burt still want him."

Did we want him? Of course we wanted him. He was three days old, and the next day, his fourth day on earth, I fearlessly flew to Nevada to bring him home. That night, when I returned home with our baby in my arms, Burt stood in the doorway crying. "Happy" was happy.

Cristopher Elton Bacharach was born on December 2, 1985. He was a beautiful baby. He had these piercing blue eyes that looked so wise to me that I was sure he was an "old soul."

I was very deliberate in encouraging Burt to have his own bonding time with Cristopher so that he would feel toward him the way I already did. And it worked. Burt would take Cris for a walk each day wearing a baby halter, talking with him and enjoying his time with him. It was a wonderful time. We were a family. And I was learning how to be a mother. I was changing diapers and rocking Cristopher in my arms for hours, singing to him.

He was so beautiful, so pure. The idea of being in a marijuana-induced altered state felt all wrong to me. I tossed out my grass and didn't use it again for years. Holding my baby in my arms, I was overwhelmed with a feeling of love I had never known. His future was unwritten, and I could be the one to help write it by loving him unconditionally and giving to him what I never had.

Burt and I kept working every day in our music room above the garage, and in addition to all the other joys that came with having Cristopher, I now had a legitimate reason to escape at regular intervals: To check in with my baby boy. To feed him his lunch, to rock him in his cradle, to just let him know I was there and I loved him.

My life was finally perfect. I had a husband I loved, a baby who filled my heart with happiness, and the ability to be actively creative with the man I adored.

Twenty-four

ONE OF MY FAVORITE records of all time is LaBelle's "Lady Marmalade." When we heard that Richard Perry was planning to produce Patti LaBelle, we played him a song we'd written called "On My Own." I give Burt the credit for pushing me to write that song, because he had a belief in it that I did not share.

I didn't hear it as a hit melody, but Burt really did, and about once a week he'd say, "Hey, uh . . . you know that song I played you? . . . I, uh, keep hearin' it. I . . . I, uh, really think it's a hit. Wish you'd take a shot at it." Finally, just to appease him, I did. At least this time he already had the melody. He also had the title, "On My Own," and it was unusual for him to hear actual words to his melodies.

Every time he'd sing it for me, whatever he was playing on the keyboard made me think it was a Polynesian melody. I could imagine a group of female singers in native costumes, leis around their necks, swaying to Burt's tune. It didn't sound current, and it didn't sound like a hit. But as I started to write the lyric, I began to like it. For one thing, Burt's melody was, for once, spacious enough to give me room to say something.

Now I know what loving you cost
Now we're up to talking divorce
And we weren't even married

On my own, on my own now
One more time, by myself

Richard wanted to produce it with Patti, so we spent a number of days at Studio 55, the studio he built below his office on Melrose near Paramount. Richard wanted Burt to play keyboards and, like Burt, Richard did not move at record speed. He took many breaks, leaving Patti downstairs while he would attend to some other business upstairs.

Late afternoon on the second day, Richard told me he had tickets that night to see Harry Nilsson at the Greek Theatre. He asked if I thought it would bother Patti, who was planning to work into the night. I told him I thought it would bother her quite a bit. Unfazed, he told Patti he wouldn't be too long—he just needed to go upstairs and change and then drive to the Greek and hear Harry, and then he'd be right back. He didn't seem to register how unhappy she looked and, patterned scarf carefully wrapped to look carelessly wrapped around his neck, he waved good-bye. 'This shouldn't take long at all," he said, and was gone.

Patti looked at Burt and me and said, "Who's the star here? I'm supposed to sit here in this studio and wait for him to do my vocals? Who does he think he is? I've had it with him. Burt, you and Carole can do my vocals."

"Oh, I don't know, Patti," Burt said. "I don't want to step on Richard's feet."

"Maybe you didn't hear me," she said. "There is no more Richard. I'm not going to work with him again, so you can either do it with me or I'll find someone else." Ultimately, we produced the record.

Richard Perry was a great producer, but his weakness was his social life and his intense interest in fashion. He was the first person who introduced me to Maxfield, a West Hollywood clothing store that remains today a fixture of style, edge, and celebrity. Art Garfunkel once told me what he said to Richard after they completed a record together: "Richard, I would work with you again if just once while we were making the record I could have seen the smile you had on your face when you were trying on jackets at Maxfield's."

My biggest contribution to the production of "On My Own" was pressing Burt to make it into a duet because, for me, Patti's voice alone, though beautiful, was very high and needed a male voice on the record to provide the bottom. I immediately thought of Michael McDonald. The moment I heard his voice alternating with hers, I fell completely in love with the record.

Richard was furious. He thought Burt had wooed Patti away from him. I reminded him of how often he played the star role while the real divas were left sitting and waiting. I think he knew what I said was true, and it didn't hurt our friendship at all, I don't think, though it was the last song of mine that he ever recorded. Hmmm.

BURT WAS OBSESSED WITH hygiene and health. Phil Ramone, a great recording engineer and producer, once remarked that Burt was the only person he knew who "washes his hands before he washes his hands." He didn't allow me to use the air conditioner. He was obsessive about the room temperature in any studio we recorded in. Having twice had pneumonia, he layered his clothing, even on a ninety-degree day, to cover a possible thirty-degree change in temperature. Scarf, jacket, cashmere sweater underneath, tee shirt underneath the sweater.

"But no air conditioning!" He unpeeled himself as the day's temperature warmed. Over the years there would be many cashmere sweater birthdays and Christmases. He looked so great in those soft mid-blues.

"BURT," I ASKED HIM when we were working late one afternoon, "what time do you want to eat dinner?"

He looked at me incredulously. "Hey," he half-whispered—his voice sounding like red wine being poured over pebbles—"I can't, uh, [count 2, 3, 4] tell you that . . . now." How crazy of me to ask him this question at five in the afternoon. "I haven't even worked out yet," he went on, "and, you know, I've gotta shower . . . Really rough when you ask me that, Carole."

What I was coming to realize was that Angie had the same Burt as me. Nothing really changes when he changes wives; his routine remains exactly the same. On my first trip to Del Mar, he asked if I'd like to take a walk with him after dinner. He'd show me the neighborhood. I gladly joined him, walking by all the houses that ran along the beach. It turns out he took this walk every night before he knew me, and he would take it after me. You could join him, or he'd do it without you.

The same with his workouts. "Hey, babe, you wanna come watch me work out?" You were welcome to tag along, but he was going to run up that hill with a jump rope, with or without you.

Twenty-five

MY MOTHER—THREE THOUSAND MILES away for most of my adult life—punctuated many a day or night with her phone calls. Even with her having given up drinking, I could always pick up just from her "Hello" which mother I'd be speaking to—the warm and friendly one or the angry, needy one. This ability didn't help me at all, because there was nothing I could do about it once on the phone, and I never quite mastered the art of "I'm on the other line, can I call you right back?" If Bad Mom was calling, a delay would only exasperate her.

She might begin with "I could be waiting till hell freezes for *you* to call *me* for a change."

"Hi, Mom!" I'd say, trying to sound glad to hear from her.

"So? What's going on out there?"

"Oh, not too much, Mom."

"How's Cristopher? How's my grandson?"

"He's good, Mom."

"And how are you? Are you feeling well?"

"Yes, I am. I feel good, Mom." Even if I didn't, she'd be the last person to confide my concern to. If my problem was big enough, she would wear it as her own and soon forget that it was me who had the problem. But the truth was she'd really rather you didn't have a concern to pass on to her. She wasn't calling for concerns. She didn't handle them well. She was calling to be pumped up. She was calling for *Entertainment Tonight*.

"Any plans this weekend?"

"Yeah, we're going to some Hollywood party."

Now she paid attention. "Ohhhhh. Will there be any notables?"

"Notables, Mom? Stars are not 'notables.' The Dalai Lama is a notable. The president is a notable."

"Well, you know what I mean."

"I'll let you know after we've gone. I'm sure there'll be some."

"And how about Liz? How's Liz?"

To my mother, one of my greatest achievements in life was having become a close friend of Elizabeth Taylor. I mean, I understand that. It was pretty amazing to me, too. How *did* I become the friend that could waltz into her house, past security, ask her housekeeper, "Where's Miss Taylor?" and, when she pointed upstairs, just go up the stairs, like I would do in my own home, and sit down on her bed. How *did* that happen?

I first met her in 1981 when Burt took me backstage to congratulate her on her performance in *The Little Foxes*. My heart started beating so fast I could barely say hello, as I looked into the world's most famously beautiful eyes. I had only seen them before on a giant movie screen and here they were, equally spectacular in real life. *Oh my God! This is Elizabeth Taylor*, I thought to myself. *Well, this is a highlight in my life.*

Then we met again at Hollywood Park, where Marge Everett, then the majority shareholder of the racetrack and a dear friend of Burt's, invited us often. Marge enjoyed hosting her "buddies," Cary Grant, Bill Shoemaker, and John Forsythe among them, and she often brought her friends together for racing events. On the occasion of the Breeders' Cup in the fall of 1985, I found myself sitting next to Elizabeth in Marge's box. We started chatting and realized that Burt and I would be moving three doors from her home in Bel Air within the month. The day we moved in, she sent down a symbolic cup of sugar and, in her extravagant manner, a cake from the Beverly Hills

Hotel and a giant box of Edelweiss chocolates, and it wasn't long before we became close. I could not imagine how significant a friendship we would develop, and certainly not what a generous, loving, and special soul she would turn out to be.

Here was the wonderful surprise: Elizabeth knew how to be a real friend. She cared about the things you cared about, she was happy when you were happy and sad when you were having a hard time, and that's pretty rare, particularly if you're as colossal a star as she was. I have found that the majority of "stars" actually see themselves as the "gift," but Elizabeth opened her house to her friends often. She saw no need to categorize them. She would easily sit Nancy Reagan next to her assistant's boyfriend and think nothing of it. I loved that.

I don't think Elizabeth was used to having girlfriends to hang out with in LA, because the two closest girlfriends she had were in London. She enjoyed spending time holding Cristopher, and as his godmother, she made sure he was heavily gifted. So was I. On my first birthday in our new home on Nimes Road, Elizabeth sent over a gift-wrapped box from Christian Dior Paris. Even the box looked extravagant. When I opened it, I saw the most unexpected breathtaking white ermine jacket. Burt's eyes just rolled back into his head.

"Jesus," he said, "what am I supposed to give you if that's what your girlfriend sends over?" he said innocently. "You know, baby, I'm not used to these stakes, I think they're a little too rich for my blood."

Burt was not free with his money. In fact, when we bought our house on Nimes Road, it cost much more than he was used to spending. Still, he agreed to pay for our basics—the food, the housekeeping, etc.—himself, and everything else was two-thirds Burt and one-third me. I would list how these were broken down, but I don't even remember what I was paying a third for. I just wanted to live bigger than Burt had in his one-bedroom apartment at the Wilshire Comstock, and he was more than comfortable with my offer to chip in and pay a part of what it cost to live the life we were living.

Sometimes I would visit Elizabeth, and she would still be in bed and invite me upstairs. Her bed had the most beautiful sheets and pillowcases, with little lavender flowers from Porthault, the famous Parisian linen shop. Her pillows had beautiful organdy frills around them and a number of loved stuffed animals sat at the foot of her bed. On her night tables were photographs, many of her with Richard Burton, with her children, with Mike Todd, intimate snapshots taken by her dear friend Roddy McDowall of her dogs, especially Sugar, her Maltese, who was probably her very best girlfriend ever. Sugar even went to the hospital with her every time she was taken ill, which was far too many times.

One day she asked me, "Would you like to see my jewelry collection?"

"Who wouldn't?" I answered. All of her jewelry was taken out of her safe and put on her bed for me to behold. It was a sight I won't forget. Imagine Elizabeth Taylor showing you, and only you, all of her favorite pieces, and telling you who gave them to her, on what occasion, and why she loved them. It's what girlfriends did, except she happened to have the most expensive jewelry collection in America, and she knew it. When her business manager would tell her she couldn't afford to buy a certain piece of jewelry she'd fallen in love with, she would say to me, "They're just being so stupid. I've been told that my collection is second only to Queen Elizabeth's. Don't they realize that because it belongs to me, it's only going to increase in value when the whole collection is sold after I'm gone?" How right she was. At the Christie's auction in 2011, the collection brought in $137 million. As an example of the frenzy her jewelry created, a single pearl necklace that Richard Burton bought her for $37,000 in 1969 sold for $11.8 million.

Other days, when she was up and going somewhere, I would get the chance—and this is no small deal—to sit in her bathroom/vanity room and watch her do her makeup. Even the greatest makeup artist in the world did not do Elizabeth's makeup. She did it. Occasionally she would let them assist her, but it was her face, and she did her own makeup even for all of her films, including *Cleopatra*. And I got to watch and to learn, though I could never do it for the length of time she did. It must have been some sort of meditation for her, because when I was going out one night, I took practically the same cosmetics out, placing them on top of my vanity, and said to myself, *I'm going to do my makeup like Elizabeth tonight*. Twenty minutes later, at most, I was finished. She would just be beginning. Our mutual friend and hairdresser José Eber would laugh at me and say in his French accent, "Dahling, you will never be able to do what Elizabeth does. I have watched her for years, and she does it as an artist, painting slowly and perfectly." Elizabeth was the most extraordinarily beautiful woman I've ever seen, even when she was completely makeup-free.

She had two nicknames for me: Little One and Mighty Mouse, because she always knew the strength I possessed underneath the smallness I projected. During the summers, when I would wear my basic uniform of white linen pants, white short-sleeved tee shirt, with a printed see-through blouse tied around me where I would have liked my waist to have been, she would say, "Little One, take that thing off. You don't need it. What are you hiding?"

"I like it, Elizabeth. I like the way it looks."

"Well, it looks to me like you're trying to hide, and I don't want you hiding anything. You're beautiful just the way you are." Now that's a good friend, even though I continue to this day to tie that same shirt around my linen pants. Now it reminds me of her sweetness.

When Elizabeth wasn't on a diet, she ate with complete gusto and abandon. One of the great treats was watching her prepare a hot dog before she was ready to consume it. She put everything on it: the mustard, the sauerkraut, the relish, and when she took a bite of it, she really bit in. One night I had fixed her up with Neil Simon in between his marriages, and the four of us went out to dinner. We went to a restaurant we had heard of somewhere in Venice. The menu had many a delicious choice on it. Elizabeth was getting excited by all of the possibilities and was having difficulty deciding what she wanted to eat. Burt didn't notice how long it was taking, because he was happy drinking his scotch on the rocks. But Neil finally signaled for the waiter to come over.

"You go first," Elizabeth said. "I'm still deciding."

I ordered. ("Can I get that grilled without butter?") Burt stuttered

through his order, making a few adjustments and speaking slowly enough
for Elizabeth to reread the menu. When it was Neil's turn, he took the liberty
of saying, "Miss Taylor will have the entire right side of the menu, please."
We all laughed, but boy, could she eat. And she made eating look like fun.
By dessert time I indulged with her, because it was just too much fun not to.
And besides, she would tease me mercilessly if I kept up my dieting lunacy
too long. I just accepted that the following day would be a starvation day, but
I could give her a run for her money on desserts. The next day I asked Neil
if he liked her.

"She's got too many fingers for me," he said.

"Huh?" I said.

"You know; all those fingers need jewelry." It wasn't his best joke but it
was honest. Neil, like Burt, was not one of the big gifters.

Anyway, back to "How's Liz?"

"Mom, she hates to be called 'Liz.' By anyone. Ever.'

"Oooohh, I see. Well, don't tell her I called her Liz.'

We would have these conversations two or three times a week, and I
would feel like she was inserting a soda straw into me, trying to suck the life
from me and make it hers. It didn't feel good, which is one reason I lived
across the country in LA.

Twenty-Six

I'M SURE THE IDEA of me writing with Bob Dylan sounds as alien to you as it did to me when he called. The whole idea of collaborating with him seemed ridiculous. If anyone felt like a self-contained solo artist to me, it was Dylan.

He changed a generation. No, he wasn't having hits when we wrote together, but he was still tirelessly releasing new records full of ambitious material and was always taken seriously because he was Bob Dylan.

I had met Bob a number of times. His girlfriend at the time was my friend Carole Childs (formerly my old friend Carole Pincus), and she suggested that Bob and I write together. Bob liked the idea, so one day in the spring of 1986 we found a day for me to drive out to his Malibu ranch and see what we might come up with.

I drove out to where Bob had lived for years now. It was farther than most homes I knew out there, but what surprised me (and yet did not surprise me the minute I put a Bob Dylan filter over it all) was the kind of rundown feeling the place had. The greenery was growing any way it wanted, and there were no gardeners shaping the plantings. It looked a lot like Bob looked to me—unkempt, frayed, and worn. His beard was growing in all directions, too.

He really was a man of few words. "Let's go out to the barn," he said. How I wished I had the self-acceptance to be in cowboy boots, but they didn't have high enough heels. The ground on the walk from his main house to his barn was more uneven than his beard or his shrubbery. A divot here, a clump of soil there; I prayed that breaking an ankle would not be part of my "writing with Bob Dylan" story. His big, musty barn reminded me of a summer camp in the middle of winter.

Two single beds faced each other, with random quilts and guitars lying around. He sat on one of the beds, and I sat myself down on the other, facing him. We were around five feet away from each other, which is unusual since I usually sit very close to where the composer is seated. He picked up one of the two guitars that were sitting against a cracked wall. An old wood upright piano was in a far-off corner waiting to be played. I had a feeling it had been waiting quite a long time.

I had to focus on why I was sitting facing Bob Dylan because there was a part of me blown away by what an unlikely pair we made—he completely disheveled from head to toe and I in full makeup, tight jeans, tee shirt, and studded leather jacket. I was wearing my faux rock 'n' roll look and failing miserably, and he could have told me he had come in from just rolling around with some farm animals and I would not have disbelieved him. He looked like he hadn't bathed in weeks.

In all truth, though he was an icon, I was not a follower. I missed the Dylan Revolution somehow, with the exception of a few classics like "Blowin' in the Wind," "Like a Rolling Stone," and "Lay Lady Lay." So I knew the hits, but I was listening more to the polished sound of pop and R&B. I appreciated Bob's thorny poetry as a lyricist, but I was always in search of a great melody. Friends whose taste in music I respect have played me some of their favorites and when I listened, though I appreciated how very good some of the lyrics were, they didn't hit me in my solar plexus because there was no melody to speak of.

Still, I sat in his barn and was completely aware that This Is Fucking *Bob Dylan*!

I had my usual yellow lined legal pad and he gave me a pen when I couldn't find mine in my overstuffed bag which included a wallet, a card case, a makeup bag in case I was sleeping over, Kleenex, Chapstick, a small collection of star crystals in a small silk pouch that I carried because I was afraid to stop carrying them in case they were protecting me, a croc case for my Lactaid and my Stevia, cards with people's names on them I no longer knew, a mirror given me by Elizabeth with undistorted magnification, my eyeglasses, a rubber tip that a dental hygienist had dropped in one day, and scores of useless other things that just kind of piled up in there.

"Thank you," I said, taking my head out of my bag long enough to take his ballpoint pen, which I wished had a thicker tip.

I refocused. "So, do you have any ideas of what you feel like writing?"

"Well, I've got a little bit of an idea."

He mumbled his words very softly. I thought he said "I godda libble bid a deer."

He started strumming his guitar. I had to admit, this was cool. Bob Dylan strumming a guitar. And then he began humming a melody. It was a simple one. He didn't ask me if I liked it but he sang,

"Something about you that I can't shake."

And he played the melody to the next line and I nervously said, "Feels like it's more than my heart can take?" I was kind of writing and asking a question at the same time. And he sang,

"Don't know how much more of this I can take / Baby, I'm under your spell."

Usually the composer waited for me to come up with the lyrics, playing the melody for me until I heard words I wanted to write. In this case, Bob was way ahead of me. "That's good," I said, feeling more like a stenographer than a lyricist.

As we continued I kept offering him lines. Sometimes he'd say, "I like that" and I would be so happy as I wrote something down.

In the middle of the song, I went over to look at his lyric sheet and I felt like an eighth grader who was trying to cheat on her English test. Bob was essentially the student you didn't try and cheat off of. He was hunched over his paper, hiding it with his left hand and his curly head of hair.

"Can I see?" I asked.

Most of my lyrics that I thought he'd liked weren't even written down— just one or two lines.

Finally, I said, "I feel like you don't really need me here writing this with you because you seem to have your own idea of what the lyric should be." I was being honest.

"No, I need you here," he said. "I wouldn't be writing this if you weren't here."

He played the same melody again. Another verse.

I was knocked out loaded in the naked night
When my dream exploded . . .

And I said, "What about 'and I lost your light'?"

He sang, "I noticed your light."

Well, that was a little something. He continued, "Baby . . ."

I said, "How about, 'Baby you know me so well.' "

He was quiet and then sang, "Baby, oh, what a story I could tell."

I would toss out a line and he would say, "That's good," and sometimes even sing the whole line, so by the time we finished I thought I had contributed maybe twelve lines to the lengthy song.

A few days later he had laid a rough version down on a cassette and sent it to me.

Of the twelve lines I thought I had written, maybe there were three or four left in the song. I immediately called him.

"Bob . . ."

"Hey."

"Listen, I don't think it's fair to you to say we wrote this song together. So much of the lyric is yours. I just don't feel right taking a credit."

"Never would have written it if you weren't here," he said again. "And you wrote some good lines."

Most of them never to be heard, I thought.

"Well, I don't feel right taking fifty percent of the song," I said, and he quickly said, "Well, how 'bout you own half of the lyric and I'll own half."

"Sure, that sounds better."

When the record came out he called the whole album *Knocked Out Loaded*, a line from "our" song. I would have been proud, but that wasn't one of my five lines. Anyway, it gave me great bragging rights, because how many people can say they wrote a song with Bob Dylan? He worked with very few writers during his career, and I certainly know why. Still, it was bizarrely thrilling.

USA Today said in the last paragraph of its review of *Knocked Out Loaded*, "It's ironic and appropriate then, that the album's best song, 'Under Your Spell,' was written with old-fashioned tunesmith Carole Bayer Sager. Dylan can't help but sing its delicate melody, and when he reaches the last line, 'Pray that I don't die of thirst two feet from the well,' old friends will be happy to give him water."

I loved that last line, too. I wished it were mine.

Twenty-Seven

DIONNE ASKED BURT IF he and I would write and produce a few songs for her new album. That same afternoon, he sat at the piano and played her "That's What Friends Are For." She loved it and immediately wanted to do it as a duet with Stevie Wonder.

I invited Elizabeth to come down and meet Stevie, since I knew what a fan she was.

Listening to the playback, an idea came to me. Since Elizabeth was so committed to raising funds and awareness for the American Foundation for AIDS Research (AmfAR), we should donate the proceeds from this record to the foundation. Dionne Warwick has taken credit for this idea in every interview she's done, and Clive Davis also claimed it to be his idea in his otherwise enjoyable autobiography. I would like to set the record straight and say that because Elizabeth was my friend, and was there in the studio when Stevie did his vocals, the idea was right in front of me. (When I asked Dionne about donating her share to AIDS research, she initially replied, "Do I have to? I just gave money for 'We Are the World.' ")

Once we knew its purpose, Burt and I thought we should add two more iconic artists to make the record that much more anthemic. Gladys Knight was perfect. She lifted it one step higher than I thought it could go. Our last thought was Luther Vandross, a great R&B singer, but his vocal, though excellent, still left us wanting that cleanup batter to hit it out of the park.

We voiced our concern to Clive, who broke the news to Luther. To Clive's credit, he then suggested—yes, *this* was Clive's idea—Elton John. More important, Elton said yes and then added a vocal so undeniably brilliant that on listening back to what would soon be the entire record, he said, "If this record is not a fucking Number One song, I am leaving the business."

Fortunately for us, he got to stay. "That's What Friends Are For" went to Number One and remained there for a month in early 1986. Everyone donated their royalties, and we raised almost two million dollars for AmfAR, something I will always feel proud of.

When it went to Number One I was ecstatic. Finally, a huge hit that Burt and I wrote together, just the two of us. I was so happy not to have shared it with a third—let alone a fourth—collaborator. It went on to be the Number One single for 1986 and it was nominated for Song of the Year. It probably meant *too* much to me, but I really wanted us to win *together*. I guess I felt these successes were much of the glue that held our marriage together. My insecurity about whether Burt really loved me often reared its head, and somewhere I believed if I could keep laying golden eggs, he'd stay with me. It made me feel horrible knowing that this was a big part of the truth of us.

On the Grammy broadcast of February 24, 1987, I introduced the performance of our song, which featured Burt, Dionne, Stevie, Gladys, and Elton. It was the last of the Song of the Year nominees to be performed, and it was received with applause that felt like it was infused with adulation. Burt and I were standing backstage afterward as Julio Iglesias and Olivia Newton-John announced the nominees for Song of the Year (all but ours by singer-songwriters): Robert Palmer's "Addicted to Love," Paul Simon's "Graceland," Steve Winwood's "Higher Love," Peter Gabriel's "Sledgehammer," and ours. I was a little nervous that "Graceland" and "Higher Love" had a chance (and in fact, *Graceland* was named Album of the Year and "Higher Love" Record of the Year). But I also knew that aside from our song being a really good one, it stood for something more—shining a light on a devastating illness while raising money to defeat it at the same time—and I felt that might be considered by NARAS (National Academy of Recording Arts and Sciences) voters.

When Olivia Newton-John called our names and presented us with the greatest songwriting award the music industry has to bestow, it was one of the purest moments of joy I'd ever experienced. The entire audience was on its feet and the applause was loud and long. It was a few things: One, an acknowledgment of Burt being back. Two, it was an acknowledgment of the song's purpose, and three, there was a deep appreciation for the four iconic voices on the song. We had a one-year-old baby waiting for us at our beautiful home, and in that moment my life was completely perfect.

I recently viewed the moment again on YouTube and was able to step back and see it as any viewer might. This attractive couple that wrote these beautiful songs together was such a romantic image, one that I lived in far more than my day-to-day not-overly-romantic life. When the two of us would perform together on stage and sing a duet of Burt's "Close to You," I along with the audience believed we were That Couple. Or when photographers stood in line to take our picture, and Burt would look at me so lovingly, I would ask for the photo, frame it, and many a day stare at it trying to believe that snapshot was who we really were. Burt was often the most romantic toward me in the music room, where sex was unlikely to happen but you could count on my lyrics flowing, and so that little flirtation I'd pick up was his way of saying thanks, more words, please! I was the only woman I know who "put out" in rhyme.

After the momentous high of winning the Song of the Year Grammy, where could you possibly go? Four nights later we hosted Elizabeth Taylor's fifty-fifth birthday party at our home in Bel Air.

I like giving parties. I like all of the details that go into planning them: the look of the room, the lighting, the table settings, the food, the mementos, and seeing it all come to life. I enjoy it when people have a good time together who might not have met if I hadn't invited them all to the same gathering.

For the invitation I found a wonderful black-and-white photograph of a ten-year-old Elizabeth with Lassie by her side. On her fourth finger on her left hand I pasted a large rectangular crystal, and sparkly crystal baubles around her neck to evoke two of the famous gifts given her by Richard Burton. I called and asked Ralph Destino, president of Cartier at the time, if he would consider making up big faux diamond rings to be presented in the famous red Cartier boxes to all the forty women in attendance, and invited him to the party to watch their reactions. He enthusiastically said yes. What president of a jewelry firm wouldn't?

I had a life-size cutout of an exquisite teenage Elizabeth on display at the valet station. Later in the evening, I handed out copies of the sheet music from our song "Turn On Your Heartlight," retitled "Put On Your Diamonds" and featuring parody lyrics. Before it was performed, the women were invited to open their gifts and wear their giant rings while singing the song.

The guest list was a mix of many of Elizabeth's friends and some of our own. I was surprised one morning to pick up the phone and recognize the unmistakable voice of Bette Davis calling to RSVP. After telling me she would be attending, she mentioned what a fine songwriter my husband was. "And you, Mrs. Bacharach," she added, making it clear that she had no idea who I was, "make a lovely invitation."

On the night of the party, Michael Jackson arrived early, bringing with him his own chef. Michael whispered in my ear, "I am so nervous. Can we go upstairs to your bedroom?"

"Well, I am hosting this party—"

"Pleeeease," he pleaded.

"Okay," I said. "Follow me."

He sat on my bed looking very handsome, dressed all in black. He had not yet gone over the top in his facial surgeries. He was quite beautiful looking in a Diana Ross way. He had not altered his skin tone and he had not yet begun to sabotage his career. Still, he was afraid.

"Can you stay up here with me?" he asked me in his breathy little-boy voice. "I'm so shy."

"Not when you're singing in front of fifty thousand people," I said.

"That's different. That's a different me. Right now I'm just so nervous."

"Well, Michael, I do have guests arriving. How about you stay here, and I'll come and get you when Elizabeth gets here?"

"Okay," he agreed reluctantly.

It was very difficult to reconcile all the Michaels in my mind. There was the musical genius, the shrewd businessman, and the self-destructive Michael at the heart of whom was the abused child who really seemed unequipped to function in an adult world. I had real empathy for him and the unlived childhood his abusive father robbed him of. As Elizabeth often said, she connected with Michael on a soul level because they were both deprived of a childhood by early stardom, yet they each looked at life at times through the eyes of a child.

Despite the fact that the Elizabeth I knew had seen everything, done everything, been everywhere, she was never jaded.

I remember this conversation at a dinner at our home.

David Geffen said to Elizabeth, "I'm thinking of going to Yugoslavia. Have you ever been there?"

"Yes, I have," she answered.

"Well, what would be the best place for me to stay there?"

"Ohhhh," she answered, "I wouldn't know. I always stayed with President Tito."

Here's a woman who stayed with presidents and was made a dame by the queen, whose legendary romance with Richard Burton almost invented the paparazzi, who I saw watch Cirque du Soleil at the Santa Monica pier with the awe and wonder of a young child. I enjoyed it. She was enthralled by it. She bought the Cirque CD of that performance, and for months it was all I heard when I visited.

Elizabeth walked in looking more exquisite than anyone could possibly be at fifty-five years old. She was accompanied by a tan and handsome George Hamilton, an actor who was also famous as an escort to some of the world's most celebrated and wealthy women. He was also the first husband of my girlfriend Alana (who later married Rod Stewart). Elizabeth and George together looked as though they had popped off the top of the most gorgeous wedding cake ever made.

I sent someone up to get Michael, and once in the room he never left Elizabeth's side, even holding her hand for most of the evening.

I have the most fantastic photographs from the party, including a shot of Bob Dylan kissing Elizabeth on the lips. I'll never forget Bette Davis's line on seeing my friend Bette Midler for the first time. "How da-a-aare she come to your home looking that way? She owes it to her public to dress like a sta-a-a-h-h-h-r," she said, turning her head away in disgust. What she didn't know is that Bette had given birth three weeks earlier and was understandably overweight and exhausted. Nothing else she owned fit, and this was way before one had to endure two hours of hair and makeup even to go on a grocery run.

I know Burt had a great time because well after most of the guests—Elizabeth included—had gone home, he was still at the piano, jamming away with Stevie Nicks on guitar, Stevie Wonder on electric piano, Bob Dylan on yet another guitar (which he signed and left for Cristopher), and Michael Jackson losing all of his earlier shyness and singing some of his hits. Stevie and Bob and Dionne joined in with Burt until the wee hours of the morning. Something I've noticed about stars: it's hard to get them to come out, but it's even harder to get them to go home.

I went to bed that night awed by the week I'd been living, and knowing that one more incredible evening still lay ahead—my induction in New York a week from Monday into the Songwriters Hall of Fame.

FOR THE NEXT FEW days, our rooms were filled with elaborate flower arrangements and the sound of ringing telephones. "Congratulations on the Grammy," "Thank you for the most wonderful party," "Would you and Burt do an interview for us?"

Life was exciting, and in a way, the best was yet to come. I was still having some difficulty believing that I would really be inducted into the Songwriters Hall of Fame, alongside names I would never think of in the same sentence as mine. My idol Carole King and her partner Gerry Goffin. Barry Mann and Cynthia Weil. Bob Merrill. Sam Cooke. It was crazy. Me and John

Lennon and Paul McCartney. I mean, that's all you really have to say to know there was a mistake.

But there wasn't. We were all going to be members of the same club. It was unbelievable. Even Burt, who'd gotten in sixteen years earlier, was excited for me. I couldn't help wondering if his and Marvin's were the two votes that carried me over the top. How could I continue to think of my whole songwriting career as a fluke? I couldn't.

I knew exactly what I was going to wear—a black Armani suit that I could dress up or down, and I decided to go up. I hired a hairdresser in New York and looked forward to our stay at the Regency.

So it came as a total shock to me when I awakened later in the week feeling complete despair.

Everything around me was bleak. I was completely unalive. I believe I was deeply depressed. Nothing mattered to me. Just like that, overnight. Crying, sad, dull, unable to eat. It felt like a nervous breakdown. I didn't relate to who I was and I didn't care. Burt said something to me like "You've got to pull yourself together. You've got the Songwriters Hall of Fame dinner Monday night." He could as easily have been speaking in Chinese. I heard the words, but they had no meaning. And the Songwriters Hall of Fame ceremony didn't even register. Wherever I was, it was a place I'd never been and pray I will never be again.

I've always maintained that my life could be crumbling around me, like bricks collapsing from skyscrapers above, and there would remain this one lane—the music lane, the career lane—that not only would I be safe in, but that not one brick could penetrate. Here was the exception. This *was* my career, its culminating moment, and not just a brick but a boulder crashed right in the middle of my clear open lane.

BURT FLEW INTO NEW YORK without me on Saturday night. My fortieth birthday was the next day, and went by unnoticed by both of us. Whatever happened during this time is lost to all memory retrieval. It's like a power outage that went on for days. Did flowers come? Did people call to say "Happy Birthday"? Your guess is as good as mine.

When Burt came back with my gold embossed plaque, he took me down to Two Bunch Palms, a spa near Palm Springs. I don't remember staying there, I just remember the two of us in a small near-empty Italian restaurant at a table for two. He was facing the door, and I was facing the wall. Recalling this detail is as odd to me as is my forgetting everything else. I remember him urging me, "Carole, please, just take a taste of the pasta. It just has a little butter on it. Can't you try?"

And I couldn't. Can you imagine? I couldn't eat. I looked at the food and it looked back at me. It was something I wanted no part of. Finally, to please Burt, I took a tiny taste.

Everything else is more than blurry. It's black. But I do remember on the ride home from the desert, I was feeling a little less awful. And within another week, I was pretty much over it, whatever it was. Believe me, I've thought about it long and hard. The closest I ever came to figuring it out was that long ago I made a Faustian bargain with the Devil: Give me a great life and much success and in return I promise not to enjoy it.

I'd already gone too far by feeling real joy at the Grammys and at Elizabeth's party, and I obviously had to pay for it. I guess whatever part of me was doling out the punishment was kind enough to believe that denying myself the Songwriters Hall of Fame ceremony, which surely would have been one of the greatest nights of my life, was penance enough for the crime of having a good time.

Twenty-Eight

I WANTED TO THINK that living and working with Burt was going to be forever, but the truth is there are always signs if you choose to see them. During the next few years, our life together was not the same as it was at the beginning. We both were relying more on our son Cristopher to keep us together. It was good for Cris because we both spent a lot of time with him. Though I had a hard time admitting it, I was aware that our married life was predominantly about the music. That might have been okay, but I was not exactly happy in the music room.

I always thought I could be doing something else with the endless amount of time Burt needed me there to be the muse in his creative struggle. It was so not fun, which is what songwriting used to be for me. I could be with Cristopher. I *should* be with Cristopher.

We didn't spend a lot of time going out on "dates," or having romantic dinners, or making passionate love. Burt's fondness for porno videos left me feeling he was more connected to the porn star he was watching than he was to me. And what at first was something that aroused me, too, was now making me feel I was not enough.

I never said any of this to Burt because I was afraid to hear his answer. When we weren't having our picture taken, or being interviewed on talk shows (where we always appeared camera-happy), I'm not sure we were having any real fun together, or even if there was any "we" at all. We spent an excessive amount of time together but only in our photographs, which I placed all over our home, were we truly happy. The intimacy wasn't there.

Burt felt like our life had gotten far too social for his taste. One night he said, "I don't want to be known for the parties I give. I want to be known for the music I write." I didn't disagree, but I didn't see them as mutually exclusive.

ONE OF THE GREAT bonuses of being a songwriter is that once one of your songs has been recorded, someone else can decide to rerecord it at any time. This happened to me a few times, but none more dramatic than when, twenty-two years after "A Groovy Kind of Love" was first a hit, Phil Collins had an even bigger hit than the original when he recorded it again for his movie *Buster*. It went to Number One on both the US and the UK charts, and remains the only Phil Collins record to reach Number One in both countries. It was also named the Most Performed Song of the Year by *Billboard*.

All this without either me or my publisher lifting a finger to make it happen.

IBM WAS HAVING A ten-day convention in Maui, flying in three separate groups of their best salespeople, and we were the entertainment. They'd rented us this beautiful condominium right off the beach, staffed by the Kapalua Bay Hotel. I remember Burt running out onto the magnificent white sandy beach before he was even unpacked so he could take a swim in the warm ocean. It was four in the afternoon. I went running out after him fully dressed, with my Nikon, taking lots of pictures of him. Later we lay by the pool where, next to us, Carol Burnett was reading a magazine.

As Burt applied sunscreen, Carol looked up and told me of the piece she was reading on teens and drug addiction. I listened and in my usual Zelig manner, nodded in agreement when she said marijuana acted as a gateway drug to substances far worse.

We didn't get off stage until one that night, and by the time we settled down, it was close to three when we went to bed. We slept in the next morning and it wasn't until early afternoon that Burt was ready to exit the room.

"Ready?" he finally asked me as he took an extra towel and threw it around his neck.

"Sure!" I said, holding the door open for him, feeling like a contest winner who'd won him as a prize. I followed him onto the beach. I had tied a great big cotton scarf around my bathing suit, covering what I considered my most serious character defect, flabby thighs. I wore white wedges, which immediately sunk into the sand, reducing me to my actual five-foot-one status. If I cheated and put a little tiptoe in, I could get to five one and three-quarters. I trailed behind him.

Burt set up our towels at the far end of the beach. This made me happy. It always made me feel happy when I had him all to myself. He removed the sunscreen from his canvas travel bag.

"Hey, baby, would you do my back for me?" he asked in his sexy voice.

"Sure," I said, squeezing the remainder of the tube into my hands and gladly massaging it into his skin.

"Be sure you get it all over. Don't forget my shoulders," he reminded me.

"Oh, no, I won't."

I might have asked him to do mine, but there was none left.

He had such a comfortable relationship with his body. He thought nothing of walking around with just a towel around his waist. He liked his muscular well-defined legs, though he told me they used to be even better when he played in the RFK Tennis Tournament. All his life he had worked out. He knew exactly how he looked.

We lay there for a minute or two, partially shaded from the sun by a big beach umbrella. Then he got up and said, "Come on, let's go in the water. It's good for us."

Water? We'd just lain down. I decided to swim with him. He knew what I looked like. He hadn't married me for my body. I swiftly followed him to the ocean, dragging a big beach towel and placing it as close to the water as possible in preparation for what would be my exit. The ocean felt wonderful, warm, and sensual. I stood, safely up to my waist in water. I wet my whole head in the ocean and tossed it back. I knew this was a good look for me: tan, white bathing suit, wet from the waist up. I let the sun play in my eyes because I knew he liked that. He looked at me.

"You know, you're very pretty," he said. "Come here." He put his arm around my waist and pulled me toward him. Was he going to make love to me right now, right here in the water? I felt so excited.

"Now, look," he said. "I'm going to show you a great exercise for your thighs. Watch what I do."

He began to run back and forth in the ocean like an old warhorse, thigh high in water.

"Follow me," he called. "Do you feel the current fighting against your thighs? Great! Great for you! Come on! Start running!"

Dutifully I began running, back and forth, back and forth. While other honeymooners were sipping piña coladas by the pool, I was doing laps as though I was in training for the Summer Olympics. He might have stayed in the water longer were it not for the two effortlessly beautiful young women in string bikinis waving vigorously and calling him from the water's edge.

"Burt, Burt! Hi! It's Cindy and Rachel."

Burt waved back. "Who are they?" I asked.

"They're two models I know," he said. "Come on, let's say hello. We'll do some more of this tomorrow."

"Oh, you go ahead," I answered sweetly. "This exercise you showed me is just so great. I'll stay here and do a few more laps. It just feels too good to get out now."

"I'm glad you're enjoying it," he said, proving definitively that he had absolutely no idea who he was married to. "We'll wait for you."

I continued back and forth, back and forth. I was exhausted and praying they would leave, but Burt looked very happy and animated standing and talking to them. They weren't going away, so I had no choice but to get out of the water. With shriveled little hands I paddled my way back to shore, ran out quickly, and grabbed my now tide-dampened towel, wrapping it—and the accompanying mud it had accumulated—around me.

"Hi, Carole," the nearly six-foot Rachel called to me. I walked over. Standing between her and the equally tall blonde Cindy, I felt like one of those baby frankfurters or a woman sawed in half by David Copperfield. I forced a smile.

"Why don't we all have dinner tonight?" Rachel suggested.

"Great!" Burt replied immediately. "We don't have any plans tonight. We'll go into town. There's a good fish restaurant."

"Oh, good," I lied again.

After what for me, though certainly not for Burt, was a long and boring dinner, he and I left the restaurant and were walking down a dimly lit Maui street.

"Hey, baby, light up a little joint for me, will you?"

Obediently I reached into my wallet and found half of a joint. I pulled it out and tried to light it, but the wind kept blowing out the match so I walked closer to the buildings and moved into a doorway to try again. Suddenly, out of nowhere, three huge Hawaiian men grabbed me and pulled me roughly to an unmarked car. I was under arrest, they said. For smoking marijuana.

In Maui?

"It's not mine," I said loudly, looking to Burt to share some of the responsibility. When he said nothing, I pointed my finger at him and said, "He asked me to light it." They were not listening to me. Burt stepped forward, hoping they would recognize him and ask for an autographed copy of "Raindrops Keep Fallin' on My Head." Instead, they wouldn't even allow him in their unmarked police car. They pushed me into the backseat and told him he had to follow behind.

In retrospect, I should have been thinking *My husband never came to my defense!* "Hey, baby, light up a little joint for me, will you?" God! He should have pulled me out of that police car and put himself in. But all I could think of as I cried and cried was how horrible this was all going to be when Carol

Burnett read of my arrest for possession of the gateway drug in the *Maui News* the next morning.

They fingerprinted me and took a mug shot. It was probably the first photo of my life I hoped I looked bad enough in that it bore no resemblance to me. I stated my name as Carole Bacharach, hoping no one would know who that was.

What would the IBM executives do when they heard the news? They were so strict they'd gone through all our songs before we performed, making me eliminate the line "your funny cigarettes" from my song "You're Moving Out Today."

Through my tears, I told Burt to call my manager, Shep Gordon. He had a house in Maui and was well wired in with the locals. Thanks to Shep, there was no publicity. I was put on one year's probation and one year later to the day my prints and mug shot were returned to me in the mail to destroy. Which, believe me, I did.

Twenty-Nine

TURNING SIXTY DEVASTATED BURT. So in 1988, in a last-ditch effort to battle Father Time, he entered therapy and suddenly discovered his anger at his deceased mother.

We were in the kitchen. Burt was having his peanut butter snack when he said, "Jack says the sleeping pills I take deaden my creative energy."

"But you've been taking them your entire adult life. They didn't seem to keep you off the cover of *Time* and *Newsweek*." I guess I felt a little threatened because the fear of not sleeping was one of the biggest bonds we had, and if he was going to try and give up his sleeping pill, I would have to do the same.

"He says with the breathing work he does and with me giving up my sleeping pills, he can reawaken my creativity."

"Well, I think that's great," I said not entirely truthfully.

"Yes. I'm going to do it," he said resolutely. "I'm going to stop. I'm going to reduce it two milligrams every week. I'm very clear about this. And I don't want you asking me how I'm doing. I don't want to report in, and if you decide to stop, too, I don't want to compare notes."

All that he left out was "I hate you and I want no part of you!"

Had the therapist promised him anything else—a deepening of his knowledge of himself, an acceptance of his age and stage of life—he would have lost him in a heartbeat; but he knew the magic words: "Restore Creative Energy."

"Well," I said, "I'd like to try and stop, too."

"You do what you want," he answered. "I just want to be separate from you on this."

On this? I thought. *He's been nothing but separate from me for the last year.*

He continued, "You know, I hate it when you make these pronouncements of what you're going to do, go on a diet, work out every day, and then you blow it, and I don't want to hear it anymore."

There was a pause.

I said, "You know, the Davises want us to come for dinner Saturday night . . ."

He let me wait.

Finally, he said, "I don't know how I'm going to feel on Saturday. I hate to commit so far in advance."

Today was Thursday. "How many times can I tell them we're in the studio?"

"I don't like their dinner parties. I don't have a good time. Tell them I'm working."

"Fine," I said.

My life was anything but fine. Just last week we had gone to a dinner party at our friends Wendy and Leonard Goldberg's house for Art Garfunkel, when suddenly Burt got up and left the table, presumably to go to the bathroom. Twenty minutes later he still had not emerged, and I was getting nervous. When he finally came out, it was almost time to leave. He told me on the ride home that he hated being there. It was too social for him.

The only thing Burt was able to commit to was Burt. Nothing mattered to him but this crisis he was going through—and his skiing. I read most men have their midlife crisis at forty. Burt was sixty, but he really didn't see himself past forty.

I kept hoping he would get it together and be there for me, but the only time he was there was when I was serving him. Now he needed to feel young and although I was nineteen years younger, being with me was making him feel old.

• • •

WHILE I WAS WRITING songs with Burt, I also wrote two screenplays with my friend Alana Stewart, the second one being optioned by producer Joel Silver at Warner Bros. She had been married to Rod Stewart, and as we became friends, we found many similarities between Rod and Burt.

I liked working in a room near Cristopher's. I just felt relief being, even if for a short time, in a room other than Burt's music room. What had once been enjoyable had become an obligation.

I WAS ALWAYS LOOKING for an external solution to an internal problem. I took the lead and convinced Burt that we should buy a beach house for the weekends. He'd sold his house in Del Mar, and I was glad because I felt very alone when I was down there. Still, he always liked the beach, so it made sense to have one closer to home. It sat on a cliff in Malibu above the water but there was an easy path down to the sand. It was lovely, homey and cozy, and surrounded by a big porch that made it feel like we were on the East Coast somewhere in New England. I couldn't wait to spend time there with him. We'd been together nine years and we were growing further and further apart. From the first weekend we spent in it, he seemed not to want to be there.

We worked together that weekend, checking different mixes of Aretha Franklin's recording of a song we wrote for her new album entitled "Someone Else's Eyes." The lyric was as autobiographical as any I'd ever written:

> This is my song
> And for too long I sang to someone else's melody
> It wasn't really me
> Somehow I took myself for granted
> In someone else's eyes

I saw reflections of the girl I was who caught me by surprise

Seeing a woman who's defined by you, I never realized

I can't love you, I can't love me

Through someone else's eyes

You were the sun; I was the one who just

Revolved around you day and night

You were my only light but if I were free

Baby, I'd take control of everything inside of me

Well you, no you're not the one to blame

I got lost inside your name

And I'll never be the same

Till I find a way back home again

We must have listened to it at least a hundred times over that weekend and never did Burt say to me, "Is this the way you feel about us?" But then again, neither did I say, "Burt, listen to the lyric. This is how I feel." It all came back to me: one of the reasons I wrote lyrics for so much of my life was for them to say what I couldn't say in the moment.

Burt only heard music, not feelings. He counted on my lyrics, but he only listened to the way they sounded, not to what they were saying.

THAT SUNDAY, BACK IN town, we were getting ready for bed. At least we would soon be sleeping in the same king-size bed and something about that made me feel connected. It also held the promise of intimacy. Burt was in his bathroom and I was in mine on the other side of the bedroom.

He was using his nightly Waterpik that preceded his nightly rubber tipping and his nightly flossing. I was doing the same, kind of. With soap and water I only half removed my makeup, because after all I wanted Burt to want me again. I did a shortened version of the Waterpik and passed on flossing, choosing instead to try on various nightgowns from my ever-growing collection. Eventually, I hoped I'd go to bed wearing something he would respond to.

He brought his rubber tip and his floss with him into the bedroom. Lying on the bed, he clicked on ESPN and began to floss methodically.

"Do you have some for me?" I asked, lying down beside him on my side of the bed.

Begrudgingly, he handed me a string. "I don't know why you always ask for mine when you have your own," he responded, annoyed. How could I tell him that I liked it when he gave me something of his, even a piece of his floss? It made me feel taken care of.

"You always used to give me your floss," I said, sounding pathetic even to myself.

Silently he flossed and watched the tennis highlights. I took my floss and wadded it up into a little ball as a memento. I began reading randomly from one of my interchangeable self-help books, feeling very, very alone. He muted the sound on the television and turned to me. "I need to tell you something so I don't get cancer."

"What?" I asked, a little startled.

"Well, Jack wants me to be more authentic. He says if I don't tell the truth I'll get sick. He says I haven't been my real self most of my life. I 'people please.'"

"I hadn't noticed."

He put his hand lightly on mine. "It's not easy for me to say this, but sometimes, [*count 2, 3, uh, 4*] when you touch me . . . Now *please* don't take this the wrong way, but I . . . I just can't stand it. It makes me feel sick, uh, almost nauseated."

What was the *right* way to take this? I pulled my hand away quickly.

"It's hard for me to say this," he continued, "but sometimes lying next to you at night, uh, I just feel so trapped. I don't know, uh, I'm working on it all in therapy, but it's important for me to just tell you the truth, so I did."

He got up and walked into the bathroom. I was searching for the little piece of floss I'd discarded to hang myself with. He was rubber-tipping his gums. On finishing he applied his night cream. "You know," he said reentering the room, "I'm really glad we can have these talks. They may be difficult, but Jack is right. I always feel better after I'm able to tell you how I'm really feeling. Don't you?"

I was unable to answer him. I'd just felt a tear drip down my greaseless face, and now I had to try and sleep with two milligrams less of Dalmane and without taking anything he said personally.

"Are you okay?" he asked, turning on his sleep machine. Without waiting for a response, he turned off the light.

Thirty

THE NEXT MORNING, I woke up and began to cry. I knew my marriage was in deep trouble. I asked myself, "Where is the part of me that should be saying, 'Hey, if you don't appreciate me, you can leave.'?"

We decided that for the moment I would live in town and Burt would move out to the beach house. He needed time to think about whether he could ever be "all in" again. He did drive in almost every day to see Cristopher, and I was grateful for that, though he was always hours later than his ETA.

Early one Saturday morning, Burt called from the beach. Could I meet him out there for a beer and a hamburger? *Odd*, I thought. *Neither one of us drank beer or ate meat, but he'd suggested we go to this hamburger bar, the Malibu Inn, where neither of us had ever been before.* As crazy as it may sound to you, I actually believed it was good news that he wanted to meet. *Maybe this was going to be a new Burt.*

I didn't want to be late, but I wanted to look good so I raced into the shower, did my hair, diffuser, blow-dryer, and flat iron (it gets humid at the beach). I should have just left it curly, but that was the way my hair was naturally, so straight had to be better.

I chose my clothes carefully.

I kissed Cris, who was now five years old and on his way with his nanny to meet his friend Jeffrey for a play date. Driving to the beach, I imagined how wonderful life with Burt would be now that he'd come to his senses and was moving back home. I felt relieved that the last painful months were finally over. I could put it all behind me. Because, when you got down to it, all the nonsense aside, he needed me, Cristopher needed us both, and we all wanted to be a family again.

I pulled into the parking lot in front of the Malibu Inn. I checked myself in the mirror and added a little more lip gloss to my already overly glossed lips.

Walking in, I spotted him at the bar. I felt my heart beat harder. Just looking at him made me feel alive. One glance and you could see which one of us took more effort getting ready. He'd arrived unshaven, hair unwashed, in sweats and tee shirt, and of course his obligatory sneakers.

"Hi, how're you doing?" he asked in his little-boy shy manner, barely making eye contact.

He kissed me on the cheek and it felt like cold air. He was drinking a beer and he ordered me a Diet Coke. I was thinking how long it had been since I had felt desirable. If only I was a little more . . . *what?* Taller? Thinner? Younger? What?

"You look very pretty," he mumbled, barely looking at me.

Oh, good, I thought, *this is going well.*

"Listen, baby," he said, "I, uh, [*2, 3, 4*] really want to work on our marriage. I really want to give it a good try."

I still loved the rhythm in which he spoke. It was original. It was a lullaby. "I know I've been, uh, kind of torn up lately, in and out . . . You know [*count 1, uh 3, 4*] I know it's been really hard for, uh, both of us. I've been in hell and, uh, I know I've put you and the little guy in a really awkward place, and it's gonna stop."

Tears started to well up in his eyes. I loved his sensitivity.

Good, I thought. *This is all good.*

He put his hand on my knee.

"I guess you know what I'm going to say to you."

I loved that he had his hand on my knee. I had to make myself concentrate. "Yes," I answered confidently. "You want to come back."

"I'm sure you have a pretty good idea," he said as though he hadn't heard me. "You know, the way it's been with us this past year."

My heart was beating hard with anticipation. This was the only thing I didn't like about Burt. It took him so long to just say. "Honey, I love you and I'm coming home."

"Listen," he said, as he took my hand in his. He looked down at the sawdust floor. "There's something I've got to tell you."

Unable to contain myself any longer I blurted out, "I know, I know. You're coming home!"

And at that exact instant he said, "There's someone else."

Because we were both talking at the exact same time, I wasn't quite sure I heard him correctly.

"Could you repeat that?" I asked, as I felt myself going totally numb.

"I didn't mean for this to ever happen." He began to cry but still continued. "Honest, it started out like nothing. It was harmless. Just a drink, in Aspen when you and the little guy got that flu . . . I was just looking to feel better . . . a night . . . a girl in a bar . . . a beer . . . I never thought it would go this far. That's why I've lied for so long. I kept hoping it would burn itself out . . . but I need more time. It's been so hard for me to live a lie . . . Can you imagine how hard this has been for me to hurt you—someone who I really love?"

Tears were streaming down his face. I wanted to comfort him, but something stopped me. I needed to understand. I felt like I couldn't breathe. I gripped the edge of the table for support as I asked the question I didn't want to know the answer to.

"There's another woman?"

"Yes. I'm so sorry." He was still looking down. "Would it help if I told you more?" Obviously needing to tell me.

I already knew all I needed. He didn't love me anymore. I couldn't speak. I felt like I was going to be ill. He didn't notice and continued.

"She's twenty-eight. I know there's a big age difference. Sixty-three, twenty-eight . . . But she makes me feel young."

My heart was beating so loudly it was drowning out everything he was saying. Something about not lying anymore, something about having to tell the truth because it was making him sick. The guilt was making *him* sick!

I actually said, I am very sorry to have to report, "You mean you're not coming home?"

"I'd really like to come home but—"

"But what, Burt?"

"Well, I feel really torn in two . . . This is so painful for me . . . for all of us."

"So what are you saying?" I screamed, getting up and knocking over the table. "Why the fuck did you make me come here? So I wouldn't go crazy in public?"

"Please, baby, don't make a scene. Calm down. I just couldn't lie anymore. You're my best friend. I love you."

He awkwardly reached for my hand.

"You fucking bastard." I threw the remaining half of my Diet Coke in his face.

This couldn't be real, I thought, as I made my way tremblingly out the door. Somehow I found my car keys. I looked back to see if he was coming after me. He wasn't. It was over. How could I have been so stupid? How could I have not seen this coming?

I started the car. I began driving and sobbing, heading nowhere. The pain was so great I thought I might die. Of all of the ways I considered dying in my life, and believe me, I'd considered them all, I never thought I could die of a broken heart.

Wouldn't most women have figured out there was a twenty-eight-year-old stashed away somewhere? Why hadn't I? What was wrong with me? He had confirmed my worst fear. I was a person who was, ultimately, leaveable.

All those months of his midlife crisis, of his needing to go away, needing to get some space. Just go away and be with her! Eight months of lying and cheating. So much for my keen intuition. All of his trips and his needing to be alone with himself. All the phone calls he made when I thought he was alone sorting out his life. He was with her: the girl who had no name but had my husband.

Thirty-One

OBVIOUSLY, THIS WAS THE end . . . unless you were me. I refused to give up. And Burt was the perfect partner to not give up with—still willing to "give it a try" without really trying, and willing to record our therapy sessions but not listen to the tapes. He left just enough air in my balloon of false hope that maybe this could all still work out.

Like a recalcitrant schoolboy, he dragged the half-filled balloon behind him, a used possession, no longer interesting but familiar. He was afraid to let it go. He was used to the string wrapped around his finger, and although he already had a new toy he thought he liked better, he couldn't be sure it wouldn't break or wear out, and then he'd have nothing. It was better to just let the balloon drag behind him. It didn't inconvenience him. He barely knew it was there.

FOR ME, THOSE NEXT months became what I call the Weather Report months. Once a week Burt would see me and say, "Uh . . . You know [*count 2, 3, 4*], if I could, uh, just take, uh, a couple of weeks, 'cause now I feel like I'm fifty-eight percent in the marriage, and about forty-two out." Or, a week later, "Hey, you know, I'm seventy in, but that other thirty . . ." He sighed. "If I could just get away and think . . ." He was processing in front of me, with no awareness of how that made me feel.

There was no way for this to end but badly. Pat Allen, the therapist we were working with to try to save our marriage—or rather, *I* was working with—told me to stay until it made me sick, and then I'd never have to do *this* again. So I stayed, and even when I felt a little ill, I still stayed. And in the end it was Burt who left, because he wanted to see what another life would feel like with Jane.

FOUR WEEKS AFTER I'D filed for divorce, the pain was only getting worse. There was no more time to screw around with shrinks crazier than I was. Dr. James Grotstein, author of a dozen books, came highly recommended, so I had high hopes. And yet after three sessions, I was already disappointed.

I lay down, trying not to be judgmental about having to put my head on the little paper napkin he clipped to the head of his couch as if he were a dentist. He obviously changed them between patients. It was like he was protecting his cherished couch from patient fallout. If he couldn't deal with a little dandruff, how was he going to handle real problems like mine?

I lay there silently, trying to like him.

He didn't say a word. For Grotstein, it was probably a few minutes of quiet time.

Finally, I spoke. "How long does it take?" I asked impatiently. "It's been a month since I filed for divorce. When does it get better?"

"It's a process. I wish I had the answer for you," he replied impersonally.

"So do I."

"What I can tell you," his voice intoned from behind my head, "is that the best way through it is right through it, right through the center."

I couldn't see his face, but I imagined at this moment he thought I was a jerk to be lying on his couch paying two hundred dollars for a fifty-minute session to hear, "You go right through the center to the center." His voice just didn't comfort me the way I would have liked it to, nor did his high-waisted pants, which I couldn't help noticing every time I entered his office.

"I just don't feel any better when I'm here," I said.

"Why should you?" he replied in his detached voice. "You're in mourning."

"Well, how long?" I said. "And don't tell me you don't know. I pay you to know. I want answers. I'm so sick of not having answers." I began to cry.

He said nothing. From above my head, a lone tissue floated down through the air and landed on my breast. He didn't even hand it to me—for two hundred dollars, no contact.

I wiped my eyes and spoke.

"It's difficult for me to say this but . . . I don't think I like you very much. I mean, aside from the fact that you're a man and most men have proven themselves to be quite disappointing in my life, I don't think I like *you*. And I swear, I have never ever said this to any other therapist I've ever had. And I have had a lot."

"Really?" he said, suddenly fascinated. He was probably so tired of hearing these patients whine about their problems, on and on, day after day. At last! Something about *him*!

"So, tell me," he asked, perking up, "what is it you don't like about me?"

"Well, everything. This kind of therapy. The rigidity of me lying on a couch, talking to a wall, going over the same stuff I've gone over a hundred times before with therapists who did it better than you. You don't seem smart enough or empathetic enough or anything enough. I get better insights on the phone with my girlfriend."

"I see. So Daddy disappointed you, and Burt disappointed you, and now you're going to add me to the list. Yes?"

"But what if you really are a disappointment? I mean, some people are just disappointing."

"Well, that remains to be seen, doesn't it?" Pause. "I'm sorry, but we really do have to stop now," he said unfeelingly.

I sat up and slipped into my wedged heels.

"One thirty on Monday," he added as I stood to leave.

Deliberately avoiding having to look at him, I made my way to his exit door. He never ushered me out the front door, so I never got to see his other patients. They were probably all as disappointed as I was. This way we couldn't compare notes.

"Oh, Carole!" he called before I closed the door behind me. Now I was forced to turn and look at him. He held his appointment book in his hands.

"I'm so sorry. I've made a dreadful mistake. I don't have you down for one thirty. I won't have that opening for another month and I don't have any other time on Monday. How's three fifteen on Tuesday?"

It was so easy to get upset with him. I blurted out, "It seems like we spend most of our time scheduling and rescheduling my appointments. You're always messing them up. I hate when you make mistakes."

"I know. I'm just your disappointing Daddy/Therapist, aren't I? As soon as something opens up I'll give you your own regular time." He shrugged apologetically. "But right now I'm all booked."

"That doesn't mean you're very good. It just means no one ever gets well here," I muttered as I stomped toward the door.

He was a big disappointment, I thought, but at the moment he was the only man I had. He would have to do.

At least I had my "little man," I thought as I drove home. I loved him so much. I started to feel sad for Cristopher. Not yet six, he was so young to have to get through this, along with being adopted.

That night, as I tucked him into bed he said, "Mommy, I'm scared. Don't go." He looked up at me pleadingly. "Rub my back." He was so beautiful.

I'm scared, too, I thought to myself.

"Mommy's right here, Baby." I knelt down next to him and began rubbing his back. He looked so sweet all scrunched up inside his Ninja Turtle sheets.

"I miss Daddy," he said.

"Me too," I said. "But Daddy loves you very much. He really does, Baby."

"Doesn't he love you?" Cristopher asked.

No, I thought. *Daddy doesn't love me. He loves a waitress/ski instructor.*

"Daddy loves me," I said. "But not the way . . . not the way a man loves a woman if he . . . uh, if he doesn't want to . . ."

I didn't want to paint his daddy as a villain.

"He just doesn't want to live with Mommy anymore," I said, hoping that was okay as a reason.

"Maybe Daddy doesn't like girls," Cristopher said, offering up a pretty good explanation.

"Maybe not," I answered, thinking Cris might have better answers than Grotstein.

"Mommy, I want to get a new Daddy," he said, very much the same way as he asked for a new soccer ball.

"You mean you want Mommy to get married again?"

He nodded yes.

"But who should Mommy marry?" I was hoping maybe he had a good idea. He was really much smarter than his years.

"The Raiders," he answered confidently.

"All of them?" I laughed. "The whole team?"

"Yeah. The Raiders, or maybe the Rams. I have a Rams helmet," he said.

"Well, I like Joe Montana." I was negotiating.

"But that's San Francisco!" He gave up, put his thumb in his mouth, and closed his eyes, holding on tight to his dependable frayed blue blankee.

"Don't stop," he said. "Keep rubbing my back."

He didn't need a pill to help him sleep. He had his mommy and he had his trusted blue blankee. Burt had been my blankee, and he'd kept cutting it down, giving me less and less. In the end, I was clinging to a shred and I still couldn't let go.

Mom and Dad out on the town

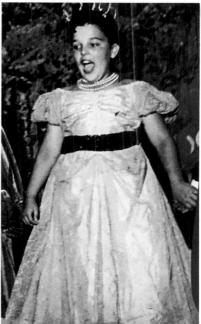

Me at age nine performing at camp
(I told you I was chunky)

With Neil Sedaka and Peter Allen in New York, 1976

With Peter Allen in LA (at my good weight)

With Marvin on our
way to the Oscars

With Marvin and Aretha Franklin

My first album, *Carole Bayer Sager*, 1977

Performing at the Roxy, 1978

With Marvin and Neil Simon

EMANUEL AZENBERG
presents
They're Playing Our Song
Book by
NEIL SIMON
Music by
MARVIN HAMLISCH
Lyrics by
CAROLE BAYER SAGER
Scenery and Projections by   Costumes by   Lighting by
DOUGLAS W. SCHMIDT   ANN ROTH   THARON MUSSER
Music Direction   Orchestrations by
LARRY BLANK   RALPH BURNS, RICHARD HAZARD, GENE PAGE
Musical Numbers Staged by
PATRICIA BIRCH
Directed by
ROBERT MOORE

STARRING   STARRING
ROBERT KLEIN   **LUCIE ARNAZ**

They're Playing Our Song
IMPERIAL THEATRE 45th STREET WEST OF BROADWAY

Three and a half years
on Broadway

With Michael Jackson recording "Just Friends" from my album *Sometimes Late at Night*, 1981

Singing with Neil Diamond, 1981

With Burt and Cristopher

With Nikki Bacharach

Winning the Oscar in 1982 for "Arthur's Theme" and receiving it from Bette Midler!! (With Peter Allen, Burt Bacharach, Christopher Cross, or, as Bette put it, "Four on a Song!")

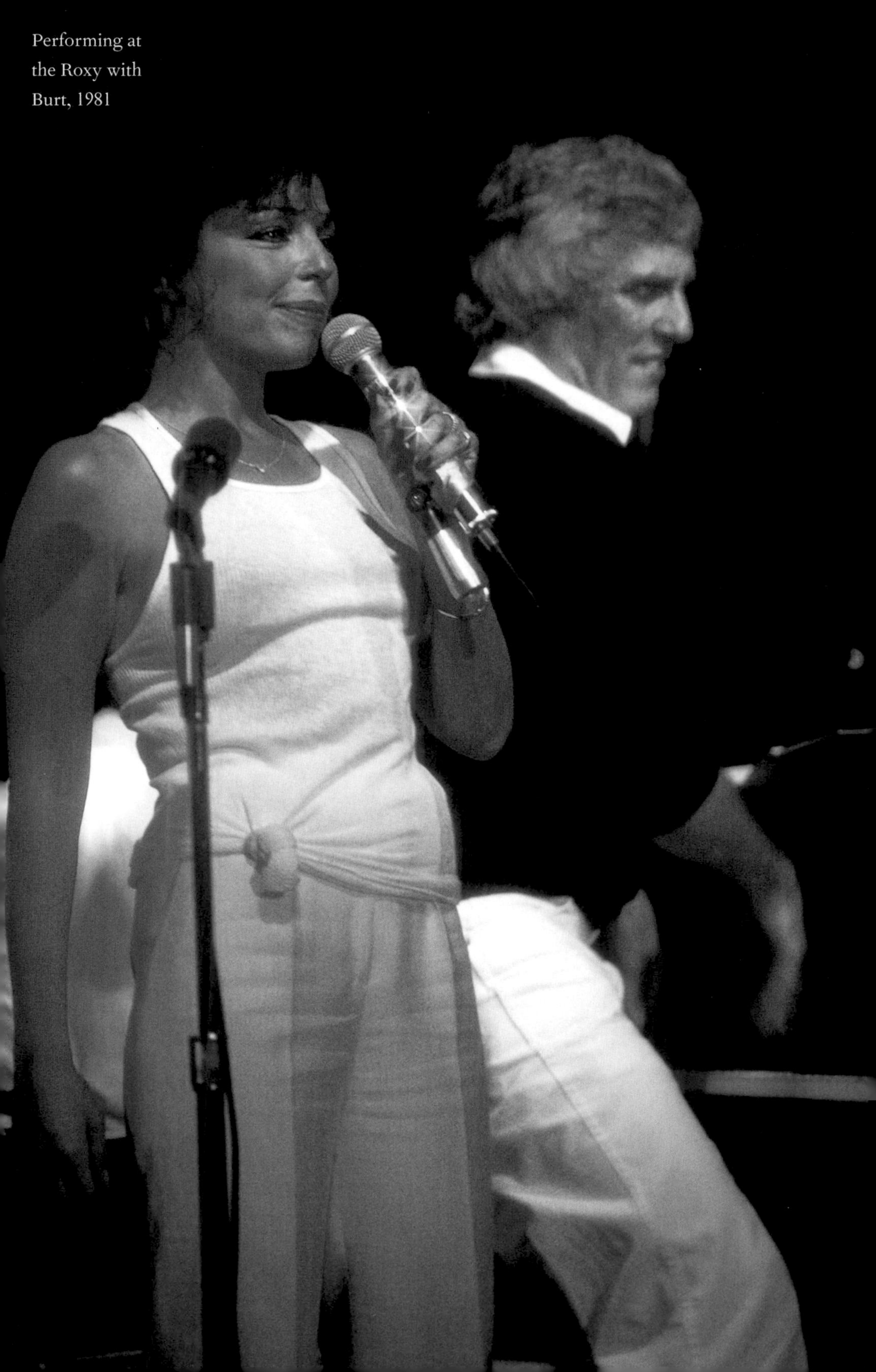

Performing at the Roxy with Burt, 1981

With Elizabeth Taylor, 1992

Bob Dylan kissing Elizabeth Taylor
at her fifty-fifth birthday party, 1987

The making of "That's What
Friends Are For": Elton John,
Gladys Knight, Stevie Wonder,
Burt, and Dionne Warwick

Elizabeth's wedding to Larry Fortensky. I was the bridesmaid (next to Michael Jackson) and fortunately not the bride. Cover of *People*, October 21, 1991

With notables David Geffen, Barbra Streisand, Elizabeth Taylor, and Sandy Gallin at a birthday party Sandy threw for me in Malibu

With Kenny "Babyface" Edmonds and David Foster in my music room

Marrying Bob, June 8, 1996

Receiving my star on
Hollywood Boulevard with
Carole King, Elizabeth Taylor,
David Foster, Neil Simon,
Kenny "Babyface" Edmonds,
and Henry Winkler, 2000

Writing with Carly Simon and David Foster. If only we'd finished it!

With my friends
Bruce Roberts, Barry
Manilow, Carole King,
and David Foster

With Andrea Bocelli,
"The Prayer," 1999

With Hugh Jackman
during my week of
performing at the
Regency Hotel,
November 2003

Enough painting people,
let's paint food! "Torn" from
my second art show

Me at my art show with
What's-Their-Names?

With Randy Jackson and
Simon Cowell, 2007

With Michael Govan
and Lynda Resnick at
a celebration of the
opening of LACMA's
Resnick Pavilion, 2010

With my cousin Joan

Girlfriends, top row (left to right): Marcia Diamond, Lauren Shuler Donner, Barbara Davis, Ann Moss, Joanne Segel, Alana Stewart, Stacey Winkler, and Mindy Seeger; bottom row (left to right): Elizabeth Taylor, me, and Margie Perenchio

My seven beautiful grandchildren (left to right): Henry, Beatrice, Robert, Julianna, Leo, Quinn, and Felix

Dogs (left to right): Devon and our three bedmates, Benny, Daisy, and Dylan

In front of Chris
Burden's "Urban
Light" for the
LACMA gala
with Cristopher
and Bob, 2012

Thirty-Two

THE LOSS OF BURT was a double whammy. Not only did I lose my life partner, my supposed soul mate, but I also lost the major collaborator in my life for the past decade. I was filled with insecurity as to how I'd start writing again. I decided to call up someone I knew, who'd be less likely to reject me.

I called my friend James Ingram, whose voice I loved, and who'd written a number of good songs. He came over and we wrote a song that day. It wasn't an important song, but what was important was the knowledge that I could write without Burt, which made it easier for me to move forward. Once I felt the music part was under control, I needed to find someone who could be the new man in my life.

The first real date I had after I filed for divorce was with Richard Cohen. Richard was a retired real estate guy who was best known in LA for marrying Tina Sinatra and dating Linda Evans of *Dynasty* fame.

Marvin and Barbara Davis—he was once the owner of 20th Century Fox—friends of mine, had taken me to Matteo's, an Italian restaurant in Westwood. It was a show business restaurant, especially on Sunday nights.

Richard appeared to be approaching our table but I wasn't sure if Marvin Davis had signaled him to come over. He was very attractive: blue eyed, well dressed, trim, blond (a first for me), and muscular. Barbara introduced me. "Carole, do you know Richard?"

"Actually," I said, "I do know Richard. I mean, we've met a few times at various parties, I think."

I didn't think. I knew. Why did I qualify everything I said? Was there nothing I was sure of? I had not only met Richard, I'd sat next to him at a large dinner party and did not have a particularly stimulating evening. As was the custom, Burt and I were seated at different tables. What was the assumption behind separating the husband and the wife? Was it that the married are tired of talking to each other? That particular evening, I remembered only wanting to be seated next to Burt, who only wanted to be somewhere other than at that dinner party, so it would be unfair to hold Richard responsible for my bad time.

"Well, it's good to see you again. You look beautiful tonight," Richard said matter-of-factly. "Good-looking friend you've got here," he said to Marvin. Bull's-eye! Score two for Richard. What better thing to say to a woman who had just been dumped by her husband?

"Thank you," I answered shyly. I wasn't very good at any of this. I squeezed Barbara Davis's hand. I felt like I could have been at my own sweet sixteen party. I looked at Richard. Now he'd passed beyond attractive to actually handsome.

Barbara, who was anything but shy, kept the dialogue rolling.

"I think the two of you make such a lovely couple. I think all of us should go out. Soon!"

"I was thinking the same thing, Barbara, you might have let me say it," Richard quickly offered.

"How's your golf game, Richard? How are you hitting the ball?" Marvin wasn't really looking for an answer. His eyes were already darting around the room, looking to spot someone else he knew, someone more famous, more interesting.

"Oh, I'm playing about the same. Hurt my shoulder last week. I have to be careful. Go a little easy on it. I played with your friend Margie Perenchio last week." He was addressing me. "She's some good player, Margie. You know she only plays with the guys." Margie was my close friend; I knew more about her than he would ever know, but of course I didn't say anything.

Marvin wasn't interested in golf. He wasn't interested in Richard, either. He didn't even bother to answer.

"What's happening in business, Richard? Oh, I forgot," he said fake laughing, "you're the one who's retired. We all want your life. Lots of money and no responsibilities."

I laughed, noting he didn't work. He seemed so young to not be working. I was trying on Richard's life in my mind, just like when I was fifteen and met a boy I was interested in. I would write my first name with his last name and see how it looked and sounded. If I were crazy about him I'd write it hundreds of times, as if writing it would make it so.

Richard bent down to whisper in my ear. "What's your phone number?"

Good. He liked me. Winning was important. This is why they called it the dating game.

"Do you have a pen?" I asked him.

"I don't need one. It's all in here." He pointed to his head. I whispered back my phone number. "I'll call you," he told me. "I'd love to stay, but I have to show up at this charity event later tonight. I'm on the board. I just stopped by because I knew you were going to be here." He grinned.

Wasn't he there because he was eating at the next table with friends? I was so bad at all of this. If I didn't know for a year that Burt was having an affair, how would I know if Richard was telling the truth?

"Oh, he likes you a lot," Barbara said later. "I can tell."

Why was everyone so anxious for me to couple so immediately? None of them looked really happy in their marriages. *Two by two they enter the ark*, I thought to myself.

When I got home that night there was a message from Richard on my answering machine. "Hi. It's Richard. I told you I'd remember your number. I'll call you later." It made me feel good—until I heard the next message. It was Burt. There was nothing particularly brilliant in it, nothing particularly anything. It was just the voice, the voice that soothed me.

"Um . . . uh . . . I just needed to ask you something about Cristopher's soccer game tomorrow." Long pause. "I hope you're feeling okay and I'm sorry to bother you but . . . uh . . . well, I'll call back tomorrow."

Of course, he didn't, but Richard did.

The first date we had was dinner at Matsuhisa, a small "in" Japanese restaurant on La Cienega Boulevard in Hollywood.

The waiter served a vegetable dumpling in a creamy brown sauce.

"Any peanuts in there?" Richard asked cautiously. Then confiding in me he said, "I'm deathly allergic to peanuts. If I eat anything with as much as a hint of a peanut I go into anaphylactic shock and I can die."

I listened compassionately.

"In fact," he added as he pulled a small kit out of his wallet, "I should really show you how to administer this just in case you ever see me blowing up in front of you." He then showed me in great detail the way you handle an EpiPen and how I was to inject him were he to find himself blowing up and unable to breathe.

Then he gave me the pen. "Keep it," he said. "I plan on seeing a lot more of you so you should have it." I didn't know what to say. I put the pen in my purse and hoped I could find it quicker than I find most anything in my over-stuffed bag should I need to save his life.

We talked about our lives. He talked a lot about how he made his money and about his former marriage to Tina. He said he knew from the start the marriage wasn't going to work out. I didn't know Tina well but I liked her. I wondered why, if he was so sure the marriage wouldn't work, did he bother to get married?

When we kissed good night, after our second date, it totally surprised me. I hadn't expected to feel so turned on.

On our third date we went to a movie. We played with each other's hands and fingers, which was better than the movie. There was nothing like the excitement of somebody new and unknown who can be a fantasy.

When I told David Geffen I was dating Richard, he reacted in his usual honest way: "You're wasting your time. He is completely uninteresting and he's not nearly smart enough for you."

Forewarned but completely disregarding his advice, I soldiered on.

For our fourth date, Richard invited me to dinner at his home. I was impressed, which he wanted me to be, when I saw how beautifully he lived. So different from Burt, who when we met was living in what looked like a one-bedroom suite in a Holiday Inn. Richard's taste, if it was his, was impeccable. He had acquired through the years a very impressive art collection. Guided in his art buying by his friend Billy Wilder, whose name he enjoyed dropping every couple of hours, Richard relished showing it all off to me. He spent hours rearranging the placement of his possessions—his Picassos, his Rodins, and his Galle lamps.

Richard had everything, I thought, as his chef served us dinner— everything except my attention. I wanted the stories he was telling me to be more interesting. He was an art collector, and I wanted him to paint with more colors.

He, in turn, wanted me to wear more color.

"Why do you only wear black and white?" he asked. He was wearing a red shirt, one of my least favorite colors.

"I don't really know," I said honestly. "I think it's just easier. It's safer. Yellow is a high-risk color."

"And those high heels," he continued. "Don't you ever just wear sneakers?"

"I like looking taller," I answered, sounding more than a little defensive.

"Well, I'd like to see you in a pair of sneakers. But you're okay with me just the way you are."

Wasn't that a contradiction?

"I'll bet you'd look terrific in a pair of sneakers and jeans instead of those . . . big shoes. You should give it a try." Richard stayed on every subject just a few minutes more than necessary. *Did everybody want to change everybody?* I wondered.

There was one of those awkward pauses between courses.

"What are you thinking?" Richard asked me.

He'd caught me thinking about Burt. No wonder I questioned his honesty as I heard myself lie.

"Nothing. I wasn't thinking anything."

Really? I had achieved the state that Zen masters can merely aspire to? *If only I could think nothing*, I thought.

He reached over and took my hand.

I felt instantly bonded. I liked it most when he held my hand and he was silent. He could be anyone I imagined. And of course, I was imagining Burt.

"I like you. A lot," he added.

"Why?" I asked him, really curious.

Clearly, he had thought about this. "You're special. You're smart and very pretty. You're talented and you're good at what you do, you've made a success of yourself. Oh, I don't know why," and then added, "if I could define it, I probably wouldn't feel it."

I felt a flush of embarrassment. If I really felt like the person he described, I'd probably like me, too. It was true I had made a success of myself. But I felt more like I had created myself. I felt like I had taken a glob of clay and molded it, bit by bit, by imitating what I saw around me that I admired.

After dinner, Richard led me into the bar. We sat on one of the large eighteenth-century sofas. The only light in the room was from the Tiffany lily lamp, appropriately dimmed, and the spots on the Pissarro, Léger, Hopper, and Hockney paintings.

Richard gazed at the softly spot-lit Matisse in the corner of the room.

"I love that painting," he said. "I waited four years to get that. Bid on it, lost it, waited till it came up again. It's beautiful, isn't it?"

I studied it with appreciation. "It really is," I replied.

"You're beautiful, too," Richard said, mellowed by the after-dinner brandy he was sipping.

If only I could believe it. I sat there, my own creation, guarded, always waiting for the well-trained eye to spot the cracks and yell, "Fraud!"

Richard reached over and pulled me to him. He kissed me deeply and it was unexpectedly hot. I let myself get lost in him. I even slipped off my shoes. Everything fit perfectly. His arms holding me were strong and muscular. My body wrapped in his felt deliciously small and female. This was what it felt like to have hot sex. He was kissing my breasts. I was responding to his every move. So far it was okay. I liked my breasts. He took my hand and put it on his pants zipper. I was secretly delighted that I still had some sex appeal left in me after the Burt bashings.

His hand moved down my body and opened the button of my jeans. He had to push his hand in. He moved it down with expertise. He was exploring my body, touching my ass, my thigh. Suddenly I became his hand. I was out of my body and inside his head wondering if my ass felt flabby to him. The spell was broken. I desperately wanted back in the moment. But I was out.

"I don't think I . . . Richard, I don't think we . . . should go to bed together yet. I don't think I'm ready," I said awkwardly.

I was forty-six years old and I wasn't ready. What was I waiting for? Menopause?

"You feel so good," Richard said heatedly. "You really get to me."

Thank you, Richard, thank you for that. Burt had done a pretty good job on my self-image through the years.

"We don't have to go to bed together. I can wait until you're ready," he said, continuing to kiss me and hold me.

I was amazed that I could feel so much so quickly. Richard was magically turning into the man of my dreams right before my eyes. And, as he became more, I was becoming less. It wasn't so much that I wasn't ready to have sex with him. I just wasn't prepared for the possibility of rejection and I still hadn't figured out how to get from the bedroom to the bathroom without my four-inch heels and without him seeing me naked. As soon as I could figure it all out, I knew I would go to bed with him.

After two more dates I found myself in Richard's bedroom. It began the same way. A Roberta Flack record was playing in the background.

Somewhere between the fondling of my breasts and the unbuttoning of my jeans, I decided not to stop him. What did I have to lose?

The sex was better than I ever imagined. It wasn't just that I had been deprived of a sexual partner for so long. It was that Richard was a really good lover, *both* times. And he was making love to me alone. No Marilyn Chambers tapes joining us from the VCR, it was just the two of us.

"You are one sexy lady," he said lying next to me in the dark.

"You too. I mean, you are a very sexy man," I said, my head nestled in his chest.

But now, how was I going to get to the bathroom? I didn't want to push my luck. I lay there trying to figure it out.

"What are you thinking?" he asked me.

"Uh . . . I was thinking . . . how good it felt. I mean, it was great being with you," I answered. I actually had been thinking that, just not at the moment he asked.

"You didn't think I had it in me, did you? I mean twice," he boasted. "You really take everything out of me, baby," he said sexily.

And the next moment, he was snoring. Loudly.

God can be so kind, I thought, as I quietly got up, went to the bathroom, came back and got dressed. I woke Richard with a kiss, thanked him for the evening, and went home to Cristopher.

I went to bed that night feeling honestly hopeful that I had really gotten lucky. A very handsome "younger" man (eleven years younger than Burt) was really turned on by me and, more important, I was turned on by him.

Maybe the pain was over.

WE SAW EACH OTHER every night for the rest of the week and we spoke a few times a day on the phone. I was just getting out of the shower one morning when Richard called from his mobile phone on the golf course. He also called from his car, and from his living room. Semi-retirement left so much free time.

"So, how many phone calls did you get today? What did the 'ladies' have to say about us?"

These were two questions I was now hearing every day. Richard liked to network, and many of his friends were women. He liked to know what the word on the street was about "us." I saw this as a minor character flaw but chose to overlook it because, well, let's face it, I was desperate. Besides, I liked drama as much as the next person. In fact, the most exciting thing about our relationship was what people were saying about it. Yesterday we'd made the *New York Post*'s Page Six, and all I could think was *I hope Burt sees this*, all the while knowing he wouldn't. I just wasn't used to a man who liked to talk about the same things girls talked about.

"Well," he asked, "does Barbara Davis think we make a great couple?" Then, "What did Alana think when you told her we're going away together next weekend?"

Was I really having this conversation? Burt hated to talk on the phone for long. He hated idle chat and morning calls. Now I was dating someone who liked the same thing I did and I was starting to hate him for it.

"Tita Cahn is finished as far as I'm concerned," he said. This was the fifth time this week he was telling me how he had reduced legendary songwriter Sammy Cahn's widow to the level of acquaintance because she badmouthed me.

"All your friends don't have to like me, Richard. I mean, we're not kids." I thought of David's dismissal of him. "I'm sure both of us have some friends who won't like the other."

"If she was really my friend, she wouldn't say nasty things about you. She is not my friend. Sammy Cahn was my friend. Tita Cahn *was* my friend, but now she is an acquaintance. If we have a party with sixty people, she can come, but if we have sixteen people she's out."

This was important information. Sixty people and she's in, sixteen and she's out. I suddenly realized I was talking to a fifty-year-old man who seemed more like fifteen. There was a world we lived in, a world with real problems and challenges, and *this* was what we were talking about? I was feeling uncomfortable and judgmental.

"I'm not so crazy about Abby Leff anymore either," he said. "For the same reason."

Richard's voice was annoying me now. I started to yearn for Burt's soft, sensual tones. I wished I wasn't having this conversation. I'd rather be making love with him.

He continued. "Soooo," letting the *O* sound linger and linger. "Monday night, what time do we have to be at the Davises?"

I hated having to answer him. It just happened. Just like that, every word out of his mouth was now annoying me.

"They'd like us to be there at seven thirty."

"Well, that means I should pick you up at about seven fifteen."

Why was this conversation making me so crazy?

"Yeah, seven fifteen sounds okay, or seven thirty? I mean, we don't have to be there at exactly seven thirty."

"Well, I like to be on time. That's when they called it for. That's when we should get there."

I didn't answer. He went on. "And what about Wednesday? I'm seeing you on Wednesday, right? We've got the Simons."

I was thinking he might have been premature telling me the details of his deathly allergy to nuts. If a person wanted to kill him . . .

"They had us," Richard said, "so we'll take them to Spago. And Friday night? What time is your friend Sandy Gallin's dinner?"

How was I ever going to get to Friday with this guy when I was having trouble getting through this conversation? I decided to be honest with him.

"You know, Richard, it's funny because in all the years I was married to Burt, I really wanted him to commit to times and dates and he couldn't. I mean, if I asked him at five o'clock what time he wanted dinner that night, it was like I was pressuring him. And now it's kind of weird because you're exactly the opposite and I feel like I've turned into Burt. I mean, all this planning. It bothers me. It feels so unspontaneous."

"Well," he answered, "grown-ups make plans. Sooooo, what time Friday?"

I answered, "Seven forty-five," with resentment in my voice.

I wondered why I couldn't be more understanding. It wasn't that I wasn't happy to have plans. It was that Richard *was* his plans. He needed them to feel safe the same way I needed Burt to feel safe. Maybe that's why it was so irritating.

I also knew that seven forty-five on Friday would be our last date. How could a man who was so insecure offer me any security? I'd just have to keep looking. I'd start at seven forty-six.

Thirty-Three

I MET MY FRIEND Mindy Seeger at an Al-Anon meeting and bonded when we found ourselves taking the same Jael Greenleaf course for Adult Children of Alcoholics. She was a recovering alcoholic who took her program very seriously—she also went to AA meetings—and when I met her she was already ten years sober. Mindy was very insightful and funny, and was willing to spend hours on the phone with me helping me process the end of Burt and the enormous bandwidth it was taking up in my life. One day I told Mindy that I was sure I was shrinking.

She told me that was impossible, but I really believed it. I showed her how my shoes were getting too big for me, and my fingers were getting smaller. I was the thinnest I had ever been, the weight I always dreamed of, and both surprisingly and not, it alarmed me.

Without Burt, I felt like I was getting tinier with each month following our split. I felt so diminished by the colossal size of the loss, and being alone felt like I was missing a limb.

Carrie Fisher fixed me up with George Lucas. She failed at first to say he lived in Marin County, but when she added that part, it did not deter me. In my ongoing search for my next Burt, what was an hour's flight? Besides, Narada Michael Walden, a hot music producer at the time, had been asking me to come up and see if we could write something together. His studio was in Marin, so a trip north seemed to be in order.

I flew up to San Francisco that Friday morning.

After checking into the Four Seasons, I quickly left to meet Narada for a writing session. Narada was given his name by his Indian guru, so that should tell you something about what his studio both looked and smelled like. Incense was wafting from half a dozen pots placed strategically around the rooms, as were Indian shawls with tiny mirror cuts all over them, usually in oranges and blacks, and pillows on makeshift couches. There were two wooden tables with prayer beads and flowers sitting on top.

The vibe was mellow, very peace and love. But as for our collaboration, it just wasn't happening. For one thing, Narada was never a hit songwriter; he was a hit producer. And second, I was too fixated on my upcoming date to center myself and write. This trip was happening for only one reason: I wanted to meet George Lucas.

Narada drove me back to my hotel, where I had two hours to get ready for my date.

I came down to the lobby looking good. I immediately spotted him waiting by the house phone. He was dressed very preppy, chinos and tweed, and the look worked.

Maybe it wouldn't work quite as well on someone else, but on George Lucas, it looked very right.

He spotted me across the lobby and watched me as I came toward him. I did make a mental note that he didn't step toward me, but I'd already traveled four hundred miles, so another twelve feet wasn't such a big deal.

"Hi," he said. I was relieved that he recognized me.

"Hi, nice to see you," I said, realizing instantly that I should have said, "Nice to *meet* you," since this was our first face-to-face encounter.

"Well, I'm glad you came," he said reassuringly. "Let's get dinner."

Oh, good, I thought. *He's glad I came.*

I was looking forward to dinner. I did notice he walked very fast. After half a block, we were not walking side by side. I was now following him up one of those ridiculously steep San Francisco streets with another two more still to go until we reached the restaurant. I had no idea why we were walking there. (Well, he was walking, by now I was almost running behind him—in heels, feeling like at any moment the wind could propel me backward down to the bottom of the hill, and he would never know what had happened to me.) *Maybe he puts all his dates through a fitness test before he feeds them,* I thought. I was completely out of breath and hoping I wasn't going to break out in a sweat.

We entered a very small French restaurant where the maître d' greeted him effusively. He helped Mr. Lucas sit down while I was left to seat myself.

George asked me if I wanted wine. Not a drinker but most certainly a people pleaser, I said, "Sure, if you do."

He asked me what type of wine I preferred.

I said, "White, please."

Had I known this was going to be the last question he would ask me all night, I would have savored it, made it last, drawn it out. In all fairness to George, I was asking him a lot of questions. Not completely out of a deep curiosity, but I had read in a recent magazine article that a man was more prone to look favorably on a new date who showed an interest in him and his work.

"So," I asked, "how did you ever come up with the idea for Skywalker Ranch?"

Two hours later, I knew more about Skywalker Ranch than I did about my own home in Bel Air. It consisted of three thousand acres, with a barn and animals, vineyards, a garden where fruits and vegetables were harvested for the on-site restaurant, a theater as well as multiple screening rooms, and parking that was mostly concealed underground to preserve the natural landscape.

He's created his own city, I thought admiringly. It did occur to me that it was going to be difficult for him to move all of this to Los Angeles. At some point he mentioned that he disliked LA and that was why he had worked so hard to make Skywalker a place he never had to leave.

I felt myself deflating as I heard his words. *This was a wasted trip,* I was thinking, when the waiter brought our desserts to the table (apple crumble with ice cream for George, berries for me).

"I really hate LA," George continued, taking a spoonful of his dessert, the smell of the warm apples distracting me from my boring berries. "The people, the smog, the traffic. The values. The business. I avoid it as much as I can. That's why I made my world here. I have everything I need," he paused, "... except the girl."

I suddenly perked up. I had been praying for a sign. Was I that girl? Because Marin County is only across the bridge from San Francisco, which is a breathtakingly beautiful city.

The check came, George took care of it, and then he was up and walking ahead of me again. A little winded, I caught up with him in the lobby. We stood facing each other.

"I probably talked your ear off," he said.

"No," I said, "it was fascinating."

There was an awkward silence.

"Well," he said, "you know my feelings about LA, but I do get down there occasionally. So maybe we can have another dinner."

"Great," I replied. "I'd love that."

"Well . . . good night." He awkwardly leaned forward and gave me a dry, mechanical kiss on my lips. It was worthy of R2-D2.

"Good night, George. Thanks again for a wonderful evening," I said, trying to hide my disappointment.

In the elevator I began to calculate the cost of this fiasco. When I passed two thousand dollars, I made myself stop. Back in my room, I noticed the fire in the fireplace was crackling on artificial logs. The king-size bed now looked big and depressing, and the thought of packing up all of my endless makeup and toiletries seemed overwhelming.

Well, he did kiss me, I told myself, taking it as a small victory and then lapsing into fantasy. *He liked me a lot. And I liked him, too.*

Fantasy was so much better than real life. I started to dwell in my newest illusion. What a brilliant guy to create such an extraordinary world. Soon I was feeling hopeful, and as I got ready for bed, I wondered how long it would be before George asked Cristopher and me to move in to Skywalker Ranch.

Thirty-four

THE NIGHT BEFORE ELIZABETH Taylor's wedding to Larry Fortensky at Michael Jackson's Neverland Ranch, I hosted a rehearsal dinner for all of the people in the wedding party at a nearby restaurant. The paparazzi were everywhere. All of Solvang, the closest town to the ranch, was swarming with photographers.

When we were leaving the restaurant, Elizabeth said to me in her sweetest voice, "Oh, Little One, I just can't stand having to deal with all those paparazzi. Will you do me a favor? Please?"

Tell me who you think ever said no to Elizabeth Taylor, especially on the night before her wedding?

"Well, if you'd just get in my limousine, I can leave here by the back door."

"Sure, Elizabeth," I said.

"Thank you, my sweet. I'll see you back at the hotel."

So I popped into the limousine, hiding inside the dark tinted windows with photographers snapping pictures as the car returned to the inn where we were staying. When it pulled up to the front entrance, there were as many photographers as you'd expect to see outside the Oscars. I felt how hard it must have been to live your life the way Elizabeth was forced to live it. They were practically falling over the car. The driver opened the door for me, and I heard a zillion voices groaning, "It's not her!" "Shit!" "Who is it?" "It's only Carole Bayer Sager!" "No!" "Forget it!"

I didn't feel bad. I felt awful. I wished Burt were in the car. At least if we had gotten out, it wouldn't have been so disappointing. Of course, the way it unfolded made perfect sense, but in my eagerness to please Elizabeth, I hadn't thought it through to its logical conclusion.

It wasn't hard to get to my room. No photographers chased after me; they parted like the Red Sea and allowed me to walk easily between them. Her plan had worked. On to the wedding.

A universal rule for anyone entering a rehab is no romantic relationships while working through your addictions. Either Elizabeth didn't hear that one or it was just one rule too many, but she came out of the Betty Ford Center sober but in love with construction worker Larry Fortensky.

Larry didn't look like Richard Burton, and he certainly didn't sound like him. His dyed blond hair hung too long from an era that had, thankfully, passed. He had a forgettable face, with bad skin that was always red, or maybe it's called "ruddy." His eyes were brown, but when you're accompanying Elizabeth Taylor, who's looking at *your* eyes anyway? Larry only became memorable because Elizabeth Taylor fell in love with him. Elizabeth did not know how to be in love with someone and not marry him.

It all looked so beautiful. We had a rehearsal during the day. Marianne Williamson, an attractive southern brunette who became famous—especially in LA—as the self-help guru of the post-EST era, turning tens of thousands of followers onto the then very popular *A Course in Miracles*, was the pastor who was chosen to marry them. I believed Marianne to be a brilliant communicator of spiritual truths.

After the rehearsal, there was a knock on the door of my hotel room. I opened it and there was Marianne, sobbing.

"Marianne, what's the matter?" I asked.

"Can I come in? I'm so upset." I ushered her in, handed her a tissue, and let her cry a bit. She collapsed on my bed.

"It's me," she said, with an almost detectable southern accent. "They're supposed to be facing me."

"Who? What?" I didn't know Marianne well. I'd learned a few valuable things from listening to a small fraction of her sixty-plus cassettes that David Geffen had insisted I buy because her message was so brilliant. Their sheer numbers overwhelmed me, sitting in their blue canvas case with the white handle.

My favorite quote of Marianne's is this one: "Our deepest fear is not that we are inadequate. Our deepest fear is that we are powerful beyond measure. It is our light, not our darkness, that most frightens us. We ask ourselves, who am I to be brilliant, gorgeous, talented, fabulous? Actually, who are you *not* to be? You are a child of God. Your playing small does not serve the world. There is nothing enlightened about shrinking so that other people won't feel insecure around you."

This was the same woman who was now falling apart on my bed. "*They're* not supposed to face the audience," she went on. "*They're* supposed to face *me*, and *I* face out to the audience."

Audience? I thought they were the invited guests. She got up to demonstrate, extending her arms out like a television evangelist, repeating, "They're supposed to face *me*. That's the correct way. That's how they've done it in all of the weddings I've ever officiated at."

"But, Marianne," I said, "this is *Elizabeth Taylor*. You've never married Elizabeth Taylor before, and if she wants to face her guests, that's how it's going to be."

"They must not know why I'm supposed to be facing outward. It has to do with the spiritual message being spread among everyone, and—"

I stopped her, put my arm around her, and said, "Marianne, you've got to get yourself together. You have a ceremony to perform, and you're going to be great. Elizabeth is counting on you." She took a deep breath and thanked me for being such a good listener. We hugged and she left.

At the ceremony, Elizabeth said her "I dos" facing her guests, against the backdrop of the roar of helicopters above, while a lone man who chose that moment to parachute onto Michael's grounds was taken away by security guards.

•   •   •

DAVID GEFFEN CALLED ME one day and suggested I drive out to Malibu to see a movie in his newly renovated screening room. He'd been waiting many months to once again be able to use it, and this was its inauguration.

"Oh, I don't know," I said, not sure I was up to making the effort to drive to Malibu.

"Stop feeling sorry for yourself. Marcia [Neil Diamond's then wife] and Sandy are coming. Get in the car and I'll see you at seven thirty."

David wasn't up for a long conversation about my feelings. He knew the best thing for me would be to do what he suggested, so once he suggested it, he got off the phone. If I wanted sympathy, his number would not be the first—or the fortieth—I'd call. If I wanted the brutal truth, there was no one but him.

I was the first to get there. David answered the door in blue jeans and a white tee shirt. I couldn't help but notice I was wearing the same thing. He looked good, very fit, and very cute. "You look great," I said.

"Thanks. You look good for someone who's falling apart. Come on, let's go wait for the others in the new room."

David had impeccable taste, and the screening room was no exception. Entering it I saw an enormous beige sofa laden with pillows in lush Rose Tarlow fabrics. It was all a cloud of pale neutrals, and I felt like the room was floating. One tier down there were two swivel chairs and a few beautiful large poufs to be used as seats, should he ever have more than eight people, which was highly unlikely. David didn't like large groups.

On the travertine coffee table sat a big red box of Edelweiss chocolates (an LA delicacy).

When Marcia and Sandy arrived a few minutes later, I was happy to see them, which surprised me, since I was not enjoying seeing anyone during this postbreakup period. It had been four months now and it wasn't getting any easier. David was immediately ready to start the film, no chitchat. The four of us sat on the couch and watched some soon-to-be-released masterwork that I cannot remember.

When the lights came up, I recoiled. Marcia had chocolate all over her face and all over her long green cotton sweater. Sandy, forever and always on a diet, was also smeared everywhere. His tee shirt looked like Jackson Pollock had been painting on it, but just in brown. David and I gaped at them both, and I think we all saw it at the same time. David's beige ocean liner of a couch was now doing a very good impression of a leopard. Fingerprints, streaks, spots of melted chocolate everywhere. Silently, I thanked God for helping me stay on my diet. My fingers were spotless. I was so relieved not to have contributed to the mess that I even held them up to David for him to inspect. Sandy and Marcia started laughing out of the horror of it all as David exploded with anger.

"Look at you both! You're pigs! Pigs!"

I think I might have thought the same thing if I were him, though I wouldn't have expressed myself quite as vehemently.

"How is it possible?" He looked at the empty candy box, with its wrappers scattered all over the table. "You ate the whole fucking box? Do you know how much money these fabrics cost? And how long I had to wait for them to be made?"

Marcia said something about sending carpet people out first thing in the morning to steam-clean the entire screening room, and Sandy got out an apology as he raced to his car and revved off.

It was the last time David ever put out chocolates. To this day he has little jars of assorted hard candies and pastel mints—nothing you'd ever really crave—just outside the screening room. Why am I telling you all of this? Because leaving his home, I laughed—*really* laughed—for the first time in ages.

CHRISTMASTIME WAS APPROACHING, AND I was still dateless for Barbara Davis's Carousel Ball, one of the city's premier charity events. I decided to call George Lucas and see if he had any interest in an experiment in sociology. He could experience everything he hated about LA all in one night.

"Who's calling?" his secretary asked pleasantly.

"Carole Bayer Sager," I answered, wondering on a scale of one to ten how recognizable my name was. *Probably a two,* I thought. *Well, depending on age, and demographics . . . older white females . . . it might be a three. George was a nine. There it was. A three was calling a nine!*

"Just a moment, please, I'll see if he's in." Basic Secretarial Training 101! "I'll see if he's in." I wondered what would happen if everyone just told the truth. "Just a moment please, I'll see if he wants to take your call . . . No, not today. Maybe he'll call you back tomorrow."

The wait seemed interminable and then there he was.

"Hello," he said. His voice sounded better than I remembered.

"Hi, it's good to hear your voice. How are you?" I asked, cringing at my fake cheerfulness.

"Swamped. The contractor screwed up my sewage system on the new building, and I've got close to a hundred guys just standing around here scratching their heads, waiting for me to figure out what I thought someone else was figuring out for me."

"I know what you mean," I said sympathetically. "That happens to me a lot." What was I talking about? "At my house . . . in a much smaller way," I added.

He was silent, making it even easier to see my pathetic neediness. It was up to me to keep going.

"Well, I just wanted to tell you I was thinking of you and the new buildings you told me about." Sure I was. Every day I found myself wondering how George's buildings were coming along. "I mean, I can't believe that I haven't seen where you work yet . . . in person," I said, like the big phony I felt like, angling for an invitation.

"Yeah," he said, ignoring his opportunity to extend one. I plowed ahead.

"How would you like to go with me to a really great Christmas party?" I asked.

"What do you mean?" he said.

Maybe if I could just sneak the name by him quickly, it would go un-noticed.

"Well," I said as fast as I could, "the Davises have this big, extravagant really beautiful Christmas party every year. It's quite unbelievable. A million twinkly lights and I thought . . ."

I thought *what?* George Lucas is going to travel to LA—a place he despises, with people who epitomize everything he hates—to see sparkling *lights?* He's created galaxies. Yeah, he's dying to come to LA to see sparkling lights.

"Are you insane!" he interrupted me. It was the most emotion I'd ever heard him express. "I'm not comfortable in that world. That's why I created my own." He added, "Honestly, it's the last place I'd ever want to be."

"Yeah, I kind of thought that was how you were going to feel. And I understand it, too. I mean, I don't even know if *I'll* go," I said, as if he cared, and knowing of course I would go. "I mean, I do like the Davises, but that life just isn't working too well for me either anymore."

Perfect. I was baring my soul to a man who wanted nothing whatsoever to do with me.

"Yeah, well . . . divorce can be a real opportunity for growth," he said. "I better be getting back to work, I'm going out of town for twelve days."

Oh. Maybe I could come, too. It was just a thought, not a real one—I promise I was sane enough to know it wasn't real. It was just one of those things that passes through my head when I've left my body.

If I was feeling bad before I called George, now I was feeling worse. It was hard to pretend I was seeing a man who didn't even invite me into his world . . . but not impossible. Here was a man so reclusive I could tell people in LA we were going together, and no one would even know it was a lie.

MY GIRLFRIEND MINDY, PROBABLY bored out of her mind with my inability to get over the loss of Burt, had urged me to write a note to his new love, Jane. She believed I needed to thank Jane for taking Burt out of the picture, which would allow something new, more loving, and healthier to come into my life. She wanted me to write it from the perspective of being well over Burt and grateful that he was gone, and then not to send it but to carry it in my wallet. Even though I didn't feel it yet, I decided to take her advice. I wrote:

Dear Jane,

I wanted to write you and thank you for taking Burt away from me even though I was his wife. To be honest, if I'd stayed with him I probably would have gotten very sick because he gave so little and took so much. I will not miss his narcissism or his inability to ever really hear or see me. I want to thank you in advance for the wonderful life I will soon be living.

Love and gratitude,
Carole

I folded it and put it in the back of my wallet. It was so hidden that I didn't find it until years later and, of course, when I read it again it was exactly the way I was feeling. Thank you, Mindy.

ALONE FOR THE FIRST time, I asked myself why I kept repeating the same dramas with the different men I was attracted to in my life. Men who never really saw me. I was the classic definition of a neurotic. I kept doing the same thing and expecting a different result. I kept choosing men I hoped would love me who could only see me as an extension of themselves. Men who loved me for my talent, but not for myself. Of course, they were all variations of my mother, who until the end of her life saw me the same way they did.

I was starting to understand that if I wanted a different result in my life, I couldn't keep walking down the same street and falling in the same hole. Recovery would mean I would have to learn to take a different street. I would have to put more value on myself and begin respecting and loving myself if I ever was going to be deserving of a man who really loved me.

Thirty-five

MY GIRLFRIEND MARGIE PERENCHIO called me on the night before Thanksgiving in 1991, ordering me to come to dinner. She and her husband, Jerry, were having small dinner parties to show their friends their meticulously decorated new home with interiors by the famed French designer Henri Samuel.

She wanted me to meet two of their friends, both bachelors: Kirk Kerkorian, owner and chairman of MGM, and Bob Daly, CEO of Warner Bros. Motion Pictures. I barely knew either of them, and I truthfully wasn't sure I could get it together, but she kept insisting.

I told her I had plans to spend the evening with a gay writer friend of Carrie Fisher's who I had recently met and liked.

"Are you crazy?" she said. "These are two of the most eligible bachelors in LA. Break that date and come to my house." I told her I would see if I could change my plans. If I had flown four hundred miles for a date with George Lucas, it seemed reasonable that I could force myself up the street to where the Perenchios lived.

Driving into Margie and Jerry's mansion past the endless manicured hedges is a sight that I still never get used to. It always feels like I could be driving into the White House. Once the former Kirkeby mansion, now renamed Chartwell, it was one of the most dramatic and recognizable mega-estates in all of Los Angeles. The front of it was used in the opening of *The Beverly Hillbillies*.

I was ushered down a very wide limestone staircase where a gleaming wood bar dominated a Giacometti table and chairs sitting beside a small sofa. It was adjacent to a huge ballroom, three steps down, that acted as their second living room and screening room. Kirk was already there. Margie smiled like a Cheshire cat and kind of thrust me toward Kirk, saying, "Carole, Kirk has never been here before. Why don't you walk him down the hall and show him some of the other rooms?"

I barely knew Kirk, but I knew I didn't want to be alone with him. He felt cold to me and austere. I knew two women who had been, or still were, madly in love with him, neither of them able, as my friend Sue Mengers used to say, "to seal the deal," and quite honestly I had absolutely no desire and even less energy to make an effort to be gracious. He was tall and slim, with a lot of gray, wavy hair and a somber face like one of the Modigliani paintings hanging on the wall I just passed. He was well dressed and looked expensive, maybe because I knew he was a billionaire. But a cheap one. I heard he lived in an apartment over his garage.

Obediently, I walked him down the large hallway as he admired the remarkable job Jerry had done meticulously renovating his mansion. "Beautiful workmanship," he said. When we turned around and walked back to the bar area, Bob Daly was coming down the wide stairs. We were introduced, though we both had forgotten that years before we'd had dinner together, invited by mutual friends. I did remember that his wife, Nancy, had once found my Lhasa apso, Hoover, when he went missing in Bel Air. The Dalys lived there as well. They returned him to me, and I sent them flowers and a very grateful note.

When Bob said hello, I immediately thought he seemed nicer than Kirk. He wasn't intimidating. He looked good in a well-tailored blue suit, white shirt and tie, and tortoiseshell-rimmed glasses. He had big brown eyes and beautiful graying hair. When he smiled, he looked a little like Jack Nicholson.

He had what would turn out to be his signature drink, a cranberry juice and soda with a touch of vodka—"just a touch"—and I had a Diet Coke. Hors d'oeuvres and caviar were always in ample supply at the Perenchio home. I was surprised when Margie said "Let's sit down," because I didn't know we were the only people coming. We walked upstairs to their beautiful smaller dining room. I remember feeling relieved to find Bob was seated to my left and Kirk was across the table, with Margie and Jerry at either side.

I had taken a Valium before I left my house because I was ridiculously nervous, and it was only now kicking in. I did like that feeling. Everything felt just a little bit easier.

In talking to Bob, I found out that he too had recently been left, by his wife of thirty years. This was similar to the bonding moment I shared with Burt ten years earlier when we both discovered we took Dalmane to go to sleep. Bob never took a sleeping pill. In fact, he told me when Nancy left him, he only slept every other night.

How coincidental, I thought, *both of us being left by our respective spouses*. Though I didn't really believe in coincidence. I believe everything happens for a reason, but I didn't share this aloud for fear he'd think me one of those woo-woo types.

The Valium gave me a sense of well-being I couldn't always count on to give myself. I think it allowed me to pass through dinner congenially, almost as though I was having a good time.

As we were getting ready to leave, Margie asked us what our plans were for Thanksgiving. I told her that Cristopher and I were going to Elizabeth Taylor's house, and Bob said he was eating at a friend's home with Nancy and his children. It appeared as though they were handling their impending divorce with much more maturity than I was mine. Margie said they were showing the not-yet-released Robert De Niro film, *Cape Fear*, at eight o'clock, after dinner, and we were welcome to come back and watch it.

Bob asked if he could follow me home. I told him I lived only six houses down the road, but he was insistent. When we pulled up to my door, I asked him if he'd like to come in for a drink. Perhaps because both of us came from families where people drank too much, we each had a bottle of water.

We sat on my long pale sofa with overstuffed beige chenille pillows in the den. For every story I had about Burt, he had a matching one about Nancy. It was so easy to talk to him, I had no idea we'd been talking for over an hour. We took turns spilling our pent-up sadness and sharing our surprise at finding ourselves alone at this stage in our lives.

I wanted to be honest with Bob and let him know who I was, so I told him, "You know, I kind of live my life waiting for the other shoe to drop."

"What other shoe?" he asked me, in complete seriousness. Oh my God, is it possible I'm meeting a man who isn't neurotic?

I excused myself to go upstairs and check on Cristopher. He heard me and sat up drowsily. I kissed him and told him to go back to sleep.

He asked me to stay till he fell asleep again, so I told him there was a very nice man downstairs who was feeling sad because he was all alone, no longer living with his wife and family, just like Mommy was no longer with Daddy. He nodded like he understood. I said I'd come up when the nice man left. He got out of bed and silently picked up his second favorite teddy bear and gave it to me. "You can give it to the man."

Returning to the den, I handed Bob the teddy bear and told him Cristopher wanted him to have it. Bob was very touched. I knew one thing—*this man will not hurt me.* I just sensed it. It was close to twelve when Bob got up to leave, asking me if I would like to meet him at Margie and Jerry's after Thanksgiving dinner and watch the movie together. I said I'd need to see if Elizabeth would be all right with that, but I thought it could work out. There were times with Elizabeth when she would become my good mommy. As it turns out, she was so happy that I had met a nice man—a studio head, no less—that she was practically pushing me out the door before I finished dessert.

Cape Fear was so scary that more than once I grabbed Bob's hand in terror of what was about to happen. Later that night he followed me home again and we talked some more.

I could be honest with Bob, and he with me. He said, "I was trying to turn myself into everything Nancy wanted me to be. It felt awful, but I tried. She wanted me to drink, I drank. She wanted me to smoke grass, I took a few puffs of grass. Whatever she wanted, I tried."

"Me, too," I said. "I went horseback riding—"

"Yeah, I went skiing," Bob interrupted.

"I cut my leg on barbed wire. The guide asked me if I wanted to go back and get a tetanus shot—me, who felt lockjaw setting in at the mere sight of rust—but I wanted Burt to see me as an adventuress so I said, 'No, later's fine. Let's just keep riding, this is so great!'"

Bob laughed. "It sounds like we both turned ourselves into pretzels."

I nodded. "Do you work out a lot?" I asked.

"No, I hate it. Nancy was fanatical about never missing a day and was always pushing me to do *something*. I hated it."

"Working out was a religion to Burt. He got endorphin highs. I have no idea what that feels like. Do you?"

"Nope, never been there." He looked at me and said, "Do you know you're very beautiful?"

"Not really," I answered. "I can't say I feel beautiful."

He shook his head. "Well, you are."

That night he asked me out on what would be our first date. Up to that point I'd only thought of him as a very decent guy. But Bob Daly was a formidable man.

He took me to Madeo's, an Italian restaurant on Beverly Drive, and we were seated in a small booth. We talked about how he got to where he was. "I was eighteen and needed a job," he told me over dinner. "I drove into New York from Brooklyn and started looking. I saw this building, I looked up, it said CBS. I said to myself, I like television, and I got a job in the accounting department. Lowest-paying job in the company. Left there as the head of the network twenty-six years later to become chairman of Warner Bros. Pictures."

"Wow," I said. "That's quite a story. You must have been very ambitious."

"No, not really. I just wanted to do the best job I could. I never had my eye on the top job. You see, I was left back in the fourth grade in Catholic school and it devastated me, so I worked extra hard at everything. All I wanted at CBS was for each boss to say, 'Good job, Bob!' "

He spoke so clearly and logically. It was funny. He didn't come in the Burt wrapping paper, but I knew that was all that was. Tear it off, and inside there was nothing of real substance, at least not for me. Bob seemed to have more of everything real.

Before dessert, he pulled out a little gift-wrapped box and handed it to me.

It was a beautiful compact. Hundreds of multicolored rhinestones made the face of Tweety Bird, one of Warner Bros.'s most beloved characters. Seeing him in living color made me smile. He told me to open it.

There was a mirror inside.

"I want you to carry this with you," he said. "So every time you don't think you're beautiful, you can look into it and know that you are."

"Oh, Bob," I said. "This is the most meaningful gift." And I meant it. How different he was from any man I had ever known before. He actually remembered how I felt and gave me a gift that could help me feel better.

Thirty-Six

BOB AND I WERE really a good match, because no normal date would allow either of us this much time to wallow in past hurts. Two "dumpees" had found each other and together felt better than they did alone. We were making a real connection.

He didn't care about me not having long legs. He wasn't tall, but he had no need for secret lifts to be hidden in his shoes. He had a wonderful acceptance of who he was, which is why he had no desire to change me.

I thought Bob might benefit from removing the little extra bit of skin I could see under his chin, but he didn't want my help. Finally, there was someone in my life whom I could not alter.

I can't say the obsession with Burt magically lifted—I still imagined him waking up one day and realizing he had made a dreadful mistake and wanting to come back—but I found myself thinking about him less and less.

My phone rang early the next day. The word was out. "Finally, you're going out with a great man," David Geffen told me. "Bob Daly is the real thing. Don't blow this!" As you know, David's opinion always carried a lot of weight with me, so I was happy he liked him. When I'd told him that Burt's leaving had devastated me, he said, "What are you talking about? You had the best ten years with him. What do you want, sixty-three to seventy-three? Let someone else have the next ten."

•   •   •

ON ONE OF OUR first dates together, I told Bob that my friend Alana Stewart and I had written a comedic script that Joel Silver had optioned and was now reoptioning. Bob said that Joel was the last producer to go to with a comedy, since he'd never made one and was only known for his big "blow up the screen" action movies. Anyway, about ten days after we began dating, Bob had a meeting with then head of production Lorenzo Di Bonaventura.

"Lorenzo," he said, "by now you might have heard I'm going out with Carole Bayer Sager. She and Alana Stewart have written a screenplay that Joel Silver just reoptioned. Lorenzo, I want you to hear what I am about to say very clearly. I do not want that script to be given one minute's more consideration than any other screenplay at Warner Bros. If you read it and want to drop it, then drop it."

Bob was adamant about not wanting anyone to think there was any nepotism at Warner Bros. I always felt that Lorenzo thought he was basically being told in some coded way to drop the screenplay.

Alana was the first to find out that our script had been canned. She called me, very upset.

"Every other studio head who was going out with you would have at least given it a tiny nudge forward," she said. "But not Bob." Later, that was to become one of the things I liked the most about him. If I ever wondered what was the right thing to do in almost any situation, I just asked Bob.

I'd been searching my whole life for powerful mythical men—white knights—all in an effort to create a world I could feel secure in. And now I might have found one. The more I got to know him, the clearer it was that he wasn't very interested in socializing with my world of entertainers and musicians, and that was the good news.

"I know that world. I service those people every day. That's my job. But I don't want to have to cater to them on weekends. That's my time off."

He ran a powerful company with thousands of employees, so he knew about power. But it wasn't what ran him. He was much more human than that.

BOB HAD YET TO meet Cristopher, so when he came over the following week for dinner, I introduced them. "Bob, this is my son Cris," I said, walking him into his room, which was strewn, like any five-year-old's would be, with little cars and trucks and Ninja Turtle toys.

"Hi," Cris said, barely looking up and then returning to his cars.

"Cris, I want to thank you for giving me that great teddy bear last week," Bob said. "And I brought you something I hope you like." He gave him a Warner Bros. shopping bag. Cris opened it and pulled out a plastic Superman. "I *love* Superman," Cris happily exclaimed, to Bob's delight. "Look at his cape and look how his arms move so he can catch people in the sky," he said, displaying the moveable arms to me.

"It's a brand-new one we made," Bob said.

"Look, Bob! Air Jordans," Cristopher said, showing off his shoes as he jumped up and slam-dunked an imaginary basketball into an imaginary hoop.

"Great shot!" Bob said. "And great shoes."

"I love shoes," Cristopher announced, sniffing his blue blankee that was never beyond his reach. "Do you love shoes, Bob?"

"Tell Bob what I call you," I urged Cristopher.

"Uh," he looked to me as if to say he didn't remember.

"You know," I said, "the story I told you about the woman who had so many shoes that—"

"Oh yeah," he remembered. "Imelda. She had to leave her country. But they let her come back . . ."

"Yes, but—"

"But they only let her come back with *one* pair of shoes because she had to give away her other shoes to the people who didn't have any."

Bob looked at me quizzically. "That is the story you told him?"

"Well," I said, "you kind of had to be there."

At dinner I watched Cristopher sniff his blankee and talk to Bob. With

Bob, he felt he could be himself. When it was his bedtime, Cris asked if I was coming up to tuck him in.

I looked at Bob, who was still finishing his pasta. "Don't worry," he said. "I'll never be jealous of Cristopher coming first. Go ahead." *I've known a lot of guys in my life, but I've never known one like Bob*, I thought, as I walked upstairs to kiss Cris good night.

Later, Bob and I lay on my bed and watched an old John Wayne movie. Bob loved westerns, especially John Wayne's. Maybe because they were so simple and life could be so complicated. There were good guys and bad guys; white hats and black hats. Bob liked things simple. My mind never shut down until some sleeping pill punched it into neutral gear. I lay with my head cradled in his arms and it felt good. When he kissed me, that felt good, too. The phone rang, and I let the machine pick it up. I alternated between watching the screen and watching Bob. I found myself studying his face. I was beginning to take great pleasure in his features. I liked his nose and his mouth. I loved his smile.

I'd never known anyone who loved John Wayne. When the wild herd of buffalo ran across the screen, I realized that Bob, like them, was the last of a dying breed, almost extinct. He was beginning to make an imprint on me and we were bonding quickly. I thought about sleeping with him, but I wanted us to really know each other before sex could cloud my thinking.

"I'm like Ajax," he told me, "but the New and Improved Ajax. In other words, I'll always be 'Bob.' That won't change, but what I can be is the New and Improved Bob." I liked that analogy because people don't change into someone else, but if they work really hard, they can become better versions of themselves.

THE CAROUSEL BALL WAS coming up and Bob and I were going together. It would be our official coming out party because all of the top executives and major talent attended. I knew I would go to bed with him after the ball, when we would go back to his suite at the Bel Air Hotel. We enjoyed being in public for the first time together. We even danced a bit, though Bob fore-warned me, "I'm not a dancer."

Back at Bob's suite I was nervous. We had two bathrooms, so we both went off to prepare for bed. I had brought the most beautiful lace nightgown, completely appropriate if I was in my thirties and on my honeymoon. But all of my concerns about how I might have looked disappeared when I saw Bob in his Brooks Brothers white pajamas with blue piping. It wasn't that he didn't look good. I just had to get used to what it looked like after seeing Burt in his boxer shorts and old tee shirts for the last ten years. My surprise must have shown.

"What's the matter?"

"Nothing's the matter," I said. "I'm not used to seeing a man in his paja-mas. Not since my dad wore them."

Bob wasn't the least bit offended or thrown off course. "Come here," he said in his matter-of-fact manner. "You look so beautiful. Come over here and get into bed with me."

I hesitated. He smiled and teasingly added, "Come on, I'm getting cold!"

"Aren't you going to turn the lights out?" I asked.

"Is that what you want? I was happy to have the lights on to look at how beautiful and sexy you are."

I didn't feel that confident. "Off, please."

In the dark we made love.

He was a very good lover. I could tell he really liked women (even if he'd only been with Nancy, and now me, over the last thirty-plus years). He was immediately turned on, and he made love to *me*. Satisfied, and relieved that we had gotten through having sex without a hitch, we both fell asleep happy to be together.

A week later, Cristopher was spending the night at his friend's house so we were at my house alone. Bob walked in when I was in the shower. "Look at that body," he said. "Look at how sexy you are."

I felt bad for him. I just had a hard time believing that someone could really love the way I looked naked in the shower. The years with Burt were sort of like being in an abusive relationship without any physical signs of abuse.

Just before Bob and I met, Joel Silver had wanted to fix him up with a Playboy bunny. I always felt he missed out. He didn't think he missed anything. He didn't want a Playboy bunny. He wanted me. That was a concept I was still having difficulty with. It was like the notice Groucho Marx sent to the Friars Club: "Please accept my resignation. I don't want to belong to any club that will accept people like me as a member."

Thirty-Seven

IT WAS HARD TO tell who was more excited waking up Christmas morning, Cristopher or me. We both rushed down the stairs. Cris couldn't wait
to open his presents. I couldn't wait for the day to officially begin. I was like
a spinning top. Burt was coming at eleven, and—terrible but true—I was
looking forward to it in spite of my new feelings for Bob, who was coming
at four.

So many presents sat under the tree, too many to count. Cris had pa-
tiently watched them pile up in the weeks preceding Christmas, keeping
count of how many were for him.

"Hurry, Mommy. I want to start."

"You can open three presents, but then we have to wait and open the rest
with Daddy."

At eleven thirty, there was Burt, half an hour late, which for him was
early. It was the first time since I filed for divorce that he was back in our living room, and it felt like he had never left. Even Agatha, our housekeeper,
was excited.

"Oh, Mr. Bacharach. You want green drink? You want tea?"

"Just a glass of water, please, Agatha," he said, with such ease, just as he
had hundreds of times before.

Cris opened his presents while I wrote down each gift. Even though
Burt and I had agreed not to exchange gifts, I had changed my mind the day

before and bought him yet one more beautiful cashmere sweater. He opened the card, sitting on the steps into the living room.

He read it to himself. It was about growing from the pain. It was about friendship and love and forgiveness. His eyes teared up. Why wouldn't they? After all, I was a writer.

Burt had kept his part of the bargain, bringing me only a token gift: a little plastic photo album. There was no card.

"I thought you'd like it for pictures of the little guy," he said.

Burt and Cristopher went outside to play ball while I stayed in and played Christmas songs, as the music played havoc with my feelings.

Someday soon we all will be together
If the fates allow
But for now we'll have to muddle through somehow.

I began to feel sad. The Push . . . the Pull . . . and the awareness that it would be impossible to step back into my old life and pretend that what had happened between us had never happened at all. Besides, now there was Bob, someone I did not want to give up.

Fifteen minutes later, Burt and Cris came back in. "Well, I guess Cris should try to get a little nap in," he said. (Translation: "I have to go.") "I'm meeting Nikki for dinner, and I'd like to try and get a little workout in first." I picked up a little gift-wrapped box and handed it to him.

"This is for Nikki. She told me she got her ears pierced."

"Oh," he said. "That's, uh, really very sweet of you, Carole." I walked him to the door. There was an awkward silence. I looked into his eyes.

"Do you feel it, too?" I asked him, wishing I hadn't heard that come out of my mouth. What was wrong with me? Though it didn't stop me. My eyes welling up with tears, I went on, "The pull?"

He looked at me. "Of course I feel it."

I knew it. I knew I wasn't crazy. There was still something there, or maybe it was just that it was Christmas.

He put Nikki's present in his pocket. "I really appreciate this, Carole," he said.

By the time he left I felt like I'd been up for days; and Bob wasn't coming over for another two hours.

Mindy called. "Would this be a good time for me to stop by? I have a little present for Cris. And one for you."

"Yes, definitely. Come by," I said, happy to have the opportunity for a reality check. When she arrived, I told her in detail about my time with Burt and feeling so inappropriately comfortable with him in the house.

"It's just Christmas, Carole," Mindy said. "I'm sure it happens to all couples in the middle of a breakup."

"And now Bob's coming for the second act of the Christmas show. No wonder they pay so much money to performers in Vegas. Two shows in one night is one too many."

Bob arrived and he kissed me hello. "Well, it's good to see you," he said, holding me close to him. Then he hugged Mindy, whom he'd met the week before.

Bob's face, too, showed the strain of too long a day. "Christmas is just not a good day for the newly wounded," he said. "I've been going through it with Nancy today. She wanted me to fly to Hawaii and join them for the rest of their vacation. I told her it was just the holiday speaking." What made him so clear and me so ambivalent?

"I brought this for Cristopher," Bob said, picking up a big present.

"Just what he needs," I said with a laugh. "Come on up and see his room. It looks like the warehouse for Toys 'R' Us."

It was hard to find Cristopher in the midst of all his new toys. He was drunk with presents.

"I don't think you have this," Bob said. "It's not on the market yet." Cristopher unwrapped it and seemed vaguely disappointed.

"It's a Looney Tunes truck," Bob explained, "with all our characters that turns into a brigade of transformers when you take them apart. It's going to be a very big toy next year."

Since it hadn't been marketed yet, Cris had no way of knowing if it was desirable. How could he want it if all his friends didn't have it or want it yet? I felt embarrassed by Cristopher's spoiled behavior. I was about to say something when, thankfully, he came through with a believable display of interest, as he began disassembling the truck. Leaving Cris to his toys, we made our way downstairs. Sitting in the kitchen, with Mindy on one side of me and Bob on the other, we laughed about the added pressure holidays bring and rejoiced that we'd all gotten through this one unscathed. That was the best Christmas present I could have asked for.

IT WAS EARLY JANUARY and Bob wanted me to meet two of his closest friends, Stacey and Henry Winkler. On the way to dinner at Trader Vic's, Bob told me that Stacey had already warned him about me.

"Why?" I asked him.

"Well, she told me to be careful with you because you traveled with a fast crowd. Sandy Gallin, David Geffen, Alana Stewart."

"I never think of myself as living a fast life," I said. "I think when the fast part came, I was already home. If I went at all."

"Well, I just want you around me," he said. "That makes me *happy*."

We got to the restaurant to find Stacey sitting alone. Henry was home sick.

Oh! I failed to mention that Stacey was Nancy Daly's closest friend. Together they ran United Friends of the Children, a foster care organization, although since the separation they were not quite as close.

The surprise of the dinner was how much Stacey and I liked each other. I told the whole horrible story of Burt leaving, and she responded with so much compassion, I felt like we'd known each other for years. We shared a similar self-deprecating humor, and I could feel us bonding as the evening went on.

When Nancy asked Stacey the next day what I was like, Stacey very unwisely made the mistake of telling her how much she liked me. That, as you can imagine, did not go over very well. Nancy ended their long and close friendship soon after. She cut Stacey off and never regretted her decision. The only thing about all of this that one might construe as odd was that within the next two months Stacey Winkler would become my new best friend.

THE FOLLOWING WEEKEND BOB suggested we go up to the Post Ranch Inn at Big Sur. The view from our terrace through the trees to the ocean made me feel instantly peaceful, though the thought did occur to me—because how couldn't it?—that in an earthquake, those stilts that our glorious room was built on would crack and we'd be swept away in the angry ocean.

We took a walk through the town of Carmel, holding hands and talking.

"No one in my family ever got divorced," Bob said. "I'm the first one in the family. I would have never left. You just don't do that. I didn't question if I was happy. We were a family."

"But were you happy?"

"Not happy like I am with you, but I figured this is how it is when you get to thirty years." I made a note to myself: Bob was a stayer.

We spotted a restaurant with a line, so long we knew it must be good. He started walking to the back of it. I wondered why he was walking the wrong way—I'd expected him to do what I thought every top executive would do, take out some cash and find the person to hand it to—but he was happy to stand there, just being Bob.

"So you don't mind standing in lines?" I said, somewhat disappointed.

"Why shouldn't I stand in line? Everyone else is." After a beat he asked, "Why, would you rather we walked right in?"

"Well, I did get used to it with Burt, and I liked the way we were treated as a result of his celebrity. But I also like the way you're happy to just stand here, because it says a lot about who you are."

"If it's important to you," he said, "I'll call my assistant and have her get us right in."

"No, this is fine. Really."

And it was. It really was. We talked, the line moved briskly and soon we were comfortably seated inside.

Bob reached into his pocket and took out a bunch of white folded cards with his name stamped on top. "These are my cards," he explained. "All of my important phone numbers and information are on here: my kids, my doctors, my medications, my employees, my Warner Bros. plane crew, et cetera." *Plane crew!* Okay, so you stand in line a little.

He pulled out another card. "This is my schedule for each day of this weekend. I have a card for every single day. When I finish the day I rip it up. But this restaurant wasn't on my card because we just came upon it."

I laughed. "I've never met *anybody* as organized as you." His voice was nothing like Burt's. He spoke crisply and concisely. What Burt took at least ten sentences to say, Bob said in less than one. He didn't give you any time to get bored.

"I don't carry a wallet. I figure it's too easy for pickpockets. So I keep my cash folded with a rubber band around it in my right pocket. I keep my credit cards and driver's license with another rubber band around them in the other pocket. I put the cards in one pocket and the cash in the other. That way, if I were to be robbed I could give them my cash and still have my cards." Who *was* this man? Who could ever think all of this through?

He had solved a problem most people didn't even know existed, as effectively as possible. I can't imagine even the thinnest wisp of such a thought ever going through Burt's head, let alone his honing in on it with such precision. I could see how Bob could run a studio.

"Easy," he said, finishing up with a quick clap. "Very easy. I like to think I make complicated problems less complicated, and when something is easy, I try not to complicate it."

"Are you always so sensible?" I asked.

"Yeah, I'm a pretty sensible guy," he said with a smile, "and I think people know it. I'm not a Hollywood kind of guy. All these years I've never gone anyplace where I've seen anyone doing drugs. My kids would say, 'Dad, didn't you smell the grass at the Eisners' clambake?' And I told them I didn't smell a thing. I didn't even know the smell of marijuana."

"Well, you do give off a kind of ethical vibe. I think people think of you as principled and would not look to include you in any activity you might feel uncomfortable in."

"When I tried it with Nancy," he said matter-of-factly, "I didn't feel a thing."

"Well, maybe we'll do it together sometime," I said, not expecting it to be anytime soon.

Thirty-Eight

TOWARD THE END OF February 1992, Peter Allen called me from New York City.

"Hey, honey, it's Peter."

"Peter! I haven't spoken to you in so long," I said, feeling a little guilty.

"Yeah, well, I've been everywhere, as you can imagine. I just did a huge concert in Australia at the Sydney Opera House, sold out, got rave reviews. Hey, I was wondering, darlin', if that fabulous Bob of yours, who just happens to own Warner Bros., I wouldn't expect less of you—"

"He doesn't *own* it," I interrupted. "He's the cochairman."

"All right, whatever. Do you think he could get me two passes to the *Mambo Kings* screening? And the party following?"

"Of course he will, Peter. And we'll be in New York for it, too, so I'll finally get to see you. I've missed you so much."

On our first night in New York, Bob, who had not yet met my family, invited my mother, my cousin Joan, and her husband, Joel, to dinner at Jean-Georges, the new restaurant that opened at the Mark Hotel.

Once seated, my mother turned to Bob and asked, "Are you divorced?"

"Not yet," Bob answered, "but we have filed."

Anita perked up and then barraged Bob with a rapid round of questions.

"Where are you living now?" "How many children do you have?" "Is Nancy seeing anyone?" "How long have you run Warner Bros.?" "And how often do you come to New York?" And finally, easily her most important question: "How did you get along with Nancy's mother?"

"I not only got along with her, I *still* get along with her very well," Bob said. "I took Nancy and her mother to Paris for her eightieth birthday."

"Oohhhh!" Anita said, duly impressed. You could hear the wheels of her mind spinning. "Would you ever take *me* to Paris?" she asked as coquettishly as she could manage, trying to temper her usually brassy timbre to sound more like my soft one.

My cousin Joan jumped in, appalled. "Anita, listen to you. You just met the man, how could you ask him such a question?"

Bob said to her, "Anita, if Carole and I are together when you turn eighty, I'll take you to Paris."

"Oh! What a wonderful event to look forward to," she said, turning to me and giving me a look that I easily interpreted as "Let's not screw this one up." As if I was the one who'd screwed up with Burt.

Joan, who dragged me to every movie she'd ever loved when we were kids—and she loved most of them—was thrilled that Bob ran Warner Bros. Her questions were more appropriate and I could tell she too was happy with my new boyfriend. Joel, who was never a big talker, stayed true to his reputation and barely said a word.

After the meal, when we were all standing in the lobby, my mother, in a failed attempt at a stage whisper, instructed me to "wrap him in cotton." In case I was deaf, she repeated herself, this time even louder, "Do you hear me, Carole? *Wrap him in cotton.* This one's a keeper." (FYI, Bob kept his word and took Anita to Paris for her eightieth birthday.)

NOT HAVING SEEN PETER in a while, I was taken aback by his appearance. He was painfully thin, and at the after-party, he took me aside and told me he had AIDS. He hadn't told anyone outside of his very closest friends because he wanted to keep working as long as he could.

I started to get teary. He put his arm around me reassuringly. *He* was comforting *me*. "I'll be fine, love. You know me."

"Is someone taking care of you?"

"Well, Liza's been amazing," he said. "Honestly. She doesn't let me be, she just wants to take care of me. And you know all my New York charity ladies—you met Judy Peabody, right? Well, she takes such care of me. I have so much food in my apartment, I could open a restaurant."

We hugged again, and I returned home determined to stay in close touch. I hadn't realized, nor had Peter wanted me to know, how sick he already was.

Two months later, he decided to drive up from Leucadia, just north of San Diego where he had a house, to try to write a song with me. He looked even worse than he had in New York, but he was still upbeat. We started a song called "Our Last Song Together," both of us knowing it probably was. It felt a little ghoulish.

We didn't finish it, as I kind of knew we wouldn't. When he left, I walked him to his car. I kissed him and hugged him and told him I loved him. He told me he loved me, too, and said, "Take care of yourself," adding, "not that I have to tell *you* that!" I smiled because he knew me so well.

Just before he pulled out I, ever the songwriter, said, "Hey, Peter, if I'm ever going through one of our unpublished songs and I find one that I think could be even better and maybe a hit, is it okay if I bring a third writer in?"

"Honey, after I'm gone, you can do whatever you want with them." He laughed.

Peter called me two weeks later, the day before he died. I was told I was one of only three people he called to say good-bye to. But I didn't say good-bye. I couldn't. I said "I love you" instead.

HOW DO YOU WRITE a song about two Saint Bernards who are in love? Of course, you don't if you are busy with other work, but my phone wasn't ringing off the hook. So when my friend Ivan Reitman, the director of *Ghost-busters*, among many others, called and asked me if I wanted to write a title song for the movie *Beethoven's 2nd*—not even the original—I said yes. It wasn't an important motion picture, but a movie is always a good platform from which to launch a new song.

I called my friends James Ingram and Clif Magness and asked them to write it with me. I hoped we would write something for James's big soulful voice.

Needless to say, I'd never written a love song for two dogs before, but all my life I've lived with and loved dogs.

The great dog whisperer Cesar Millan once observed me with my dogs and said, "Carole, a dog needs three things equally. Exercise, discipline, and love. You give them three things: love, love, and love. Then you wonder why they don't respect you." The story of my life.

I think I love dogs as much as I love people, with a few exceptions. I love that I can ascribe my feelings to my dogs. When I'm feeling a little sad, Daisy, my little Bolognese, looks forlorn, and when I'm happy I can see a big smile on my Maltese Dylan's face. As for Benny, my baby Yorkie, wherever I am, he is within two feet of me. These little beings adore me unconditionally, and they literally look up to me. Whatever I say to them, they always look at me as if to say, "Wow, you're so smart." So it was with a smile that I sat down to write the song that became "The Day I Fall in Love," which did turn out to be a duet for James Ingram and Dolly Parton.

The song needed to be happy, leave a smile on your face, and work if you imagined people as well as dogs. It was not a hard song to write. The image of two happy dogs stayed in my head as we wrote it.

I wonder where's that great big symphony?
Roll over, Beethoven
Won't you play with me?

I was not completely surprised when it was nominated for a Golden Globe in 1993. Well, let's just say I helped some of the small group that constituted the

Globe voters become familiar with our song. Unlike with the Oscars, you're allowed to throw press events for the Globe members. I opened my home to them, throwing a beautiful luncheon with four surprise guests: the two giant Saint Bernards from the movie, James Ingram, and an unmistakable life-size cutout of Dolly Parton, who could not be there—okay, three surprise guests and some cardboard.

At each seat lay giant chocolate bones engraved with the movie's logo. (Hopefully the members knew it was for them and not their dogs, as chocolate is known to kill dogs.) The curvaceous cardboard Dolly was placed strategically next to a piano where James performed his side of the duet live over Dolly's recorded vocal, embellishing the track with flourishes of chords.

Each guest had his or her picture taken standing next to James and "Fake Dolly" along with the two very real dogs—so real that they were urinating anywhere they saw fit. Three days later, each guest received their individual photos and the sheet music, all autographed by the three of us.

After the Golden Globe nomination, we received an Oscar nomination as well.

The thing for me about being nominated for an Oscar is even when I know in my heart that I have no chance of winning, on the day of the Oscars, I start to imagine that just maybe through a series of impossible circumstances, I might end up holding that golden trophy in my hands.

David Geffen called me while I was getting dressed.

"What are you doing?" he asked chattily, forgetting that Bob and I were going to the Academy Awards.

"I'm getting ready to leave for the Oscars," I said while finishing up my evening makeup at two thirty in the afternoon, and expecting to feel very overdone, to say the least, in the bright sunlight awaiting me.

"Please," he said. "Why even go? You realize you have absolutely no chance of winning."

"You're right," I said, "but you never know for sure."

Well, that was it for him. "Are you *out of your mind*?" he said, raising his voice. "*Bruce Springsteen*, who has never written a song for a motion picture, is nominated for the *Tom Hanks* movie *Philadelphia*, about a man who has *AIDS*, and you think you are going to win with a song about two Saint Bernards in a totally forgettable movie? Are you *completely* crazy, Carole?"

"You're absolutely right," I said, as whatever small balloon of hope I had popped above my head. "I think it was more of a fantasy."

"Well, don't tell it to another soul. Have a good time," he said, hanging up.

It's just nice to be nominated, I thought a few hours later, watching and applauding from my seat as Bruce Springsteen walked up to the stage of the Dorothy Chandler Pavilion to accept his Oscar for "Streets of Philadelphia."

Thirty-Nine

ON THE EARLY MORNING of January 17, 1994, with Cristopher away for the weekend with a friend, Bob was sleeping at my house on Nimes. At 4:31 a.m., we were jolted awake, my heart pounding instantly. The house was shaking violently. Bob, instantly clear-headed, said, "This is a big one. Get under a doorway." Finally, the rumble subsided.

We both walked into my bathroom. It looked like the epicenter was right there at my vanity. All my mirrored walls had cracked and some of the mirrors had fallen down. Was there a message here for me? My toilet had separated from the wall and was hanging on lopsidedly in its stall.

"I don't want to sleep here ever again," I said, knowing Cristopher was coming back from Aspen in a few hours.

"Don't worry. I'll send Tony" (a lovely, loyal man who had worked for Bob for years) "over today to help all of you move into my house on Carolwood. It's on flat ground. It'll be safer."

The universe was conspiring to move us closer together sooner than we had planned. Stacey and Henry Winkler, who sustained a lot of damage, too, were also coming over to spend the night with their children, Max and Zoe. It was so funny that all of us inherently believed that Bob's was the safe place to be.

When we got there, I saw no damage in his downstairs at all. The kitchen and the family room were perfect. It wasn't until we went upstairs to what was now going to be our master bedroom that I stopped in my tracks. Nancy had chosen to put a giant chandelier right over their king-size bed. It had come away from the ceiling and shards of glass were in slivers all over the duvet cover.

"Oh my God, we could have been killed if we slept here," I said out loud. Despite evidence to the contrary, we still all believed Bob's house was the safest place to be, and he was the safest person to be with.

All the newscasters were saying how lucky Los Angeles was that it struck at such an early hour, for although thirty-three people died and eighty-seven hundred people were injured, the numbers would have been infinitely higher if the quake happened during working hours.

There were aftershocks and more aftershocks, but Bob, Cristopher, and I were now a family living in Carolwood, and it wouldn't be long at all before my house on Nimes Road was put up for sale.

The earthquake, defined as "a sudden and violent shaking of the ground," was for me exactly that—a seismic shift causing me and Cristopher to be thrown together suddenly with Bob under his roof. Life was demanding that I change and that Cristopher change as well. He could no longer talk to me disrespectfully without Bob saying, "Excuse me. That's no way to talk to your mother. Apologize to her."

What? I'd never heard that before. Burt would drift away, hating conflict even more than I did. I was left to handle Cris's outbursts on my own, and my difficulties stemmed from never wanting to be my mother, the stern disciplinarian, so I overgave and overforgave more times than I should have.

When Burt left, I thought it important for Cris to see a really good child psychologist to help him process whatever feelings he was having as a result of our impending divorce. We sat in the doctor's office for the first time. Cris and I were seated together on a couch, and Dr. Wasserman was sitting behind a brown desk. He asked me why we were there. I began to tell him about the split-up and the eight months of trying to keep the relationship together. I felt a hard tap on my head but kept going. He asked me questions and I answered them. How was Cristopher handling the divorce? As I spoke, I felt an even more significant tap from Cris in the center of my head. I looked at him, smiled understandingly, and continued. What, Wasserman asked, was I hoping that Cristopher would gain from seeing him? Did I envision it as a short-term or long-term relationship?

Cristopher knocked me in the head yet again.

"Are you aware," Dr. Wasserman slowly said, "that your son has been hitting you in the head this entire time?"

"Oh. Yeah," I said, semi-aware.

"Three times now," he added.

"Well, you know, he's understandably nervous."

"So that gives him permission to hit you in the head?"

I had no answer.

"Hitting you in the head, Mrs. Bacharach, is a complete boundary violation. Your son is violating your boundaries."

Oh, I thought, realizing that I wasn't really sure what boundaries were, or if I even had any.

That night, before it was time to put Cristopher to bed, I wanted to hug him and tell him how much I loved him. I went into his room and started to embrace him. He pushed me away. "Stop," he said. "That's a boundary violation." How was it possible that a six-year-old understood and embraced the doctor's message so quickly that he was able to use it against me, while I continued to struggle with the very idea of boundaries?

Here I was, living with a completely functioning adult male who showed up for life on a daily basis. On time. Maybe it was just seeing this and feeling this shift in energy around me, but I found myself waking up earlier in the morning and driving Cristopher to school, picking him up, taking him for a snack, making *him* my priority instead of leaving it all to a nanny.

Bob got up every day at a set time, regardless of how late he'd been up the night before, and that was all very new for me.

Unlike so many other times in my life where my writing and relationships were intertwined, there was no confusing why Bob was with me. He just loved me.

He certainly didn't love me for my music, which often amazed me, because every other man in my life had. I don't even think Bob loves music. In any car I've ever been in with him, regardless of what's playing through the speakers, his first words are "Turn the music off, will you?" To him, it's extraneous sound that interferes with his thinking. Until he met me, the FM button on Bob's radio had never been pushed. But being loved by a really good man beats having a music partner. Hands down.

Being present in my own life is something that I had not been for far too long. This new me was going to take some getting used to, and I knew I needed to imagine it as a long-distance run and not a sprint.

So the gauntlet had been thrown down. Not by Bob, but by me, because I could have just said, "You know what? I can't do this. It's too high-functioning for me," and found another barely present guy to distract me from examining my own behavior. But instead I stayed, and I welcomed the opportunity. It was already way past the time to have a different life, which is to say, to be fully alive.

NIKKI BACHARACH HAD BEEN living with Angie again since she'd gotten out of the Wilson Center. Bob and I would have her over periodically for dinner, and Cristopher loved discovering a new sister. Though she was eighteen years older than he was, he seemed to understand that she needed to be treated gently. I was happy when Burt started taking her and Cristopher out to dinner to spend more time together.

She'd been officially diagnosed as suffering from Asperger's syndrome once the medical community became aware of it in 1992. In light of this news, the Wilson Center recognized that they could not help her in any meaningful way and released her. I apologized to Nikki for my part in her having been at the center.

Nikki was obsessed with earthquakes for as long as I'd known her—all she wanted was to feel one—and at one particular dinner she spoke incessantly about her misfortune of having been in Tahiti when the Northridge quake hit LA. She mourned the fact that she missed it; it pained her that she didn't get to experience the shaking.

"But, Nikki," I said, "people died in that earthquake."

"I know," she said, "but that doesn't change my pain at having missed it."

She was also phobic about noise. The sound of a helicopter overhead or a leaf blower from a neighboring garden would drive her to despair.

But what consumed her the most as the years passed was the crippling fear of her mother eventually dying and leaving her on the earth alone. This was unbearable to her. She would say, "If Angie dies, I'll kill myself."

I felt tremendous compassion for Angie, who seemed to have given up any chance for a life of her own to care for her daughter. It had gotten to the point where she had to discontinue her weekly card game at her home, because even that much noise would make Nikki crazy.

Angie got Nikki an apartment in Thousand Oaks and enrolled her in a college nearby where she could take one geology course each semester and study the earthquakes she loved. On the weekends she went home to Angie.

Sadly, as Angie got older, Nikki's fear of being left alone became more intense, and in January 2007, at forty, she committed suicide.

It was all a tragedy, her death and her life. Cris felt the pain in his own way. It took two years for him to show me he had tattooed a heart on his wrist with Nikki's name below it. When I asked him why, he said, "Because she was my sister."

I called Burt to tell him how sorry I was, and he told me she left him a note. I asked what it said, and he said he didn't read it.

"You didn't read a suicide note from your daughter?" I asked incredulously.

"I let Jane read it and decide if I should read it, and she said I shouldn't. It was just rehashing all the things I already knew: her anger at me for putting her in Wilson and leaving her there for nine years."

Today there is so much more understanding, support, and coping strategies for someone like Nikki with severe Asperger's. I certainly would have been more accepting and compassionate, and would have clearly seen the futility of sending her away from home for help.

I felt guilty that instead of helping her I added to her burden. I never could have changed her situation, but sometimes out of the blue I'll think about Nikki and feel anguished that I just didn't do enough to try and save her.

forty

ALTHOUGH I NEVER DOUBTED my unconditional love for Cristopher, through my close girlfriend Stacey I did come to see the big difference between me, who was always a working mother, and Stacey, who was a full-time mom. I was almost never with Stacey for any length of time before one of her three children *needed* to speak to her.

Sometimes I wished I had that relationship with Cristopher. When I would call Stacey at night, her son Max would often pick up the phone. Until he was well past sixteen, he would almost always say, "Could she call you back later, Carole? Mom and I are spending some quality time together." I wanted Cristopher to want to share his feelings with me, and want to watch television with me, and basically spend more time with me, but maybe I hadn't put in enough time with him. In any event, Cristopher once very wisely said, "Mom, I'm not Max. Stop comparing me to him."

ONCE I WAS LIVING in Carolwood, I was in the process of becoming everything Daly: up early, no sleeping in, go go go all day, and at night, tear up the card. That was the Bob Daly way.

Now, with me being an only child, you can imagine my surprise when I finally met all of the family. There was Linda, Bobby, and Brian. I felt like I instantly went from *Mame* to *The Sound of Music*. With the Dalys and their closely knit family, all of whom I liked, I expected Bob to blow the whistle and for me to get in line with the von Trapp children and break into a chorus of "Edelweiss," the perfect Austrian song for a Jewish girl.

Cristopher loved the concept of "more." Thus, he loved being part of a big family.

As I tucked him into his new bed in his new home, he started to count his family members much the way he counted his prized sneakers and hats.

"I have Linda, who is a new sister, and Bobby is a new brother, and Brian is another new brother. That's three more family."

"Well, you know, Bob and I are not married yet."

"Marry Bob," he said. "I want more brothers and sisters."

"Okay, sounds good to me," I said, rubbing his back. "Let me work on that."

It took another two years, and his daughter Linda's marriage, before Bob asked me to marry him. There was something about his getting engaged before Linda that struck him as inappropriate, and Bob always listened to his gut.

He gave me free rein to make the wedding of my dreams. As my first two weddings left so much to be desired—the first saw me going down the aisle in need of smelling salts, and my second had four people witnessing Burt saying "I'll try"—I wanted this to be the real thing: beautiful, enchanted, and romantic. I felt that by planning all the many details of our wedding, and surrounding us with people we loved, our commitment to each other would be more meaningful and this time it would last.

Of course it's exceedingly dangerous to give me free rein, because I'm as impractical as I am creative. Even a set designer has a budget, but without one, this is how my first meeting with our team went:

"I would like it to be tented down below"—they began to take notes— "but I want the tent to disappear," I said.

"Disappear?" the wedding planner asked with some concern.

"Yes, I want it to look like you've walked into an enchanted forest, with wisteria and lilies hanging at various lengths from the branches above. I'd like a faux brick and wooden entrance so people have no idea what they're stepping into or where they are. Oh, and I'd like not to have a pole in the middle because I don't want anyone to even know they're in a tent."

Bob's longtime trusted aide, Marissa, asked, "Well, how is the tent supposed to stay up, Carole, if there's no support in the middle?" The others, wanting to please me, because I was after all to be Mr. Daly's wife, said they were sure they could figure out a way to make me happy.

Bob wanted a "traditional" white cake with white icing. Well, you have no idea how many white cakes are not completely "white" or don't "taste like traditional white cake," whatever that taste is. He sampled nine different cakes before he found the one he loved. If I'd had to go through as thorough an investigation as those cakes did, I might not be Mrs. Daly today.

For days before the Saturday evening wedding (June 8, 1996), hordes of people were setting up the sound system, the lighting, and of course the construction of the pole-free tent. Late Friday afternoon, we did a final lighting check, and when I walked inside I was standing in this magical forest that was everything I'd imagined and more.

Two hours later I was upstairs reveling in the fantasy setting we had all created when Bob burst into the bedroom. "Your tent with no center pole just collapsed," he said. "It's gone. It's lying in a pile."

"You're kidding, right? That's not funny, Bob."

"You want to see not funny? Come downstairs and look."

With no center pole, the weight of the flowers and the twigs and the branches and the wires was too much for the structure to bear and down it came. The tables that had already been beautifully set were now covered with debris and piles of now-all-visible canvas.

I started to cry. Marissa told me not to panic. They would fix it. I couldn't imagine how, yet unbelievably, with a double crew from Warner Bros., they worked overnight like an army of elves and managed to put the tent back up with the all-too-essential center pole, now disguised—as it always should have been—to look like a magnificent tree reaching up toward the sky.

It was the most magical night imaginable. Our families, our children, our close friends, all gathered to celebrate two people who had found each other later in their lives. It was a middle-aged fairy tale.

Cristopher walked me down the aisle. He was now ten years old, and I couldn't have loved him more. After we said our vows outside our living room, golf carts took the guests down to the enchanted forest. Once everyone was seated, Bob said, "Some of you may be wondering about what you are sitting in tonight. It was all Carole's vision. She dreamed this and I wanted to give it to her because she makes every day of my life magical."

I had tears in my eyes.

He said, "Carole is known to some as a woman who has many names, but tonight she has one name, and I would like to ask Mrs. Daly to have this dance with me."

If I were any other woman sitting there, I would wish I were me. Bob was the most romantic man in the room and he loved me.

Bob's turn to get teary came when his two sons, who were his best men, made their toasts.

Brian thanked me for "bringing our Dad back to us in a way we never had him before, more open, more fun-loving, more available to his family."

And Bobby said, "I always knew I was going to be the best man for one of these guys, I just never dreamed it would be my father."

James Ingram, David Foster, and Melissa Manchester performed. "Oh, Carole and I go back a long way," she said between songs. "Even back then, this girl knew what she wanted—big furniture." Huh? I felt a little confused, but then I remembered how reluctant she was to leave my big-pillowed couch back in the Seventies. Then David began to play an intro and Melissa said sweetly, "Pretend like you're singing this to each other," and sang "Come In from the Rain" so beautifully I rushed to the stage to hug her and thank her.

The greatest gift Bob has given me in our years together has been the gift of really being loved, which allowed me, for the first time in my life, to feel safe. And on our anniversary every year since, we have this tradition of eating the same meal and the same cake—thank God the bakery is still in business—and then watching the full-length video of our wedding. The last few years it became more depressing, as we'd lie in bed and sadly comment: "Dead, divorced, dead, dead, Alzheimer's, divorced, dead" as we watch each couple enter the man-made forest. Finally, this year we couldn't take it anymore. We went directly to the three-minute highlight montage, edited to "That's What Friends Are For."

No marriage is perfect. One constant area of contention that plagues ours involves time, as in "What time do we have to leave for . . . ?" So used to being late with Burt, it was not easy to make the 180-degree switch to Bob's need to be more than on time. I would accuse him of wanting to get to a party so early he could help the waiters set up. He liked being early better than being on time. I still beg him sometimes, "Drive around the block. I'm not going in yet. There's not one car here." We have the same little argument over and over.

"God, we're going to be too early."

"What's the difference if we get there a little early?" he'll answer. "We can sit and talk. You always say we don't talk enough!"

"Yeah, but I didn't mean sitting and talking in an empty restaurant while the waiters are still setting up."

While I'm finishing dressing, Bob will walk in and say, "Ready?" I'll say, "Not yet," and he'll say, "I'll be downstairs."

"What does that mean, 'I'll be downstairs'?" I'll argue. "You said we don't have to leave for ten more minutes."

"That's right. And I'll be waiting downstairs."

This lets me imagine him waiting in the car, going crazy, causing me to move more slowly. Sometimes the phone will ring.

"I'm in the car. Where are *you*?"

"Where you called me. Here."

"Hurry up, there's going to be traffic."

I enter the car trying to shake off the annoyance of knowing I'm going to be too early. And then, somewhere along Sunset a few extra cars will be stopped at a light and he'll say, "Didn't I tell you there was going to be traffic?" And it never changes. We repeat the same scenes, knowing exactly who'll say what, and when. Why do we do that?

Forty-One

DAVID FOSTER HAS WOVEN in and out and around my life like the thread of a fine tapestry so effortlessly and for so long that I sometimes forget to notice his many contributions to it, both professionally and socially.

I can't recall ever asking him for help when he hasn't said yes, whether it's putting talent together for my wedding or other major events, or performing with me for certain charitable organizations, or playing keyboards on various records I was involved with. Though we didn't write together nearly as much as I did with others, he is one of my favorite collaborators. As with a few others I've mentioned, I had to be wary because he, too, could make anything we wrote sound like a sure hit.

David is handsome, quick, funny, irreverent, and oozing with musical talent. Burt once said he thought David was possibly the most musical man of the baby boom generation. He was a brilliant composer, producer, and arranger, and his work with artists including Josh Groban, Chicago, Earth, Wind and Fire, Céline Dion, and Barbra Streisand earned him forty-seven Grammy nominations and sixteen wins, including Record of the Year and Album of the Year in 1992 for Whitney Houston's "I Will Always Love You" and the soundtrack to *The Bodyguard*.

David is so inventive and so able to arrange records on the spot that there was a certain producer who was said to put the best session musicians in a studio, get Foster to play keyboards, and just sit back knowing David would produce the record and he'd take the credit.

"Hey, Caaa." That's how David has said hello to me for as long as I can remember. And then, because he probably likes the cadence he'll usually add in perfect rhythm, "Carole Bayer Sager Hamlisch [where I then interrupt and say "Not true, never married him"] Bacharach Daly."

I spoke to David a short while ago. He knew I was writing this book and asked me, with still a trace of his Canadian accent, "Did you put that story about us in this book?"

"What story?"

"You know, that time when we were both between spouses and I laid my head on your lap, and you looked down and asked me, 'What are you doing?' without a thought that I was looking to get something going between us." I guess the reason I didn't pick up on it is because David has a type, and I was so far away from that type—tall, blond, big breasts—it would never have occurred to me that he was being flirtatious.

In fact, he was so completely without filter during most times that we worked together that he once held up a photo to a few studio guys of his soon-to-be (and now ex-) wife Linda Thompson. "Look at this picture. Does she not have a body that goes on for days?" When it was passed to me, I felt like I was just another guy in the recording studio. Anyway, his mentioning this to me thirty years later was flattering.

David played keyboards on my first two records. We wrote a song for my second record, . . . Too, "It's the Falling in Love," which Michael Jackson later recorded on Off the Wall, the first of his brilliant trilogy with Quincy Jones, followed by Thriller and Bad.

When Warner Bros. approached me to write the songs for what was to be their first animated musical, I said yes and immediately asked David if he had any interest in collaborating with me. He did, so we signed on together to try our hand at Quest for Camelot.

Quest for Camelot? The title alone should have been a red flag. It sounded like something everybody had already seen on television as a kid and hated even then. The pitch meeting in which the story was described to us was not reassuring, leaving me wanting something more, something better. *Much* better. Still, the idea of being given this large canvas on which to write a half dozen songs clouded my initial instinct, which was flashing: "Not Good Enough, Not Good Enough." You would think I'd have learned something about trusting my instincts from *Georgy*, but no. I completely ignored the signs and moved forward.

It reminded me of Steve Martin's movie *The Man with Two Brains*, where he is about to marry this horrifying gold-digging woman and he looks up at a painting of his dear dead wife hanging over the fireplace and says, "Becca, if there's anything wrong with my marriage to Dolores just give me a sign." The room spins, the painting falls off the wall behind him. Lights explode and the portrait of Becca spins and spins. Horror music plays, underscoring the scene. Beat. "Just any kind of sign—I'll keep on the lookout for it. Meanwhile, I'll just put you in the closet."

David and I began to work on the songs for the movie. The director was very young and, it turned out, singularly untalented. He'd grown up in Belgium, so I'm not sure how familiar he was with American music, but the whole process felt very disorganized. There seemed to be no one in charge who knew what they were doing. In fact, except for me, no one involved had ever worked on a musical of any sort.

Our job, writing the songs, was easy. David and I always worked well together, and this project was no exception. We wrote most of the required songs and they were really quite good, one or two of them maybe even excellent. They were easily the best things in the film thus far.

In the story line, the heroine of the movie is about to embark on a dangerous adventure into the treacherous woods, and her mother is worried for her safety. I suggested to David that we write "a prayer" in that scene, where the mother prays for her daughter's protection. David began playing different melody ideas until I interrupted with what had become my signature line, "Play that again." That led us to "The Prayer":

> *Lead her to a place*
> *Guide her with your Grace*
> *To a place where she'll be safe*

The leads of the film were unknowns, totally different from the brilliant star casting on the big Disney films (and then subsequently the Pixar and Dream-Works movies). We did have the wasted talents of Gary Oldman as the villain and Eric Idle and Don Rickles as the comical two-headed dragon, which only looked good as a stuffed toy (and I would have made those differently—more plush, not so stiff).

The only other stars were artists David and I cast to sing the songs, including Céline Dion, Andrea Corr from the Corrs, and Steve Perry, the lead singer of Journey. Not to mention Andrea Bocelli (an opera singer whose greatest success was his duet with Sarah Brightman on "Time to Say Good-bye") singing the end credits in Italian.

QUEST FOR CAMELOT WAS the only thing that *almost* threatened my marriage to Bob.

Many times during the making of it, David threatened to quit, not to be difficult but to disassociate himself from what we both had little faith could ever turn into a good film, even for little children.

Lorenzo Di Bonaventura, who seemed to be overseeing the project from his post as Warner Bros. head of production, was no fan of musicals. If it had been up to him, he would have taken all the music out and just let things explode for no reason at all. I came home one day and said, "Bob, you have no idea how crazy things are in the animation department. It's horrible there. No one has a clue what they're doing."

"If you weren't my wife you wouldn't be able to tell me this," Bob said. "I don't want to hear this information from *you*. I want to hear it from the people who are *supposed* to tell it to me."

"Well, *they* are the problem, so they're not going to tell you. They don't even know anything's wrong. *I'm* telling you this thing is a disaster. You need to get involved. Maybe even shut the whole thing down."

"If you were at Disney," Bob continued, "no matter how famous you and David Foster are, you would still be 'songwriters for hire' and would need to go through the proper chain of command. You would not have access to Michael Eisner."

Unfortunately, this was not the last time we would have versions of this exchange, and both of us invariably ended up annoyed and misunderstood. One night, Bob said, "I am not going to have this conversation anymore." His voice and his face were conveying a certain level of anger I hadn't seen until then. "Consider me *out* of this project. I don't want to hear about it again. *Ever*. You know Terry Semel. Call *him*." And so I did.

I told Terry I had two big issues. One, there was no musical person other than David and me attached to this project, so how did they think it was going to be a musical? We needed to bring another person or two on board who knew about musicals: their structure, their storytelling, choreography, etc. Second, he needed to override Lorenzo, who thought that Céline Dion—the biggest star in this whole film—singing "The Prayer" stopped the story line. As if there were a story line. I didn't like Lorenzo, who, if you remember, killed my script with Alana. Now he was trying to take the best song in the movie *out* of the movie.

"Let me get this straight," Terry said. "You're saying that we don't have a musical person working in production other than you and David."

"Yes," I answered. He agreed to bring in someone from the outside who knew musical theater. "And don't worry," he added, "I'm not going to lose a Céline Dion song from the movie."

Terry brought in Kenny Ortega, the choreographer of, among other films, *Dirty Dancing*, but the movie was already unsalvageable. How could he choreograph what was already animated? It was all too late.

Finally, the premiere was upon us. The Warner Bros. lot was decorated to re-create the look of the movie, and families were invited to view it and celebrate afterward with food, games, and giveaways. But I didn't feel very celebratory.

When we got home, Bob went into his office. I followed and sat down on his big blue sofa looking very unhappy.

"What's wrong?" he asked. "Didn't you have fun?"

"Fun?" I started to cry.

"Why are you crying?"

"It was awful," I said. "I hated the movie. It was everything I was afraid it was going to be. I feel so terrible."

"Carole, you're not responsible for the whole movie," Bob said empathetically. "You're only responsible for your songs, and they came out great. What are you getting all upset about? You need to let it go."

The movie opened to very mixed reviews, grossed under $7 million in its opening weekend, and that was that. It was the beginning and the end of Warner Bros. going into the animated musical business. They realized they had no structure in place to make these types of films.

The irony for me is that out of this rubble came one of my most important copyrights and one of the songs I am proudest of, "The Prayer." The duet with Céline Dion and Andrea Bocelli found its way out of this silly movie to be nominated for the Golden Globe and the Oscar.

This was the song Lorenzo wanted to cut.

Over the end credits, having secured Andrea Bocelli to sing with Céline, we added a bridge that musically opened up the song even further, giving both artists a place to display their phenomenal voices, with all the inherent money notes they were both capable of hitting with ease. And the last verse of the song was sung jointly in Italian by Andrea and English by Céline:

> *We ask that life be kind*
> *And watch us from above*
> *We hope each soul will find*
> *Another soul to love*

It was easy for me to write this lyric. It fit the story perfectly, and it was also about the thing I had prayed to feel during so much of my life. Safe. David Foster and I flew to New York City, where he produced Andrea singing the song.

On meeting Andrea, I was struck by how handsome he was. His wife came with him. She spoke very little English and was extremely beautiful. David, who I mentioned often has no filter, was taken with her beauty. Later in the evening, he took Andrea aside and said, with the help of a translator, "Andrea, you're blind. How did you choose such a fantastic-looking woman as your wife? Is there some sixth sense that blind people have?" Andrea laughed and said, "I asked my brother!"

CÉLINE DION WAS DOING a Christmas special for CBS called *These Are Special Times*. Her guest star on the show was to be Andrea, and they planned to sing "The Prayer." Lightbulb! We should invite the members of the Hollywood foreign press to come and watch the rehearsal. Afterward, they'd enjoy a Q&A with Bocelli.

About thirty members showed up, sitting happily in the theater alone with the crew. Luckily, Céline was not happy with the first take, so she and Andrea sang it three more times before the rehearsal was completed. This meant that the Golden Globe members heard it three more times. A song can grow on you by the second time you hear it, so imagine a good song sung by two of the world's greatest voices *four* times. I couldn't have felt happier.

The members of the Hollywood Foreign Press Association were genuinely excited to meet Andrea, and to their collective delight, Céline joined all of us soon after. I had arranged for each member to take a photograph with Céline and Andrea. When the photographs were returned, both singers signed each one, along with an autographed copy of the sheet music signed by all four of us. I wasn't all that surprised when David and I were nominated for "The Prayer."

On the night of the awards, a few of the Golden Globe members were photographers from different countries, and were working the red carpet. When Bob and I walked in, one of them winked at me and another gave me a "thumbs-up" sign. I saw this, correctly as it turned out, as a good omen.

Having won the Globe for Best Song, the question for me instantly became how to get Andrea to come to the Grammys and sing the song with Céline so that it could be heard again, and thus help it be nominated for an Academy Award. Remember, we're not talking about *Titanic* here. This was a movie seen by maybe four hundred children and their disappointed parents.

Unfortunately, this came at the precise moment that Andrea had convinced himself he was here on earth to sing only opera—"no more pop-era"—so he had no desire whatsoever to come back to America and sing this song again.

Tony Renis, who wrote the Italian translation for "The Prayer," was Andrea's friend. David sent him to Italy to convince Andrea to come and sing at the Grammys, but Andrea was adamant: "No more pop-era."

I stayed up nights trying to figure out what it would take. There had to be something that would get Andrea back to America. Finally, it hit me. I'd offer him half of my share of the publishing, which after deducting David's quarter and Warner's half, amounted to an eighth. Still, as my friend and famed entertainment attorney Alan Grubman always says, "It's not about the money, it's about the money."

Bob, always seeing the bigger picture, pointed out that whatever deal I was going to make to get him to sing at the Grammys had better include singing at the Oscars as well. God, I was glad he was in my life.

Andrea showed up at the Grammys and he and Céline got a three-minute standing ovation. I felt so proud to have helped create a song that lifted people's spirits so dramatically. The Grammy performance led to our being nominated for an Academy Award for a film most of the Academy did not see. We were up against the hit DreamWorks film *The Prince of Egypt* with its theme "When You Believe," sung by Whitney Houston and Mariah Carey shouting over each other.

It's customary for all the nominated songs to be performed live during the Academy Awards ceremony. Ours was the last, and when Céline and Andrea finished, the audience in the enormous Dorothy Chandler Pavilion leapt to its collective feet and gave them a deafening standing ovation, the only one of the night in the Best Song category. I was sitting next to Bob, who you know by now is not a man who tends to assume anything. If he says, "Give me your bag, I'll hold it for you," you can pretty much see yourself polishing your Oscar. And that's exactly what he said to me.

When Jennifer Lopez opened the envelope and read, "The winner is 'When You Believe' from *The Prince of Egypt*," I thought, *Wait. That's wrong.* Tony Renis's reaction was even worse than mine. He actually jumped up and headed toward the stage. He had to be pulled back by David, who was seated behind him.

Bob whispered in my ear, "If they'd heard the song tonight and seen the standing ovation before they voted, you would have won."

If I had a choice today between winning my second Oscar or being the cowriter of "The Prayer," I would choose the latter. While many Oscar winners find their way into oblivion, the ongoing life of this song even surprises me. It has found its way into our musical culture, becoming a classic without having spent any real time on the American charts. "The Prayer" was the Number One single of the entire year in Australia, renewing my fondness for that country.

Today "The Prayer" is sung at both weddings and funerals. It has been recorded by great artists including Josh Groban, Charlotte Church, and Yolanda Adams. It touches the hearts of people looking for safety in an unsafe world. To me, hope is one of the greatest gifts you can give.

BOB DOES NOT ENJOY celebrating his birthday. He does not appreciate parties because he doesn't like a fuss being made over him, and, more importantly, he hates when friends make toasts about the birthday man or woman, which he finds "redundant and embarrassing after one heartfelt toast. People say the same things over and over again." He forbade me to ever make a surprise party for him. It almost derailed his first marriage when Nancy attempted to give him a surprise fortieth.

He truly disliked presents, he opened them each year almost with disdain, wishing no one had brought him anything, with the exception of family photos, which he loves more each year as our family grows. Other than that, there was not much you could give him: unless he needed new Brooks Brothers pajamas, white with blue piping, he wanted for nothing. He was not a shopper, not a consumer, and his presents would often sit piled up in his bathroom, still in their gift boxes.

"Bob," I'd say to him each year, "you really need to learn how to show some appreciation when someone gives you a gift. They went to the trouble of picking it out for you, and you give them nothing back. Learning to appreciate a gift is as important as giving one." He would answer, "But I don't need anything," completely missing my point.

Warner Bros. owned the rights to Superman, and I had the idea to replace the image of Superman with Bob, in his usual business garb but wearing a red cape, several watches, and with a briefcase in hand. This was "Schedule-man." One of the WB employees was kind enough to help me create this image.

And so I threw him a birthday party. Not a surprise party. Just a surprise theme! Guests (only family and a few very close friends) were each given Scheduleman watches, agendas, and whistles. The entire party ran On Schedule. A minute-by-minute agenda, with a drawing of Bob as Scheduleman on the front, was given to each guest. Sample entries:

7:30—ARRIVAL

Please enter home promptly and with a minimum of small talk and please deposit your gift on the gift table. This is not a sightseeing tour, so please stay focused on your objective. Get your gift to the table.

7:40—You should now be in the living room, enjoying approximately 1½ hors d'oeuvres. Reminder: Those of you who require medication for mood regulation, please dose yourself before arrival, as there is no time allotted for mood swings that may slow down or speed up our schedule. *Henry, stop eating the hors d'oeuvres.*

7:50—Enter dining room and take your assigned seat. Please place your stopwatch around your necks so you can pace yourself, as you only have ten minutes to eat your salad, which should be arriving momentarily. After eating and enjoying your salad, please pick up your special pencil and cross it off the list.

8:10—Even though you are still eating, at this point you might want to shoot loving glances and make a few gratuitous statements to the Birthday Boy, to remind us of why this night is so rigid.

8:20—Arrival of surprise guest Elizabeth Taylor, amazingly ON TIME!!!!

8:28—Cake comes out. Sing "Happy Birthday" as quickly as possible. Bob hates it anyway.

8:29—Make a toast. "Yeah, yeah, he's a great guy. Wrap him in cotton."

8:44—Please remove yourselves to the living room where we will open presents and make appropriate "oohs" and "ahhs." If you have written a lengthy sentimental card, can it!

8:50—Prepare to go home. Explain that the babysitter has to leave, you have an early meeting, any bogus excuse will do. Just go.

Upstairs afterward, Bob thanked me for his party, and particularly for keeping it to just under ninety minutes. This gave him time to watch the nightly news and his obligatory late-night shows. (Because of his years at CBS and now at Warner Bros., Bob was able to get the East Coast feeds, so when most people in LA were starting to watch *The Tonight Show*, we had seen it, crossed it off our list, and were ready to fall asleep.) Before he turned the light out, he tore up his card for the day.

Forty-Two

ONE OF THE HIGH points in my songwriting came when I got to write with Carole King, whose music I'd loved since I was a teenager.

Carole hadn't written in years—she'd moved to a ranch in Idaho in the late Seventies and had become very active in the environmental movement. I ran into her at some industry thing and, decades after she'd turned me down the first time, I again suggested that we might collaborate. Maybe it was because she had just started going out with director Phil Robinson (*Field of Dreams*) and might just have been looking for a reason to spend more time in her Malibu home, but she agreed to give it a try.

This was another one of those moments like Dylan for me. Here I was sitting next to Carole King! *She* was at *my* piano. My mind went back to when I first heard *Tapestry* and I realized I was sitting next to a genius.

And we still looked like polar opposites. I took time with my hair; Carole was wash and wear. I fussed over makeup; Carole barely bothered. She lived on a rural ranch in Idaho; I lived in Bel Air. She was the true definition of her famous song "A Natural Woman." She enjoyed communing with nature; I liked to admire it from a distance. Carole never tried to be anyone other than herself; I was trying always to be something more than myself.

She began to play a few chords on the piano and started to hum. I immediately heard words. "I like that," I said. "Keep playing those chords." I offered a few words, and she liked them. It's not important what they were, because the song, "I'd Do It All for You," turned out to be unextraordinary. Still, I fell in love with it because it was the first one Carole and I had written. And to hear her voice, a voice I'd adored so much for so long, singing our song, delighted me.

For me, the blush of infatuation with anyone's music—even Carole's—only lasts so long, and soon my ears begin to hear the difference between melodies that feel like hits and ones that don't. I'm not sure either one of us were in our hit zone at this juncture in our lives, but I was very pleased with the songs we wrote together.

In 1998, Carole and I wrote two film songs. One, written with David Foster, "My One True Friend," was recorded by Bette Midler for the film *One True Thing*:

> *For all the times you closed your eyes*
> *Allowing me to stumble or to be surprised*
> *By life, with all its twists and turns*
> *I made mistakes, you always knew that I would learn*
> *And when I left it's you who stayed*
> *You always knew that I'd come home again*
> *In the end*
> *You are my one true friend*

It was quite beautiful and I loved the way Bette sang it.

The second song, "Anyone at All," was a little more daunting to write. It was for the movie *You've Got Mail*, and Nora Ephron was the director. She was very clear in her music choices, and it took our writing it twice to satisfy her. I'm not sure which version was really better but I did love when Carole King sang it in the film.

> *You could have been anyone at all*
> *A stranger falling out of the blue*
> *I'm so glad it was you.*

We were on a roll. A few days later I said, "I think we should write for *you*, not for other people. I think you should be making another record."

"I had a feeling that's what you'd think I should do, and I'm not ruling it out. But it requires so much of my time. I need to decide if I want to devote myself to making and promoting a record."

"Well, why don't we just write as though you might make a record, and if you don't, we can show the songs to other artists," I offered.

"Okay."

CAROLE AND I AGREED that I'd invite Kenny "Babyface" Edmonds to write a song with us. I had met Kenny at one of Clive Davis's pre-Grammy parties. He was the "Face" half of LaFace Records. (The other half was L. A. Reid, a fine record producer as well.)

LaFace had artists such as Bobby Brown and Toni Braxton (Kenny had written and produced her hit "Breathe Again"), and Kenny had his own hit as an artist with "When Can I See You Again." He also produced my favorite Eric Clapton record, *Change the World*. Along with all of that, he was handsome and sexy in a cute way (thus, "Babyface"). He was smart, well dressed, and had a very smooth positive energy to him. His album was called *For the Cool in You*.

Kenny came over, and the three of us wrote a song called "You Can Do Anything." It was a really likeable song and the demo was great.

Don't you know that you can do anything
You can take anything and make it your own
Don't you know that you can do anything
And you don't have to do it alone

I think it may have been that song that convinced Carole to make her own record. We began spending time in the recording studio with engineer-producer Humberto Gatica at the helm. It didn't take long for Carole to gain

back her confidence as an artist. I set up a meeting for Carole to meet Phil
Quartararo, then president of Warner Bros. Records.

The first thing Phil asked her was what her tour plans were to promote
the record. "Well, Phil, I can't really see myself touring at this time." Within
the first two minutes she'd uttered the worst sentence any record company
president could hear. And she wasn't finished.

"And you should know, Phil, that there are very few television appear-
ances I'll do. Maybe *Good Morning America*—but only with Diane Sawyer—
and I'll do *one* of the late-night shows." I think my mouth might have been
hanging open enough to catch a basketball, and yet I can't say I was shocked.
Carole acted as though *Tapestry* was a year ago and she was still twenty-nine.
Was she actually expecting a record company to spend major money on an
artist who had no interest in promoting her work and who had forty years
behind her instead of ahead?

When I told Bob about how uncompromising Carole was with her
boundaries, he said, "It's Carole King," as in "She's just being who she is."
Which is one of the things I admire about her—her inner sense of knowing
and self-worth. Through the years, "It's Carole King" has become a short-
hand between us that means "Why should anyone surprise you once they
show you who they are?"

Ultimately, Carole decided to make her record independently, so there'd
be no big record company telling her what to do. She went on to release *Love
Makes the World* herself and Starbucks promoted it heavily. You could pick
it up when you paid for your café latte. And as a bonus from our writing together, Bob, Carole, and I have become really good friends.

Forty-Three

MY MOM HAD A terrible flu for well over a week. She kept telling me she was getting better while she was sounding worse. Then came the shocking call. "I haven't told you anything because I didn't want you to worry." She had been in a terrible mood on the two phone calls prior, but I attributed it to how you get when you have the flu and a cough and a fever.

"I didn't want to worry you . . . until I knew."

"Knew what?" I asked, knowing the answer was not going to be a good one.

"Until I got the biopsy back."

"Biopsy? What biopsy?" I felt my heart begin to race.

"I think you should maybe fly in and talk to my oncologist. I have stage-three lung cancer."

"Oh my God. Lung cancer."

"What, you're surprised? I'm not surprised. I've smoked every day of my life since I was twelve."

She certainly had. She hadn't even given it up after her quadruple bypass more than two decades earlier. I remember walking into her hospital room just at the moment she was moving her oxygen mask to the side and offering a nurse five dollars for a cigarette. If the nurse had complied, we could have all just blown up right there.

"What are you going to do?" I asked. "What's the plan?"

"Well, the doctor wants to do lung surgery, but I don't think I'm going to do that. I think it just spreads it. I think I'll do the chemo. We'll make a decision when you come in."

"Oh my God. Does Aunt Lucille know? Or Joan?"

"No, I didn't want people around me getting hysterical. You're my first call."

That was amazing to me, that she could go ten days knowing she might have cancer and share it with no one. The other amazing thing was my reaction once I knew my mother had a life-threatening illness. I flipped from being the daughter who avoided her neediness to the daughter who'd do everything in her power, leaving no stone unturned, to make sure she didn't die.

Bob and I flew to New York. "Look," she said to us as we sat in her bedroom on Central Park South, where she was resting. "What did I expect, smoking like a chimney for sixty-five years? Listen, I have very good doctors, and if I'm meant to get through this, I will, and if I'm not, your mother had a very fine seventy-seven years, thanks to you."

That was the thing about Anita. Part of her could be so angry and so crazy, and the other part could be so realistic and so brave. She was filled with contradictions, and where she was concerned, so was I.

After consulting with the head of oncology at Sloan Kettering and my mother's doctor at New York Hospital, I found them to be in complete agreement that the treatment she would be receiving—a combination of chemo followed by radiation—was the right one.

I wished I could stay in the city indefinitely to be there for my mom, but my son was on the West Coast, and we both knew that I needed to go home. I would monitor her illness by phone.

SIX MONTHS LATER, TO everyone's surprise, my mom was in complete remission and came out for a visit. Still smoking on the sly, and still bigger than life, she arrived talking away as Johnny, our house man, carried her luggage up to her room.

"You see my jacket?" she asked me. She was wearing a green and yellow Looney Tunes WB jacket with Bugs Bunny embossed on the back. "This jacket got me from coach to first class," she said with her schoolgirl giggle. She was so enamored with herself and her ability to manipulate just about anyone.

"When I got to the airport, my little friend Linda who works the counter at American loved my jacket, so I told her my son-in-law would get her one, too, and just like that, your mother was seated in the lap of luxury, on a coach ticket!" She laughed again. "How about those apples! You gotta give me credit."

"I'm so glad you're here, Mom." I went over and hugged her.

"How do I look?" she asked before she could even take in my hug. Her synthetic wig was a tiny bit crooked on her head, and she had tied one of the Hermès scarves I'd given her around her neck.

"You look great, Mom. Really. I'm so happy you're better." Now I gave her a big hug.

"Yes, thank you, my sweet daughter. I must say I liked everything about having cancer except the cancer. Everyone was so wonderful to me, including you and Bob. I got presents and calls from everyone. There was this lovely woman seated next to me in first class, who asked me how long I was staying in LA. And I said, 'I'm staying till the first fight breaks out.'"

Cris, who was back from school and was in his room, which was right across the hall from where Anita always stayed, heard her as she approached.

"Cristopher, Grandma's here," she said loudly, not even knowing if he was home. "Is my grandson even here?"

"I'm here, Grandma," Cris said, not yet coming out of his room.

"Is this any way to greet your grandmother who had cancer? I'm coming in for my kiss." She barged into his room and gave him one of her wet kisses, squeezing his cheek till it hurt. "Look what Grandma brought you." She reached in her bag and took out a Bugs Bunny watch that Bob had given me and I had given to her. "Here, sweetheart."

Cris took the watch, a little underwhelmed. Warner Bros. swag was not exactly hard to come by in the Daly household.

"Thanks, Grandma."

She whispered in his ear, "Now do you have a cigarette for your grand-mother?"

"Grandma, I just turned thirteen. I don't smoke."

"Come on, I'll give you money, go find Grandma a cigarette. Ask one of the guards."

"No, Grandma. You shouldn't smoke, either. You had lung cancer."

"All right," she said, dismissing him. "Maybe Mindy will come visit soon. I'd love to see her. Don't tell Bob I asked you," she said as she went back to her room, continuing to talk, but now to herself.

Five minutes later, she called out, "Cristopher, be a sweetheart and set up Grandma's computer for her."

A few years earlier I'd bought my mother a laptop and spent hours teaching her how to use it. It took her a while, but once she mastered it, she had no patience for any of her contemporaries who hadn't become "computer literate." She saw it as a serious character flaw. Sometimes when I'd walk past her half-closed bedroom door, I could hear her raising her voice on the phone to her sister.

"Lucille, what do you mean, you don't do e-mail? Do me a favor. Don't call me until you can send me an e-mail."

Pause.

"Well, you're an idiot. You could find someone to teach you, that's how. Pay someone! We could be playing gin now on Yahoo."

Pause.

"Lucille, you're wasting my time. Get wired or get lost!" She hung up on her sister—no good-bye—and returned to playing gin with some stranger on Yahoo.

My mother, who once installed closet systems to try to make a living after my father died, wanted her online name to be Closet Queen, but that name was, naturally, taken. She tried many variations and in frustration she settled on Closet Person Stuck, meaning she was stuck for a name and would have to settle for that one. That name got her into many fights with online gamers, most of them asking, "Why don't you come out of the closet and be true to yourself?" To which Anita would shout to the screen, "I'm not *in* a closet, you moron," and then, in anger, disconnect them from the game.

Anita had acquired more enemies on Yahoo than most people ever could. Having a hefty record of unfinished games made her undesirable to play with, kind of like a kid who gets a D in Works and Plays Well with Others. Why would anyone want to start a game with someone who famously quits in the middle? But for Anita, if they played too slowly, she disconnected them. If they tried to engage in unwanted chatter, she would get annoyed and switch to another opponent.

My mother had her routine in LA. She would see one or two members of our family—my father had a sizeable number of relatives living in LA who all got a kick out of their Aunt Anita—and a few times a week someone from our house would take her to and from Neiman Marcus. She would wait to be picked up on the bench outside the store, enjoying whatever small exchanges she would have with the folks of Beverly Hills.

"People are so friendly in your town," Anita said at the dinner table. "One man in front of Neiman's told me what a flair I had for putting myself together." Bob was shaking his head, more with amusement than exasperation.

"And your woman on the second floor"—she tapped me on the arm—"the one who helps you buy all your *expensive* clothes"—if you knew how to listen, you could hear judgment sprinkled with jealousy—"I never shop on that floor. I go to three, where the prices are at least reasonable and you can find some bargains." My mother was looking for bargains at Neiman Marcus. "Anyway, your woman always tells me how *adorable* I am. She *loves* me!"

Bob had to interrupt her monologue. "She doesn't *love* you, Anita, she *likes* you! All of those people you talk about *like* you. They don't *love* you. They don't even know you."

She laughed. "You know, I tell anyone who'll listen that if you and Bob ever break up, I want him to have joint custody of me." Even Bob laughed.

She went on and on and on about nothing of importance and finally landed on her little friend Irene (whom I hardly knew and Bob never heard of) until, bored and exasperated, he interrupted. "You're filling the air, Anita, you're filling the air."

"What does he mean?" she asked me.

"I mean," Bob said, not without affection, "you just seem to need to fill the air. Not even *you* care what you're saying."

She laughed. "What, we should all just sit here without talking? Very nice. We'll have a séance." Anita got up. "I'll be right back. Don't worry, I'm not leaving yet." She walked out of the kitchen door to try and find someone to sneak her a cigarette.

Forty-four

IN FEBRUARY 2000, MICHAEL JACKSON was starting to make a new record. He asked for my thoughts on possible collaborators. The first name that popped in my head was Rodney Jerkins. I told Michael how talented I thought Rodney was and how much I loved "Say My Name," the record he wrote and produced for Destiny's Child, the three-girl group led by Beyoncé Knowles. Michael asked me if I would introduce him to Rodney and if he could meet him at my home.

Easily the hottest producer of the day, Rodney was beside himself with joy. Michael Jackson was his idol. He was "the one," and for Rodney, the greatest opportunity of his life would be making a record with him.

We met in my music room about a month later, after Rodney had time to work on some tracks for the King of Pop, who wanted me in the room with him because he didn't know Rodney and was shy. I introduced them, and Michael asked Rodney to play him some song ideas. Rodney took out a CD and began to play it through my sound system. They were all tracks, ideas for songs not yet complete, still missing vocals and melodies.

I thought they were great. They all sounded like Michael, but Michael in 2000, not 1987.

I knew Michael loved what he was hearing, but now, without Quincy helming the project, Michael was insecure. He had waited too long between records. Instead of saying, "Great. Let's finish these tracks and let's record them," he said to Rodney, "These are good, but now I want you to dig deeper! Go in the studio and try to go even *deeper* and come up with your very, very, *very* best work." I thought that what Rodney had just played him *was* his best work, but Michael always wanted more.

Poor Rodney had no idea what was in store for him. Even I didn't. Month after month making track after track; Michael stopping by the studio, liking one or two tracks but still wanting him to go further. "Dig deeper, Rodney. Give me more," he said in his famously breathy voice.

As much as I was Michael's friend, I started to feel guilty about what I saw happening to Rodney. He was giving all his time, all of his creativity to Michael, who probably left the best tracks months behind him, and Rodney was going to blow his time as the top R&B producer in America. I had seen it happen to other producers with Michael (Teddy Riley, Jimmy Jam, and Terry Lewis).

Michael was exacting and elusive and mysterious in both his work and his life. He never told me *anything* straight out. Who else was working on the record? Who was he getting counsel from? He amassed so many more songs than he needed to complete this record—neither of the two songs I wrote with Rodney made it on—but at least Rodney had written many of the songs when the album finally came out.

One night I got a call from John McClain, Michael's manager at the time, saying they were missing one last key song and they wanted me to write it with Babyface. We only had three days to write and record it.

And we did it. Our "three-day" song, "You Are My Life," joined the same album with songs that had taken more than two years to complete (not to mention all of the unused partly finished tracks and vocals scattered in recording studios across the country). Michael named the record *Invincible*, and to my surprise he and Rodney wrote, on the first page of the booklet, this dedication: *To Carole Bayer Sager: Without you this album could not have been possible. We truly love you from the bottom of our hearts.*

The record went to Number One, but in terms of his career, there was no comparison to the Quincy trilogy.

•   •   •

AFTER YEARS OF FIGHTING an often losing battle with drug addiction, Whitney Houston was supposed to be making her comeback album. It was 2002, and the aftereffects of her cigarette and cocaine use left her voice not quite as brilliant as it once was.

I knew Whitney through her aunt, Dionne Warwick, who had collaborated so closely with Burt. Whitney was still a young girl when I first met her, and she was in awe of her famous aunt. Whitney's mother, Cissy Houston, was one of Dionne's backup singers for many years.

With over 170 million sales of albums, singles, and videos combined, Whitney's success had eclipsed every other female artist ever. But that was all then. The last ten years had been all downhill and her life was chronicled weekly in the tabloids.

With this as background, Kenny Edmonds called me about writing a song for Whitney. What was her voice like now, and what was she like physically? I asked. He said she was clean and really sounding very good.

Two years prior, she'd shown up late and disoriented at the Academy Awards rehearsal. She was to sing "Over the Rainbow" and didn't know the words. Burt, who was the musical director that year, met with Lili and Dick Zanuck, who were producing the show. They told him to fire Whitney. "No one will remember who won Best Picture," they said. "They will only remember that Whitney was a train wreck." They replaced her with Faith Hill with only twenty-four hours before the show went on the air.

That was the last I'd heard about Whitney until Kenny's call.

I loved her voice. To me, she was one of the greatest singers of our time. Like millions of other viewers, I was heartbroken watching her disastrous exchange earlier in the year when Diane Sawyer interviewed an anorexic-looking, clearly stoned-out Whitney who denied using any drugs at the time—yet another tragic moment in a career that was spiraling out of control.

Believing, or wanting to believe, that she was better, Kenny and I began working on a song for Whitney. She was separated from her husband, Bobby Brown, at the time, and her family was helping her stay sober and clean. I thought a lot about what Whitney might want to say if she was writing her own song. I gave Kenny my title, "Try It on My Own." I wanted to write a lyric that would empower her. He liked it. I wrote the following to his melody.

> *And I am not afraid to try it on my own*
> *I don't care if I'm right or wrong*
> *I'll live my life the way I feel*
> *No matter what I'll keep it real, you know*
> *It's time for me to do it on my own*

Kenny produced the record, and Whitney did sound great. I also loved the video, which parodied her being fired from the Oscars, spoofed *American Idol*, and had her pushing Bobby Brown away, and then singing the song her way with a large gospel choir in front of a live audience at the Lyric Theatre, one of the oldest black-owned theaters in Miami. I don't know if the video was Whitney's idea or the director's, but she owned it. The album sold more than three million copies. Good, but as with Michael's *Invincible*, not outstanding, and nowhere near what she did at her height.

The problem was that Whitney had not truly recovered, and every time she sang live, her performances got worse. Her pitch was off. She struggled for notes that were once easy for her. She was still lost in her addiction, and her rail-thin appearance was difficult for audiences, including me, to see. This might have been what prevented the song from being a much bigger hit on the scale of some of her others. But for me, as her fan, the sight of her unraveling was the worst part.

I HAD ALWAYS WANTED to write with Carly Simon and I finally got that opportunity in 2002 when Freddy DeMann (co-owner of Maverick Records with Madonna) asked me if I'd consider writing a song for a Broadway play he was producing called *Take Me Out*. It all took place in a sports locker room, with five teammates exploring the underbelly of baseball as a metaphor for life.

Carly and I had met before in 1978, when she recorded my song with Marvin Hamlisch, "Nobody Does It Better." It was a great success for all of us, but like so many people you have the opportunity to work with, you don't necessarily stay in touch after the project is complete.

Twenty-four years later, before Bob and I went to New York, I called Carly and asked her if she would like to try and write the song for the play with me. She was still living on Martha's Vineyard, and said she'd come into Manhattan and stay overnight in the city.

So here was my Carole King experience happening all over again. I was excited to see what we might come up with. I loved everything Carly—her albums, her songs, and her voice—and in that way that I can do, we bonded instantly. She looked like an exotic bird, tall and graceful with the most charismatic smile and piercing blue eyes that made her instantly beautiful.

Being in a hotel room high above the city, hearing Carly's sultry voice singing in my ear while strumming her guitar was nothing short of heaven. The song we wrote was called "In the Bigger Picture."

> *I've been feeling this weight on my shoulders*
> *Thinking it belonged to me*
> *I've been holding this perfect photograph*
> *Of how I am supposed to be*
> *But what if it is all a lie*
> *What if that's not who I am*
> *Can't I be a million things and still just be a man*

In the middle of our writing session, Carly mentioned she was feeling particularly nervous. Of course if she was feeling nervous, I soon noticed that I, too, was feeling the same. She excused herself and ran across the street to

Zitomer's (a large pharmacy that sells almost anything you can think of), to purchase some calming tea for both of us. When she returned, the water was boiled, and we began downing cup after cup of Koppola Tea, certain we were feeling its benefits within the first fifteen minutes.

"Carole, I think this is really working. Don't you?"

"Yes! It's almost like taking a Valium," I answered. The label promised us "CALM-fidence—to calm mental or emotional anxiety, relieve physical tension and refocus our sluggish energy." So impressed was I with this miracle tea that I ordered boxes and boxes of it online. Within a week the owner himself called me, asking if he could use my name on his website in return for some free tea. Let me say, long after Carly was home at the Vineyard, I had enough Koppola Tea to supply all of LA's health food chains. Sipping it without Carly just wasn't the same, and I quickly returned to my green tea and coffee.

Back at the piano, I loved our lyric but I noticed our melody rambled a little. Carly was a really fine lyricist, so it was challenging to bring something to the lyrics she couldn't do on her own. Like me she had a notebook where she jotted down potential lyrics or ideas when she thought of them. I wasn't completely honest about how I felt about the chorus melody because I wanted to continue writing with her and besides, maybe it really was good; it takes me a while to decide.

Carly was known for not liking to fly, something I easily related to, but after much coaxing, she agreed to fly back to LA with Bob and me and write together for six days. We invited her to stay in our guesthouse and she accepted.

We started writing every day at about eleven. With or without music, Carly was fun to be with. We wrote a song I loved, "Leap of Faith":

> *That would take a leap of faith*
> *Bonds that I would have to break*
> *Chances I've been scared to take all my life*
> *I'd be absolutely safe*
> *With just a simple leap of faith*

No wonder I loved writing with her. We both carried deep scars from our childhoods; you always know when you've found a kindred spirit. I loved the cadence of her voice and the poetic phrases she would use in conversation. No doubt I had a "friend crush" on her.

David Foster joined us one afternoon to write a beautiful song called "Heading Over Heels":

Make it like the first time
As if there was no past
Take me like the first time
But this time make it last
Love me like the first time
Heading over heels

Eventually Freddy decided the play did not need a song in it but I didn't care. I was so happy to have had this time with Carly. She was charming, smart, literate, very seductive, and a little crazy in a poetic way. As Neil Simon wrote in *They're Playing Our Song*, "In this business aren't we all a little rococo?"

Carly seemed freer to me than I was with myself, her flowered long skirts ready at all times to dance in the wind. I enjoyed all of the stories of the dramas in her life, her complicated relationship with her then husband Jim Hart. It seemed that when she was deciding to come out to be with me, he was deciding to come out, period. We could talk for hours in our non-writing time.

We haven't seen each other in over ten years but I think if I were to see her tomorrow, it would feel like no time had passed. It's odd that you can feel so connected to someone for a period of time and then disconnect. I don't know if it's a show business thing, or if it has more to do with creative people having busy lives, living on different coasts and eventually losing track of each other. I do know that when either of us picks up a phone to talk, we're immediately connected without missing a beat.

Forty-five

IN 1998 BEN GANNON, a theater producer from Australia, came to Los Angeles to talk to me about a musical he produced that had opened to raves in Australia called *The Boy from Oz*, based on the life of my dear friend Peter Allen. Peter was a huge cultural hero in Australia, having written its unofficial theme song, "I Still Call Australia Home."

I was so happy to hear that there was a successful musical about Peter and was surprised when Ben told me he wanted to bring the musical to New York and coproduce it with Robert Fox.

"Wow! New York," I said, duly impressed but still dubious about the commercial Broadway prospects of the life of an Australian singer-songwriter who was never *that* famous in America. "What songs are you using?" I asked.

"Well, you've written at least half of them with Peter."

"Oh," I said, suddenly feeling more interested. What I didn't know is that it was going to take another four years before Ben would visit me again to tell me that indeed they were moving forward with *The Boy from Oz* in America. They were going to be workshopping it in New York. I almost died when they told me they'd signed Hugh Jackman to play Peter.

The commercial prospects had just shot from ten to one hundred. Hugh Jackman was a big star.

"I'd like to get your feeling on it," Ben said. "The music. Maybe you could be helpful to Hugh."

"Yes, I'd love to come to the workshop, and I would love to help in any way I can." I was thinking since I wrote so many songs with Peter and knew his style so intimately, I could protect them and make sure they would sound the way Peter would have wanted them to sound.

Bob and I flew to New York for the workshop. One thing I knew immediately. Hugh Jackman was fantastic. We were in a small rehearsal room, and I was dumbfounded at how charismatically he brought Peter back to life. He had watched his videos, listened to his songs, and studied him carefully, and through his gifts as an actor he found all the little poses and nuances that made Peter *Peter*. In bringing him back to life, he became my friend instantly. When I watched Hugh I saw Peter. It's almost like I didn't have to miss him; he was with me again.

Hugh is so easy to like—warm, friendly, open—and so gifted as an actor and singer. He transformed into Peter while I was watching him. After the run-through I was able to share with the keyboard player how, if he wanted the piano to sound more like Peter's, he needed to create a steady 4/4 rhythm in his right hand while his left played chords at the beginning of each measure. I also told him not to rush the tempos, which many pianists, especially when performing in live theater, have a tendency to do.

It was surprising to hear songs that Peter and I had long given up on ever being heard now being used to help illustrate Peter's interesting and complex life story. They were now going to be heard nightly on Broadway, and on a cast album. I couldn't have dreamed this one.

Songs like "Quiet Please, There's a Lady on Stage," which we wrote as a tribute to Judy Garland, and "Continental American," about the nightclub scene in New York in the Seventies, and "She Loves to Hear the Music," which we wrote about a friend of mine who was a music groupie, all found their way to the stage after going unnoticed between the better-known hits on Peter's albums. I ended up having cowritten nine out of the eighteen songs in the show and was given the title of musical consultant as well.

At the first preview of *Oz* on Broadway, Sandy Gallin was on my left and Bob on my right. We were all mesmerized at seeing Hugh play Peter. It was uncanny. I just knew the show was going to be a hit. After the applause died down and before we went backstage, Sandy turned to me and said, "You know, if Peter Allen *looked* like Hugh Jackman . . ." He paused, making me wait for more. "*And* if Peter Allen *sang* like Hugh Jackman . . ." Another pause. "*Peter* would have been a *gigantic* superstar." I wasn't sure I was hearing right. "In other words," I said, "if Peter Allen had been Hugh Jackman, he would have been a bigger star!" I looked at Sandy in disbelief.

"That's all true," I said, "as long as Hugh Jackman *wrote songs* like Peter Allen."

"*You* know what I mean," he said.

Hugh easily won the Tony that year for Best Performance by an Actor in a Musical, and if he had wanted to stay in the show, it could have run forever. In one year, not missing a single performance, Hugh made all of the money back, with even a little profit for the investors. There were fans that called themselves OZalots who'd seen the musical four or five times.

He was so brilliant in the part that when the producers tried to think who could replace him, the answer was absolutely no one. For me as a songwriter, the longer it ran on Broadway, the longer the checks kept coming in, so I had added incentive to find a way to keep the performances going, but in truth, I totally agreed. For any actor to even attempt the part would have been foolhardy. Hugh owned that role. Forever.

I loved Hugh so much for giving me that extra year with Peter. I can almost hear Peter saying, "Who'd ever think the two of us would end up with our lives portrayed on Broadway? In two different musicals. Honey, we lucked out."

Forty-Six

ONE DAY CLINT EASTWOOD called. I'd gone to dinner with him and his then girlfriend Frances Fisher when I was still married to Burt, but I got to know him even better once I was with Bob because Clint had made a fortune for Warner Bros., and Bob was very grateful to him.

"Hey, Carole," he said in his classic, slow-raspy voice. "How are you?"

"I'm doing really good, Clint," I said, thinking he was calling for Bob. "It's so nice to hear from you."

"And how's Bob doing?" he asked, still making small talk.

"Bob's great. Hold on, I'll get him for you."

"No, no, I called to talk to you. I'm doing a movie now, *True Crime*, and I have this little melody that I hear for the theme of the film, and I was wondering if you want to hear it sometime."

That was one of the surprises of Clint. This rugged cowboy possessed a sensitive side that wrote beautifully melodic film themes. He wasn't a trained musician. He played his melodies almost with his right hand alone. But he worked with a very fine orchestrator, Lennie Niehaus, who was able to fill in what Clint heard but could not play himself. "Of course I would," I said. "I love your melodies."

"Great," he said, "then we'll do it." I was at my desk and looked down at my calendar to see what might be a good day. There was a pause. "So, are you busy now?"

"Now? No, I'm not."

"Well, what if I come by in about fifteen minutes or so?"

Of course, that had been his plan all along. Ten minutes later, Clint was standing at our front door, his blue pickup truck parked outside. He and Bob spoke for a few minutes, and then we went downstairs to my music room.

My music room was—and is—a wonderful sanctuary, hidden away in what feels like the woods but is really one side of our driveway. The main room opens into an alcove, where I have a little table for six to have lunch, and a separate smaller alcove, which houses a recording booth.

The walls are lined with gold or platinum records, cassettes, and CDs and various awards, all of it reflecting my many years as a songwriter. Some records are propped against the walls because I ran out of space to hang them. Behind the piano, which centers the main room, is a recording console and multiple speakers and monitors. You could easily make a record here. Clint took it all in, admiringly I think.

"So let me play you this," he said, as he sat down at the black Yamaha grand, his long and lanky legs almost not fitting under the piano, and picked out the melody for me to hear. Even in its raw form it was beautiful. We talked about artists he liked and he told me how much he loved the jazz artist Diana Krall; I too was a fan. He wanted a bittersweet lyric that would be great for Diana to sing and that he felt would work well on the end credits of his movie. He wanted a "torch song." And the wonderful thing about writing with the director is, if he likes it, that's it. Ordinarily, you would have to go to the director for final approval, but here was the director sitting with me.

I suggested to Clint that David Foster might be the perfect person to produce the record. Clint left a tape with me that was made by Lennie and was a professionally arranged version of the melody he had just played me.

We agreed to meet later in the week, when I would play him the lyric. David drove in from Malibu with his then wife, Linda Thompson Foster, and listened to the song. I had more than half of it written. Knowing Linda was a lyricist, I asked her if she wanted to finish it with me because I was feeling a little stuck, and we did it in under an hour. "Why Should I Care" practically wrote itself, as she offered some very nice lines, and it was, I thought, very beautiful.

And will someone else get more of you?
Will she go to sleep more sure of you?
Will she wake up knowing you're still there?
And why should I care?

When Diana Krall put her sumptuous, hickory-smoked voice on it, it became magical. It not only went on the soundtrack of *True Crime*, Diana put it on her album as well.

Eight years later, I would write a second song with Clint, this time for *Grace Is Gone*, a film he was scoring but not directing. It was nominated for a Golden Globe in 2007, marking the ninth time I was nominated by the Hollywood Foreign Press. And it was with Clint, which made it doubly cool for me!

IN 2003, I DECIDED to accept an invitation to perform for a week at Feinstein's, an intimate club at the Regency Hotel in New York. Performing once held a lot of fear for me, and I wanted to try to do it again, but this time, hopefully, with more grace.

Bob and I decided the best time would be in late November. New Yorkers would still be in town, not yet caught up in the pre-Christmas madness. Next was figuring out how I wanted to present myself on stage.

The person I knew who could best help me decide was Marvin Hamlisch. He was so adept at knowing exactly how to show the best of the performer and keep the audience engaged.

I called him.

"Marvin, hi, it's Carole."

"Ah, the Carole of oh so many names, mine not being one of them."

We both laughed. When I told him about the upcoming show at the Regency, he said, "Fantastic," not at all surprised that I'd be performing again after a break of more than twenty years. "Hold on while I get my calendar. When will you be in New York next?" He knew what I wanted before I even asked. "We should talk it through before we start to rehearse."

Start to rehearse? "Marvin," I said, "you are so amazing. I was hoping for a little help, but this is beyond. I'm so grateful." When Marvin was your friend, he was your friend forever. At least that's how he was for me.

"Why wouldn't I help you? Hey, weren't you the one who wrote 'That's What Friends Are For'?"

We picked a day we could meet in New York and brainstorm what I'd do on stage. Then he added, "I'm supposed to come out to LA in late September, so if I stayed a couple of days, I could rehearse with you and your band and help you pull it all together."

We met at Marvin's apartment a few weeks later when I was in New York. The place still looked the same as it did more than twenty years ago, minus me living there. I didn't feel any nostalgia for my old life, but I did feel tremendous warmth for Marvin. It was like old times. He and I together, talking over each other, bursting with ideas.

In Los Angeles, Marvin kept his word, flying in to work with my musicians at a rehearsal hall in the Valley, six hours a day for three days. He spoke with each one of them, explaining what he needed from them, and to keep in mind that I didn't have a big voice and not to overpower me with volume. All of the musicians were deeply respectful of Marvin and wanted to please him. Bob was genuinely impressed with the time and effort Marvin put in. It was nice to see them bond over their shared love of baseball.

The first night in New York was great. Marvin changed his schedule so he could play keyboards on opening night. It was the first time we'd performed together, but looking over at him made me feel instantly safe.

During that week, Hugh Jackman came by and sang with me after *The Boy from Oz* let out, as did Lucie Arnaz, who twenty years before had sung "me" in *They're Playing Our Song*. I felt totally comfortable singing my songs for a roomful of friends and strangers. I felt a lot of love in the room.

Here's the only problem. I was traveling first class with three background singers, a piano player, bass player, and a drummer. They were some of the best session musicians in LA and the same players who traveled with Barbra Streisand when she was on the road Just one thing: they charged me the same amount of money they charged her, but she was playing major venues, and I was playing an intimate club that seated 150 people tops!

You can understand why Bob, after I completed what Feinstein's said was their most successful week, said, "You have finally found the one profession that could bankrupt us if you do this full-time."

For me, the best news was, I finally figured out that the remedy for stage fright is preparation. As a thank-you, I gave Marvin a Cartier watch because I treasured his time and brilliance. He was a gift.

It was worth every moment I put into it, because I got to experience myself as a fully alive, confident woman, able to talk and make jokes with the audience and have a good time. So different from the terrified, insecure performer of many years ago.

Forty-Seven

I HAD MINIMAL CONTINUITY with Michael Jackson. He would be in my life intensely for a time and then disappear. I hadn't seen him since helping him with his 2001 album *Invincible* when the phone rang one day in 2006.

"Carole? It's Barbara."

Barbara Davis—a lovely, gracious, and generous person—has been a friend of mine since 1986, when Burt and I performed in Denver for her and her husband Marvin.

"Do you think you could come for dinner this week?" she asked me in her slightly singsong voice.

"Ummm . . ." I knew Bob wouldn't be big on dinner at the Davises', or dinner at anyone's, for that matter.

"I really hope you'll come because I have Michael Jackson coming, and I want him to be comfortable, and I know how much he likes you. It's just us. Would you ask Bob, please?"

With a little coaxing from me—because I couldn't find one reason not to want to go and spend an intimate evening with Michael—Bob said yes. At this time, the Davises were living at the Knoll, one of Beverly Hills' most palatial estates. Entering the big gated doors to a large round marble entryway (the Rockettes had once danced down this swirling staircase and performed there), my attention was instantly captured by two young children who were driving around their huge foyer in child-sized replicas of a red Mercedes convertible and a yellow Ferrari like they were in the Grand Prix. I saw a blond boy and a dark-haired girl.

Barbara entered. "Hello!" she said. "Oh, I'm glad you're here. Did you see Prince and Paris in their new cars?"

How could we miss them? They almost ran us over, speeding around right in front of us.

"Aren't they cu-u-ute?" she asked. "They call me Grandma." She smiled a big smile. "Michael said they could call me Grandma." With a Mercedes and a Ferrari as an opening gift, who wouldn't want this billionaire lady as their "Grandma"?

Sometimes I would have a moment of disbelief that I was actually leading this life. This was such a moment.

We were ushered inside to their smaller dining room, which was still very large. And there was Aaron Spelling (producer of, among dozens of other shows, *Dynasty*, one of my guilty pleasures) and his wife, Candy (lovely and overjeweled for a family night). And there was Michael.

He looked a little more fragile than when I'd last seen him and a little more surgically enhanced, not that there was much left to enhance. He had come to wearing a little plastic holder, almost invisible, on the tip of his nose that, I'd been told, was holding what little nose he had left onto his face. Can you imagine? Look what this poor man had done to himself.

I knew him when he was Michael, and then I knew him when he was the New and Improved Michael. And then I knew him when he was the Okay, Now I'm Beautiful in a Diana Ross Sort of Way Michael. And then, when he should have stopped right there, he kept going. And going.

"Oh, hi, honey," I said. "Look at you." What could I say after that? *What did you do to yourself now?* No, maybe a little less honest. *You look great!*

Once the table was seated, I had Prince on my right and Michael on my left. Next to him was Paris, and going around the round table, Candy, Marvin, Aaron, Barbara, and Bob. The adults engaged in the usual feigned interest in what everybody had been up to, though, of course, if they cared, they'd have known. Prince and I had our own conversation comparing our favorite foods. I couldn't help thinking how crazy it was to have a six-year-old as my dinner partner. The light was bright, which was fine for the children, less so for the women at the table and Michael.

Aaron was famous among his friends for a distinctly peculiar trait. He hated to eat. This was a man who simply did not like food. Unimaginable, I know. He'd been ill for a while and now had zero appetite. I watched him as he continued to push one lone string bean around and around his plate as I sat salivating at mine.

I looked around the table and noticed that Marvin had fallen asleep. He literally had his head down and was breathing heavily, yet nobody said a word about it. Barbara was slowly eating a baked potato, but she was slumped over so you could have made the incorrect assumption that she, too, was dozing. Bob was giving me looks like, "How could you have done this to me?" When I turned to talk to Michael, I saw that he, too, was sound asleep. My instinct was to laugh hysterically, but I didn't want to wake anyone. Was it in the water?

Eventually, something awakened Michael. He tapped me on my shoulder and said in a whisper, "Come with me. Over here." He pointed to the billowing yellow satin drapery behind him. I got up and walked two feet to Michael which, somehow, made enough difference to him to feel he could speak privately. He whispered in my ear, "Do you think anyone saw that I was sleeping?"

Only if they happened to have their eyes open, I thought. What I said was, because let's face it, he was the King of Pop, and as such, expected to be lied to and shielded from harsh truths, "No, I don't think anybody was looking, honey. Don't worry."

"Good. I'm so tired," he whispered slowly. "I just got back from the Middle East. I am so jet-lagged." According to Kenny Edmonds, Michael had been home for three weeks and was on some heavy narcotics that caused him to slur his words, or worse, as I'd just witnessed, nod off. I worried about him on the ride back home. Bob felt bad for him, too, but there was nothing in the evening that he cared to ever experience again.

Forty-Eight

I WAS NOT EXPECTING *American Idol* to ask me to be a guest judge on their 2007 New York episode, but I said, "Yes, absolutely," because I was a fan. I had my favorites each year and enjoyed the Simon-Paula-Randy panel and the seemingly substance-induced unpredictability of some of their—well, Paula's—behavior.

It was odd sitting on the panel between Simon Cowell and Paula Abdul. I was so used to seeing them from a horizontal position. I certainly found how very popular the show was when over the next week I kept hearing, "Weren't you just on *American Idol?*"

In what might have been a mistake, I had once signed up for Google Alerts, which does just that. It alerts you when something about you appears anywhere on the Internet. I clicked and read on, of all places, a website called Cooking Light the following comments on its community message board:

Guest judge on American Idol?

MaryMorph
01-25-2007, 10:01 AM
I missed the beginning of AI last night—who was that Joan Collins lookalike guest judge? We came up with all of the carols we knew, but couldn't identify her!

01-25-2007, 11:11 AM

Miss_Liss

The consensus in my office is Elizabeth Taylor, but I guess that's another dark-haired woman who obviously has a really close relationship with her plastic surgeon :D

01-25-2007, 12:38 PM

cocoa's mom

Under what rock did they find that throwback from the 80's Carole whatever? She looks like if she gets another facelift it will disappear all together. Why do they have this has-been from yesteryear on? Watching Paula Abdul is bad enough but at least the years have been kind to her.

01-25-2007, 12:49 PM

Gracie

Thank you for asking this. I meant to post this very same question this morning! DH and I were going nuts trying to decide. We both knew it couldn't be Joan Collins but man she was a dead ringer for Joan.

I have no idea who Carol Bager Sayer is.

Loren

And then, this small reward the next morning, when I was considering not getting out of bed:

charley

01-26-2007, 07:08 PM

Back on topic—call me crazy but I think Carol Bayer Sager looked beautiful on American Idol the other night, and I loved her hair style.

EVERYONE WANTS TO LIVE a long life, but no one really wants to get old. That's a bit of a conundrum. There are two choices as you age. Either you can do nothing, look completely natural, let your hair gray and your chins multiply and wear your age, or you can have a facelift and Botox and filler and *look* like you had a facelift, Botox, and filler, but look good to yourself.

I never debated which road I was going to take. I'm opting to look as good as I can for as long as I can, while believing if I jump the shark, someone I trust will tell me. And the fact that I haven't heard that yet from David Geffen or Sandy Gallin—neither one of whom would hesitate for a second to say, "Carole, you've got to stop whatever you're doing and leave yourself alone"—makes me trust I'm still on the safe side of the line.

Jennifer Aniston came up to me at a pre-Oscar party a few years ago and said, "God, you look great. You know my friends and I all want to look like you when we're your age." I can imagine that. A group of forty-something women terrified of being fifty-something sitting around making lists of who over sixty still looks good. I used to do it. I take it as a compliment of course, but always with a tiny bit of surprise that they know I'm old. I thought I hid it so well. A friend recently told me anyone who met me would take me for someone in her fifties, and I thought to myself, *Fifties? I'll take it.*

Recently I watched, as perhaps you did, too, the two-hour *American Idol* finale. I found myself very emotional watching all the former idols and judges reunite for what was for me fifteen years of viewing history. I was completely surprised when Jessica Sanchez, now only twenty years old and long one of my personal faves, came out and performed "The Prayer" (which she had done in the past), but this time she knocked it out of the ballpark. The judges all stood, as did the audience, in the longest standing ovation of the night. It lit up Twitter and I'm hoping this performance reignites her career. Once again, the power of the right song coupled with a great performance equals magic.

THOUGH BOB AND NANCY were on speaking terms, particularly when it concerned their children, a lot of damage had been done during the three and a half years leading to their divorce: dueling lawyers, words spoken that should never have been voiced, hurt feelings, and a fractured family.

But when Nancy was taken ill in 2006, after Bob and I had been married for ten years, her diagnosis of pancreatic cancer was so devastating that it became clear to me almost immediately that we all needed to be a family. Nancy and her husband, Los Angeles mayor Dick Riordan, were legally separated in 2007. It was easy for me to reach out to Nancy and offer her my friendship, which she accepted with gratitude. Her children Linda, Bobby, and Brian were all grateful to have their father back caring for their mother, and it was such a large challenge to get through, we were all better getting through it together.

I have nothing but profound respect for the way Nancy handled her illness, and the way her children all rose to the occasion. Nancy's lung had collapsed but she feared if she went into the hospital in New York, where she had traveled to meet "John of God," a revered Brazilian healer, she would die there. She was very definite that she wanted to drive back to her "home," California. Perhaps very much aware she might not survive the road trip, Bob organized an RV where her nurse and all of her children could be by her side. They were crossing the country in a trailer; they made it only as far as St. Louis when Nancy died on October 4, 2009. I always felt, somehow Nancy arranged that, because there was no one she loved more than her children. In the end, they were all together on their mother's final journey home.

Forty-Nine

THIRD ACTS ARE OFTEN filled with loss, and loss is never funny. It doesn't feel good not to be able to see or call loved ones who've carried your history with them. Third acts shoot bullet holes through the fabric of who we were, making us who we are today.

My mother was thankful for the extra years she had received after her stage-three cancer diagnosis, but it eventually returned and spread to her liver. When her treatment options in New York ran out, Bob suggested we bring her to LA to live with us, and that's when I had an epiphany. I finally realized Mom wanted not just attention, as I'd always thought, but *my* attention. And the more I gave it to her, the less she needed it from everyone else.

In the months that followed, there was no appointment to which I did not drive her—no chemotherapy, no scans, no checkups. I was there for her whatever she required, and that made her happy.

But she was still Anita. Once, halfway through her battle, I was wheeling her through the halls of St. John's Hospital for a blood transfusion when she said, "You know, all the years I sat at the desk at New York Hospital as a volunteer, directing people which way was which, most times sending them in the wrong direction, I would see a lot of people wheeling their mothers or fathers through the hospital. And I would think, *That's never going to be my Carole. She'll send the money, which is very nice, but she's not going to be wheeling me around.* My God, I never thought I would see this."

I was touched, but before I could speak, she added, "Now, before you kill me, would you please get me an attendant to wheel me who knows what he's doing?!"

ALONG WITH THE METASTASIZED lung cancer, she had survived a quadruple bypass and gastric surgery. I made an agreement with myself to love her unconditionally in her final months.

One day her cardiologist came to the house to see her.

"Carole," my mother said, a tiny figure that no longer loomed so large in the queen-size bed in her room, "I am a lucky woman to have such a young, handsome doctor."

"Yes, you are," I said.

"Look how he's here in the evening with me," she continued, "while he should be home with his lovely wife and their three little children."

He smiled. "I wanted to check on you before I went home."

"What a wonderful doctor!" She looked at me and said matter-of-factly, "You should give him Benny."

Benny is my four-pound Yorkshire terrier whom I love as though he were my other child.

"Benny?" I exclaimed, startled. There was an awkward pause.

"Give him Benny," she said again. "They have little children, and they would enjoy playing with him, and he would have a lovely home."

Dr. Natterson seemed embarrassed by her outrageous suggestion. Bob, forever the realist, said, "Anita, are you crazy? We're not giving Benny away, so just stop it. Benny is Carole's dog."

It was classic Anita. She loved making a grand gesture, but her resources were sketchy, and she never did grasp—and never would—the difference between what was hers and what was mine. Benny stayed.

She would buzz me on the intercom. "Do you wanna play gin?"

"Yeah, I'll come in."

"No, no, on the computer. Let's play on the computer."

Sometimes we did this when she was in New York, which at least made sense. But two rooms apart? But we would start playing. My mom was a pretty good gin player, and I guess so was I. We'd be halfway through the game and she'd say, "What do you need?"

"What do you mean?" I'd ask.

"Do you need a jack? I'll give you one."

"Mom, I want to play an honest game. Just keep playing."

"Do you need a king?"

"Mom."

"But I want to give you something. Let me give you something to help you win."

IN THE LAST SEVEN months of her life, I never once heard my mother ask "Why me?" In fact, she used to say "Why not me?" She never felt sorry for herself, and she would tell me over and over how happy she was to be in our home and how wonderful her son-in-law and grandson were to her. It makes me sad to relive this, but it pleases me to know she was mostly happy at the end. She would tell me, "Who needs heaven? It's right here with you." She rarely lost her humor, unless she tapped into her old anger, exaggerated by the steroids she needed for the pain.

She didn't go out much after December, but she still played her gin games. It was when she stopped trying to get up and play online that I knew she was losing her fight to stay alive.

I now see that my mother didn't know how to leave me. On the day before she died, she seemed cheerful. I was lying on her bed while she was eating frozen yogurt, and out of the blue she asked me probably the most amazing question I had ever heard. "Do you want to come with me?"

Come with her? It was shocking, but I knew exactly what she meant. "No, Mom," I said quietly. "I can't. Not now."

"I know you have Bob and Cristopher to care for," she replied, then waited a few beats and said, more to herself than to me, "But how will we ever separate?"

Today, I am so grateful for that time. I learned what my mother wanted. There was hardly a day that I did not tell her I loved her and she didn't tell me the same. It wasn't as if all those years ago didn't happen, but they were part of the past, and our last days together became the memories I now cherish.

She e-mailed this to me from two rooms away, shortly before she died:

I love you for all your depth. It is a deep, deep love I have for you. We are being given this extraordinary extra time. Most can never realize this time together. It is truly a gift from our Higher Power. Save this note and maybe when reading it back, you can feel I am near and saying these things to you. OK?

My mom, Anita Bayer, died on March 3, 2008. She was eighty-six—certainly a more than reasonable number of years for a person to live. But she was my mother, so there is no such thing as enough time.

My mother was a true original. No one who met her ever forgot her, usually because she had said something so outrageous or inappropriate it was seared into their memory for life. She was funny and bright, and she had little patience for people who didn't grasp things quickly, which often resulted in behavior she regretted. And she was a champion, always, for family and friends in need.

If I could send her an e-mail today, it would read:

My heart is opening now. It needed to shut down after you died because I was afraid of being flooded with too many feelings. You occupied so much space inside of me. To me, you were always bigger than life. I still hear your voice—I know what you would say to me and how you would say it. You are still here, yet now the critical voice has softened, and your courage and your big heart and, most of all, your authenticity, have moved to center stage. Thank you for allowing me to love you during those eight months, and thank you for allowing me to discover the lovability beneath your booming voice. You will live forever inside my heart.

fifty

I WAS TIPPED BACK in the chair at my dentist's office, which happened to have a television playing in the room, when they interrupted whatever I was paying no attention to with breaking news: Michael Jackson was dead. It was not shocking, just terribly sad. This tortured genius child-man was gone.

I immediately called Elizabeth, who was inconsolable. She adored Michael. She mothered him and flew across the world when he was in crisis to be by his side. He was the last "man" in her life—the last one who truly loved her, who showered her with the extravagant jewelry she'd come to equate with great love. Theirs was a special relationship. Two of the world's greatest superstars, with lives that were lived on stages or on movie screens since they'd been children. How could either of them find anyone else who could understand their lives?

I've thought a lot about Michael's life, while he was alive and since his death. So many people have asked me how he could be so brilliant and so crazy at the same time. I see it now like this.

Imagine surfing the channels on your television. One channel is so clear, colorful, and vivid you can't take your eyes off of it. This was Michael and his extraordinary talent. No one else performing in his time came close to challenging the totality of him as a singer, songwriter, dancer, and entertainer. No one. There were artists who could challenge maybe one aspect of his talent, maybe even two, but none could challenge them all.

Now switch the station. It's his emotional channel. All you see and hear is static. No brilliant picture, no pristine sound. Occasionally a glimpse of him comes through but never past his adolescence. After that, just static.

Some channels came in and went out. For example, when he bought the Beatles' music publishing catalog, the picture was intensely clear. When he spent so much money that he had to sell half of that catalog to Sony to cover his debts, the picture got very blurry.

He was, to me, a phenomenon. Singular in his stunning talent and stunted beyond measure in the rest of his life. And to the extent that he was capable of love, I believe he loved his children, his mother, and he loved Elizabeth.

ELIZABETH DID NOT GO to Michael's funeral. She didn't want to be part of the spectacle, as she surely would have been, so I didn't go either. I went instead to Elizabeth's bedside and sat with her, holding her hand as she cried through the whole telecast. I can't help but feel that losing Michael accelerated her decline.

Elizabeth and I became friends soon after she'd come out of the Betty Ford Center, and being her friend in sobriety was a privilege and a treat. She was present and alive and fun, and as down to earth as anyone I'd ever known. Years later, when she became so ill with viral pneumonia that they had to perform a tracheotomy (for the second time in her life) and there was a chance she could die, I visited her every day in St. John's Hospital. It was necessary for her to be on many medications during this time, some of them highly addictive.

Surviving that crisis, and all the many others before, including a surgery to remove a benign brain tumor, had taken its toll on Elizabeth's body. Her back was completely shot, and her heart was beginning to fail. She now had nurses around the clock, even on her good days. Often when we would speak or I would visit, I knew she was altered from her medications and that was painful for me to experience.

•   •   •

ON FEBRUARY 9, 2011, Elizabeth was admitted to Cedars-Sinai Medical Center in LA due to heart problems. She had had surgery for a leaky valve, but that did not help to turn around the heart failure that, along with a number of other conditions, all suggested her body was beginning to shut down at seventy-nine. I was told she was very ill, but probably because she had been ill so many other times and had always recovered, I kept hoping against hope she would survive this hospital stay as well.

Bob and I canceled plans to travel to London because I refused to go anywhere with Elizabeth in the hospital. I visited her often. She was on oxygen, and I saw no sign of her getting better. She looked tinier and tinier with each of my visits, but week after week she was still there trying to will herself well.

On one occasion I just held her hand. I told her how I knew she could get better, and she squeezed my hand. She barely talked, and when she did it was in a whisper. She was losing the fight.

On March 22, I went to the hospital in the early evening. Her two daughters, Liza and Maria, were sitting in the room, and I wasn't sure if I was intruding. They signaled for me to come in and sit down. Elizabeth no longer looked like herself. The life force, which was so much a part of her essence, was fading away. I felt overwhelmingly sad and began to cry. After sitting there for a while, I went over to my sweet friend and kissed her on her cheek. I knew I was saying good-bye for the last time.

This woman who loved me unconditionally and took me under her wing, as she did with all those she loved, was so much more to me than what people saw on the big screen. She was nurturing and loving and fierce in her loyalty. When I was devastated over Burt, she comforted me, and when I found Bob, she rejoiced that here was a man who was going to take good care of her little friend.

In the morning, I switched on the news and heard that she had died. To this day when I think of Elizabeth, I can only remember the largeness of her spirit and the generosity of her heart. And, of course, her breathtaking beauty.

What made Elizabeth great? As huge a star as she was, throughout her life people felt her humanity. They felt her passion, whether in her greatest roles on the screen (never better than in *Who's Afraid of Virginia Woolf?*) or in her role in real life as the first star to use her power as a celebrity to shine a light on the horror of AIDS.

THE STRING OF LOSSES started with my mother. Then Elizabeth. And one ordinary day, while I was talking on the phone to my friend Stacey, Bob wasn't even fully through the doorway of my room before the words were out of his mouth. "Carole, Marvin Hamlisch died. I just heard it on the news. Marvin's dead."

I might have told Stacey that I had to go, or I might have just hung up the phone. I don't remember; I was in shock. "What? How?" Bob didn't know. I looked at the date on my computer. August 6, 2012. I started a Google search with shaking fingers. *Hamlisch dead. Collapsed after a brief illness.* Illness? What illness? It was impossible, nobody was more alive than Marvin. Tears were already welling up. There's no way to prepare for news this shockingly sad.

I saw his face in my mind's eye. He was smiling at me from the piano, his easy confidence making me feel safe on the stage at Feinstein's.

I called Alan and Marilyn Bergman, the two great lyricists who wrote "The Way We Were" with him and remained good friends. They'd know what had happened.

"Marilyn, it's Carole."

"Oh, honey," she said, her voice quivering, and then she started to sob. "I'm devastated."

I cried with her.

"Do you know what happened?" I learned that Marvin had undergone a kidney transplant earlier in the year, had been frail, and was looking seriously ill. I couldn't understand why he hadn't called me, but I guessed he didn't want me to see him weakened. Just months before, he'd been named director of the Pasadena Philharmonic Symphony Orchestra, and I'd been looking forward to seeing him in California more.

He was just sixty-eight years old. He was always so animated; my brain was trying to comprehend his absence.

We flew to New York to attend his memorial at the Juilliard School where, at the age of seven, Marvin was the youngest student ever accepted. All nine hundred seats were filled. Barbra Streisand sang "The Way We Were" and Marvin's and my song, "Looking Through the Eyes of Love," and Aretha Franklin sang "Nobody Does It Better," adding, "Marvin, you're the best." Along with my grief came pride when it was announced that of all the songs that Marvin had written during his lifetime, his favorite was ours from *They're Playing Our Song*, "If She Really Knew Me."

The whole memorial was a testament to the magnificence of Marvin and how much he was loved, not just by me, but by so many people. The *New York Times* called him "America's Composer" and I will always miss him.

Fifty-One

PEOPLE SOMETIMES ASK ME, "Are you still writing songs?" My answer is simple. I got spoiled. I wrote lyrics with some of the greatest musicians of my generation. So when my publishers would send me a new composer who had one hit and a fraction of the musicality that I'd become accustomed to, it became increasingly difficult to get excited. And the new artists that I loved—Ed Sheeran, Beyoncé, Lady Gaga, Adele—were either self-contained or had their own cadre of producers and writers. And I was no longer the hot writer in town. If I for a moment believe I can be young while writing, my good friend David Geffen will happily remind me, "Sweetheart, you're old."

There's a time—or, if you're lucky, times—in every successful songwriter's life when you're in the zone. It all goes right. The hits, the opportunities, the requests all line up. I hit that zone twice—in the Seventies and in the Eighties, with some nice momentary highlights after that. But I got tired of writing a new song and not knowing where it was going, or if it was going anywhere, so I took myself out of the game. Or maybe the game just decided to go on without me.

There's a naïveté I once had, where I believed that if a writer or an artist was hot, they would stay that way forever. It's simply not true. I'm sure there's an exception somewhere, but I'm not it. The only time I miss writing songs is when I hear something so great on the radio that it makes me want to write again. But the feeling quickly passes.

•   •   •

ABOUT SIX MONTHS AFTER my mother died, I started to paint. My girl-friend Margie convinced me it would be a great distraction for me in my sadness. She challenged me to paint a self-portrait and, never one to shrink from a challenge, I started taking lessons from a teacher of hers, Manny Constantino. I told him, "I want to paint a self-portrait."

"Okay," he said, "but it's not going to be easy." And so began my crash course in drawing and painting. I saw Manny three times a week and painted seven days a week, and after two months I had my self-portrait. I looked very serious in the painting, but I did it. And during that time that click happened where I was completely in it. And, as I don't know how to do things in half measures, I was completely absorbed in painting. I know myself. I have to do something creative almost every day. That is the key to me being an artist. The medium is almost irrelevant, as long as I can practice it fully.

With that encouraging beginning, I continued to study, painting as I went. I completed a portrait of Michael Chow, the restaurateur, who paid me $15,000 in cash and $10,000 in credit at Mr. Chow's restaurant. (Bob took many a business associate to lunch on my credit.) When I told David Geffen about it, he said, "Sweetheart, it's a hobby. It keeps you busy. You should give the paintings away. Don't charge people for them."

Needless to say, I gifted David the portrait I did of him. I believe it sits in the guesthouse of his palatial estate in Beverly Hills. Since I have rarely known him to have a guest there, I imagine it has been seen only by the staff that keeps the house free of dust. I hope they dust my painting every so often.

I STARTED STUDYING WITH Vietnamese artist Tien Ly. After eight more portraits I found my way to my true obsession: food. They were still portraits, but now they just happened to be of grilled cheese or peanuts or kernels of caramel corn that looked like the universe colliding. I would photograph the foods I wanted to paint and then crop them in a way that unhinged your perception, altering and abstracting them so that they looked realistic from a distance, and less so as you moved closer to the subject.

Once I believed these paintings were good, I immediately wanted them to be shown in a gallery, and my expectations were suddenly higher. I don't know if I've ever done something creative just for myself, something I didn't need others to approve of to give it value. So I ended up with three art shows and good reviews. Gallery owner William Turner wrote of my grilled cheese painting "Torn," "These micro and macro views dislocate us from familiar perspectives allowing apparently representational images to become surprisingly abstract."

It was by no means a cure-all for my food obsessions. If anything, it made it harder to spend the day painting galaxies of candies ("Galaxy") and shredded candy wrappers ("Shredded") and come upstairs to my dinner of flattened chicken, broccolini, and spinach. After four years of painting nothing but, I was done painting food. I've always believed that when there's a void the universe will fill it. So I'm hoping when I go back to my studio, I'll find what it is I want to paint.

ALONG WITH EXPLORING NEW areas of creating, I believe that third acts are about giving back and there are many causes I care deeply about. Putting music and art back in the public schools is why I joined the board of DonorsChoose, an online charity where teachers ask for what their students need and you as a donor become an instant philanthropist at any level of giving you choose, which is the perfect way to use the Internet for good. I also joined the board of the Los Angeles County Museum of Art (LACMA) after Michael Govan shared his vision of the world-class museum it held the promise of being in Los Angeles. I created public service announcements (PSAs) for DonorsChoose and for LACMA. And until we end AIDS, I continue to be an ambassador for the Elizabeth Taylor AIDS Foundation.

•   •   •

SO MANY OF THE fears and anxieties that drove so much of my life are now dormant. I hop on a plane like a cheerful flight attendant. Wherever I am, if one of my crazy "symptoms" pops up, I flick it off. And when a crisis arises in the world, which seems an almost daily occurrence, I no longer expect to be annihilated by it. Which is kind of amusing, because in the past my fears were highly unlikely to be realized, while today, when worrying would be far from unreasonable, I'm at relative peace.

Bob and I have been together since November 1991—at this writing, almost twenty-five years. It's the longest relationship that I've had by far, and I still cannot conceive of how the time went so quickly.

When we met, not one of Bob's children was married. Today, all three are, with seven fantastic children among them. What a transformation for me, coming from a small family. I embrace them all and love being called Grandma Carole.

My son, Cristopher, is now thirty years old. He works for Universal Music and is smart and funny and kind, and I love him dearly. I have not written about his adulthood, or about my three wonderful stepchildren, Linda, Bobby, and Brian, because I want to respect their lives and their journeys. Their stories are for them to tell in their own time. I waited until now to tell mine.

Many years ago Neil Simon told me something that must have resonated with me, because here it is again. He shared the story of the first time he ever went to a group therapy session in the early Seventies.

He found ten people sitting around in a circle, ranging in age from the midthirties to about eighty. The male therapist began with "Okay, who wants to share first?"

No hands went up, and finally the therapist said, "How about you, Sophie?" He was looking at the eighty-year-old woman sitting with her arms crossed, holding her pocketbook on her lap, and seeming a little lost. "Why don't you start?"

Sophie was reluctant, but finally she said, "Vell, it vas Mother's Day last veek and none of my children came to spend the day vith me. I vas all alone vatching television."

"And tell us, Sophie," the therapist asked, "how did that make you feel?"

"Vell, they vere busy, I know my daughter had to go vith her husband's family and my son had to go vith his vife's mother, so I stayed home alone, and—"

"And how does that make you *feel*, Sophie?" the therapist pressed.

"Vell, it makes me feel a little sad, a little disappointed. I vould have liked to maybe have seen Rachel."

"And tell us, Sophie, what do we say when we are disappointed, and maybe a little angry?" Sophie whispered something no one in the group could possibly hear.

"Louder, Sophie, louder! What do we say when we feel a little sad?"

Sophie shrugged her shoulders and said in a voice still too quiet to even be heard, "Fuddoo Izerve."

"I'm sorry," the therapist said, "we still can't hear you. Sophie, what do we say when we're feeling sad?" he asked again, raising his voice.

She whispered, "Fuck you, I deserve."

"Louder, Sophie!"

Now in a voice that could be heard in the next apartment, she shouted, "Fuck you, I deserve!"

I don't know why this story struck me, except that at the time I must have thought I could wind up like Sophie—that age and still in therapy, still complaining about my life.

Thank God that's not the way it turned out.

Much of my aliveness came from meeting Bob. Much came from spending years and years working on myself with different therapists, psychoanalysts, rebirthers, workshops, Kabbalah teachers, self-help groups, psychics, and healers. I got something from each of them that I needed at the time. And much came from just getting older and finding out so many of the things I feared never came to pass. The moments I thought would kill me clearly didn't. I wish I could have lived more bravely. When my fears prevented me from participating, my life continued anyway.

•   •   •

HAVING WRITTEN ENDLESS NUMBERS of songs in my life (at last count over four hundred) some certainly ring truer to me than others. There are songs that I've written that feel like strangers to me. I've completely forgotten about them. I think of a line from a song I wrote with Peter Allen:

All my lines ring but some of them ring truer.

If I never heard some of my songs again, I wouldn't feel deprived. I wrote them, I may have enjoyed the process, but were I to hear them today, I wouldn't feel they were a part of me. And then there are the songs that define me, that remind me why I wrote in the first place. My best songs made people feel connected, better, hopeful. Even a shared sadness can help to heal someone who's feeling completely alone. And that someone was often me.

Just as my very early songs reflected an immaturity that can only be altered by the passing of time, through the years I learned that life never stays the same. For every high there will be a corresponding low. Time heals, and there are no shortcuts to wisdom.

I learned that music is a universal language. When a song reaches its fullest potential it has the power to cross lines and cultures like nothing on the written page can. It's almost unfair that a love song created sometimes in less than a few hours can hit a common chord across the world, while a book or a play can be slaved over for God knows how long and not have a fraction of that impact.

I learned that people want to be in love. They long to be in love, they pretend to be in love, they think they're in love, and sometimes they are.

I've always believed that the best songs come through us, not from us. In cases where I couldn't open my heart in real life, I opened it in song, sometimes giving others what I couldn't give myself. There are songs I've written that are my soul songs. They touch my heart: "Come In From the Rain,"

"Looking Through the Eyes of Love," "If He Really Knew Me," "Someone Else's Eyes," "It's My Turn," "On My Own," "That's What Friends Are For," and of course, "The Prayer."

Are they the best songs I've written? Some are. But they're the ones that ring the truest to me. I see my lyrics today as lifesavers, feelings I was able to release and put to music rather than have them fester somewhere in my psyche and manifest as anxiety. They gave me life, they gave me an identity, and I gave them my tears, my heart, and my truth.

MY FRIEND MINDY ONCE told me, "You are holding rhinestones to your breast and God is waiting to give you diamonds." I didn't know it then, but it turned out to be true.

Bob takes care of the ones he loves, and he loves me, and I take care of him. He has brought family into my life and into Cristopher's, and he has made me feel safe. I live a life of privilege that I never dreamed would be attainable. In my world I have access to almost everything and know so many people I never would have imagined I'd ever meet.

I look back now and see all the times that something outside of myself became the only thing that made me feel alive—when I was so hungry to do more, accomplish more, or when I thought the person I was with made me feel like more. Today there is nothing outside myself I covet. I've come to a point in my life where I've made a delicate peace with myself. That is not to say there might not be border skirmishes, but I've learned that external validation is like cotton candy. As you taste it, it bursts into nothing.

Getting off the hamster wheel, I've found that happiness comes from within, and multiplies when shared with others. A friend asked me, "How do you get to that place sooner?" My answer is, you don't. Life is a process and you go through it, and hopefully, one day, you get that aha! moment. Or you don't.

For so much of my life I only lived on one channel, the creative one, and though I believe this will always be necessary in my life, I know now how much I value connection, compassion, family, deep friendships and love, and how they've gained importance through the passing years and nourish my soul.

Every day I wake up grateful to be alive. Every morning I get down on my knees, though since my knee surgeries I now use a pillow, and say my prayer. It sets an intention for the day; it allows me to express my gratitude for the life I am so privileged to live, and to turn my life over for that day to a power greater than me. I thank God for all my blessings and I ask that I go through the day doing what it is He would have me do.

It was very important to Bob that at some point I put this fact in the book. "Why?" I asked him.

"Because I've seen you do it every morning since I've known you, and sometimes I tell people about it, and they're always surprised."

"Why would you tell people about it?" I asked.

"Because I love that you do it. And it just doesn't sound like something you would do."

"You love that I do it and it took you twenty-five years to tell me?"

"I had to. I want you to put it in the book."

Okay, Bob, this is for you. And now, I guess, it's for anyone who reads this.

Acknowledgments

BOB, YOU ENCOURAGED AND supported me throughout the process of writing this memoir, as you've done throughout our life together. Thank you. I love you so much.

Cristopher, you are your father's and my best collaboration. I love you dearly and always will.

Mom, I still hear your voice, and know exactly what you would say under any circumstances. You gave me life and I'm ever grateful.

Dad, you loved me unconditionally before I could love myself, and I love you for that.

Linda and Mike, Bobby and Krishna, Brian and Cindy, and my beautiful grandchildren, Leo, Julianna, Quinn, Beatrice, Felix, Henry, and Robert, I cherish that you are my family, and love each of you for being exactly who you are.

Joan Berlly, you are my cousin/sister. We share each other's history. I love you.

To my extended family: Michael, Anna, and Ben Berlly, Brendon, Lauren, Jordan and Brady Blincoe, Ceil Berman, Eleanor Carley, Trina Greitzer, Lorraine Sinskey, Bobby Nathan, Susan Nathan, and Cecille Krevoy, thank you.

• • •

THERE ARE PEOPLE THAT you write a few songs with and never see again. And then there are people that you write with who become lifelong friends, whether or not you ever write with them again.

Melissa Manchester, your magnificent voice and melodies made a tremendous impact on my musical life at its formative stage. Our songs connected us with women who felt as if we were writing just for them. Thank you.

Peter Allen, we shared so much of our beginnings together. You became a *great* performer and you were special in your songwriting, your wit, and your originality. You remain completely alive within me today.

Marvin Hamlisch, "America's Composer," my gratitude could fill this whole section. You were the musical genius I not only got to know and love, but to share such a peak of creativity with in the years we were together, and well beyond. Some of my favorite songs are ours, and I miss you with all my heart.

Burt Bacharach, you are so much a part of this book and of my life, and are a true musical legend. (And yes, genius.) We shared some of my highest musical moments together. You remain today a wonderful father and some-one dear to me, and you provided me with some of the best material for this book.

Bruce Roberts, we met in New York in the Seventies. You were young and marvelously musical. Writing together was always fun. I'm so glad we got to share so many wonderful memories from back in the day and laugh with the comfort and knowledge that we will always remain friends.

Bette Midler, I am so awed by your extraordinary talent. Even before we met at the Continental Baths, I was your biggest fan. And now, forty-odd years later, I still am that fan who adores you and feels grateful that you are also my dear friend.

Carole King, you know how inspired I have always been by your ex-traordinary talent. The time we enjoyed writing together, and the friendship that was forged, means the world to both Bob and me.

Carly Simon, writing with you allowed me to hear your ch-so-famous voice right next to my ear, and our half-written songs are waiting right here for you to come back and help finish them.

David Foster, you are one of the few effortlessly musical people I have ever known. You inspire me with your melodies, you make me laugh with your wicked sense of humor, and you humble me with your constant generosity. One word I've never heard from you is "No," and you occupy a very special place in my heart.

Kenny Edmonds, I love you for your voice that sang "Silent Night" and transported me to someplace that felt close to heaven, for your great songwriting and producing skills, and for your keen intelligence and insight into so many things other than music, all of which make you and Nikki so essential in my life.

With all of the above, it's not about the level of success we achieved, it's about the connections made that have woven through the fabric of my life, and have made each of you part of my family.

Sandy Gallin, you are the brother I never had. Talented, funny, and kind, you welcomed me into your world and embraced me with your giant heart, and to this day serve as an example to live every day completely, squeezing out as much pleasure as possible. I will love you forever.

David Geffen, you are my touchstone for reality. Aside from Bob, there is no one whose left-brain opinions and insights I have ever trusted more. So much of the wisdom you've shared with me through the years has become tenets by which I live, and my life would be infinitely diminished without you in it. I love you.

Mindy Seeger, you have seen, helped, and shared my struggle from the earliest incarnation of this book. You embody every aspect of what a great friend should be. And my love and thanks are endless.

Stacey Winkler, Margie Perenchio, Alana Stewart, Lynda Resnick, Ann Moss, Lauren Shuler Donner, Marcia Diamond, and Joanne Segel, you have been the supportive sisters who have held my hand and laughed and cried with me on this journey called life, as were these women who left my world too early and live inside my heart today: Elizabeth Taylor, Evelyn Ostin, Nora Ephron, Marci Lakos, and Madeline Kahn.

Jane and Terry Semel: Terry, you are Bob's best friend and will always be. Nobody ever understood how the two of you *did it* but you did it with ease, mutual respect, and love. And I have additional respect for you, Jane, for taking on challenges that would defeat many others and still finding what's funny inside of them. We are always here for you.

Jerry Perenchio, you are one of the most incredibly caring and ethical people I have ever known, and I love you very much.

Brad and Cassandra Grey, you enrich our lives with your kindness and friendship, and you have honored us more than words can say by making us godparents to your beautiful son Jules.

Michael Govan, your vision and passion inspire me to help do what I can to make Los Angeles a world-class center of art, and in doing so you and Katherine have also become dear friends.

Carole Childs, my high school girlfriend, you were my original fan and supported my songwriting before I'd ever even had a hit.

Barbara Davis, you and your late husband Marvin showed me love and kindness from the day we met long ago in Denver, and I value you in my life.

Henry Winkler, you have always taken up my cause and have never been anything but kind and loving to me, and I will appreciate that always.

Tien Ly, thank you for teaching me so much more about being an artist than I could have ever learned alone, and thank you for being one of the kindest men I've ever known.

Laurie Gonlag, Maybelle and Johnny Yap, Ann McDowell, José Eber, Fran Cooper, Waldo Fernandez, Cary MacMiller, Gary Stiffelman, Katja van Herle, Peter Lau, Piero Morovich, I thank you for taking care of me and making my life infinitely better just by being in it.

And then there are so many other friends, old and new—too many to list in this limited space—who have touched, and continue to touch, my heart. I hope you all know who you are, and if you're not sure, call me.

•   •   •

AMANDA URBAN, YOU MADE me understand that writing is rewriting, and believed I could dig deeper. I'm very lucky to have you in my life.

Courtney Hodell, you helped me, long distance, to really understand the nature of writing a memoir, and taught me a rule I will never forget: Don't Tell Us, Show Us. I thank you for that.

Paul Slansky, you are not only a great editor, you are the man who was able to access in me a part of myself I didn't know how to find, and then helped me to bring it to life, and find *my* voice on the printed page. I am forever grateful. And through it all we enjoyed the by-products of laughter and friendship.

Megan Hogan, Larry Hughes, and Dana Trocker, thank you for making the road from manuscript to finished book easier for me by being so available to answer all of my many questions.

And lastly, to Jonathan Karp, who as a boy saw his first Broadway musical, *They're Playing Our Song*, and, luckily for me, loved it. Thank you for stewarding my memoir so enthusiastically. I feel ever grateful you were at the helm of it all helping me to make it even better. As an added bonus, I loved our entertaining e-mails, and how quickly they flew back and forth. When Binky Urban sent you my book to read, I was blessed.

Appendix

2016

"Stronger Together"

Jessica Sanchez

Carole Bayer Sager/Kenny "Babyface" Edmonds/Bruce Roberts

2008

"So Many People to Love"

Carly Simon

Carole Bayer Sager/Carly Simon/Wade Robson

2007

"Grace is Gone" (MOVIE SONG)

Jamie Cullum

Carole Bayer Sager/Clint Eastwood

"Thankful"

Josh Groban

Carole Bayer Sager/David Foster/Richard Page

2005

"State of My Heart"

LaToya London
Carole Bayer Sager/David Foster/Linda Thompson

2004
"A Mother's Prayer"
Céline Dion
Carole Bayer Sager/David Foster

"The Prayer"
Anthony Callea
Carole Bayer Sager/David Foster

"We've Had Enough"
Michael Jackson
Carole Bayer Sager/Michael Jackson/Rodney Jerkins/Fred Jerkins III/
    LaShawn Daniels

2003
"If You Wanna"
Justin Guarini
Carole Bayer Sager/Justin Guarini/Wade Robson

"When I Need You"
Clay Aiken
Carole Bayer Sager/Albert Hammond

2002
"Try It on My Own"
Whitney Houston
Carole Bayer Sager/Kenny "Babyface" Edmonds/Jason Edmonds/
    Aleese Simmons/Nathan Walton

2001

"I Wasn't Gonna Fall in Love"
Carole King
Carole Bayer Sager/Carole King

"It Could Have Been Anyone"
Carole King
Carole Bayer Sager/Carole King/David Foster

"You Are My Life"
Michael Jackson
Carole Bayer Sager/Michael Jackson/Kenny "Babyface" Edmonds

"You Can Do Anything"
Carole King
Carole Bayer Sager/Carole King/Kenny "Babyface" Edmonds

2000

"Why"
M2M
Carole Bayer Sager/Marion Elise Ravn/Marit Elisabeth Larsen

1999

"On My Father's Wings" (MOVIE SONG)
The Corrs
Carole Bayer Sager/David Foster

"Why Should I Care?" (MOVIE SONG)
Diana Krall
Carole Bayer Sager/Clint Eastwood/Linda Thompson

"The Prayer" (Golden Globe Award for Best Original Song, 1998)
Céline Dion and Andrea Bocelli
Carole Bayer Sager/David Foster

"Without You" (Emmy Nomination for Outstanding Music and Lyrics, 2000)
Liza Minnelli
Carole Bayer Sager/Albert Hammond

1998
"Anyone at All" (Golden Satellite Nomination for Best Original Song in a
    Motion Picture, 1999)
Carole King
Carole Bayer Sager/Carole King

"I Stand Alone" (MOVIE SONG)
Steve Perry
Carole Bayer Sager/David Foster/Steve Perry

"My One True Friend" (MOVIE SONG)
Bette Midler
Carole Bayer Sager/Carole King/David Foster

"She Says That She Needs Me"
Brian Wilson
Carole Bayer Sager/Brian Wilson/Russ Titelman

1997
"Don't Say You Love Me"
The Corrs
Carole Bayer Sager/David Foster/The Corrs

"I Never Loved You Anyway"
The Corrs
Carole Bayer Sager / The Corrs

"If I Didn't Have You" (MOVIE SONG)
Eric Idle and Don Rickles
Carole Bayer Sager / David Foster

"Looking Through Your Eyes" (MOVIE SONG)
LeAnn Rimes
Carole Bayer Sager / David Foster

"One Man"
Sheena Easton
Carole Bayer Sager / Clifton Magness / Sheena Easton

"Still It's You"
Phil Perry and Wendy Moten
Carole Bayer Sager / Michael Gore / James Ingram

1996
"I Do" (MOVIE SONG)
Dave A. Stewart
Carole Bayer Sager / Dave Stewart

"It's Still Okay to Dream"
Babyface
Carole Bayer Sager / Kenny "Babyface" Edmonds

"You Love Who You Love"
Alannah Myles
Carole Bayer Sager/Paddy Moloney

1995
"Forever Yours" (MOVIE SONG)
Wendy Moten
Carole Bayer Sager/Bruce Roberts/James Ingram

"When You Love Someone" (MOVIE SONG)
Anita Baker and James Ingram
Carole Bayer Sager/Marc Shaiman/Anita Baker

1994
"Once Before You Go"
Klymaxx
Carole Bayer Sager/Burt Bacharach/Joyce Irby

1993
"Any Kind of Love"
James Ingram
Carole Bayer Sager/Bruce Roberts/James Ingram

"Colors of Love" (MOVIE SONG)
 Lisa Fischer
Carole Bayer Sager/James Ingram

"The Day I Fall in Love" (Oscar Nomination for Best Original Song, 1994;
     Grammy Nomination for Best Song, 1995)
Dolly Parton and James Ingram
Carole Bayer Sager/Clif Magness/James Ingram

"Look What Love Has Done" (Oscar Nomination for Best Original Song, 1995; Golden Globe Nomination for Best Original Song, 1994)
Patty Smyth
Carole Bayer Sager/James Ingram/Patty Smyth/James Newton Howard

1991
"Everchanging Times"
Aretha Franklin and Michael McDonald
Carole Bayer Sager/Burt Bacharach/Bill Conti

"Hang Your Teardrops Up to Dry"
The Stylistics
Carole Bayer Sager/Burt Bacharach/Gerald Goffin

"Someone Else's Eyes"
Aretha Franklin
Carole Bayer Sager/Burt Bacharach/Bruce Roberts

1989
"Take Good Care of You & Me"
Dionne Warwick and Jeffrey Osborne
Carole Bayer Sager/Burt Bacharach/Gerald Goffin

"Why Can't We Be Together"
June Pointer and Phil Perry
Carole Bayer Sager/Bruce Roberts/Burt Bacharach

1988
"A Groovy Kind of Love" (BMI Top 100 Songs of the Century)
Phil Collins
Carole Bayer Sager/Toni Wine

"Love Light"
Barbra Streisand
Carole Bayer Sager/Burt Bacharach

"One More Time Around"
Barbra Streisand
Carole Bayer Sager/Burt Bacharach/Tom Keane

"You and Me for Always"
Barbra Streisand
Carole Bayer Sager/Burt Bacharach

1987
"Heartbreak of Love"
Dionne Warwick and June Pointer
Carole Bayer Sager/Burt Bacharach/Diane Warren

"In My Reality"
Natalie Cole
Carole Bayer Sager/Burt Bacharach

"Love is Fire (Love is Ice)"
Gladys Knight and The Pips
Carole Bayer Sager/Burt Bacharach

"Love Power"
Dionne Warwick and Jeffrey Osborne
Carole Bayer Sager/Burt Bacharach

"The Minute I Saw You" (MOVIE SONG)
John Parr
Carole Bayer Sager/David Foster/John Parr/Marvin Hamlisch

"Over You"
Ray Parker, Jr. and Natalie Cole
Carole Bayer Sager/Burt Bacharach/Ray Parker, Jr.

"Overnight Success"
Gladys Knight and The Pips
Carole Bayer Sager/Burt Bacharach

"Split Decision"
Natalie Cole
Carole Bayer Sager/Burt Bacharach

1986
"I'll See You on the Radio (Laura)"
Neil Diamond
Carole Bayer Sager/Burt Bacharach/Neil Diamond

"Love Always"
El DeBarge
Carole Bayer Sager/Burt Bacharach/Bruce Roberts

"On My Own"
Patti LaBelle and Michael McDonald
Carole Bayer Sager/Burt Bacharach

"They Don't Make Them Like They Used To" (MOVIE SONG)
Kenny Rogers
Carole Bayer Sager/Burt Bacharach

"Under Your Spell"
Bob Dylan
Carole Bayer Sager/Bob Dylan

1985

"Finder of Lost Loves"
Dionne Warwick and Glenn Jones
Carole Bayer Sager/Burt Bacharach

"Love (It's Just the Way It Goes)" (MOVIE SONG)
John Farnham and Sarah M. Taylor
Carole Bayer Sager/Quincy Jones/Clif Magness/Glen Ballard

"Sleep With Me Tonight"
Patti LaBelle
Carole Bayer Sager/Burt Bacharach/Neil Diamond

"That's What Friends Are For" (Grammy Award for Song of the Year,
    1987)
Elton John, Gladys Knight, Stevie Wonder, and Dionne Warwick
Carole Bayer Sager/Burt Bacharach

1984

"A Chance for Heaven" (1984 OLYMPICS SONG)
Christopher Cross
Carole Bayer Sager/Burt Bacharach/Christopher Cross

"Moonlight Lady"
Julio Iglesias
Carole Bayer Sager/Albert Hammond

"Turn Around"
Neil Diamond
Carole Bayer Sager/Burt Bacharach/Neil Diamond

1983

"Blame It On Me"

Peabo Bryson and Roberta Flack

Carole Bayer Sager/Burt Bacharach

"Maybe" (MOVIE SONG)

Peabo Bryson and Roberta Flack

Carole Bayer Sager/Burt Bacharach/Marvin Hamlisch

1982

"Girls Know How" (MOVIE SONG)

Al Jarreau

Carole Bayer Sager/David Foster/Burt Bacharach

"Heartlight"

Neil Diamond

Carole Bayer Sager/Burt Bacharach/Neil Diamond

"Making Love" (Golden Globe Nomination for Best Original Song, 1982)

Roberta Flack

Carole Bayer Sager/Burt Bacharach/Bruce Roberts

"One Hello" (MOVIE SONG)

Randy Crawford

Carole Bayer Sager/Marvin Hamlisch

1981

"Arthur's Theme (Best That You Can Do)" (Academy Award and Golden
  Globe Award for Best Original Song, 1982)

Christopher Cross

Carole Bayer Sager/Burt Bacharach/Peter Allen/Christopher Cross

"Easy to Love Again"
Carole Bayer Sager
Carole Bayer Sager/Burt Bacharach

"Fool Me Again" (MOVIE SONG)
Nicolette Larson
Carole Bayer Sager/Burt Bacharach

"Just Friends"
Carole Bayer Sager
Carole Bayer Sager/Burt Bacharach

"On The Way to The Sky"
Neil Diamond
Carole Bayer Sager/Neil Diamond

"Roses & Rainbows"
Julie Budd
Carole Bayer Sager/Marvin Hamlisch

"Some Changes are for Good"
Dionne Warwick
Carole Bayer Sager/Michael Masser

"Sometimes Late at Night"
Carole Bayer Sager
Carole Bayer Sager/Burt Bacharach

"Stronger Than Before"
Carole Bayer Sager
Chaka Kahn
Carole Bayer Sager/Burt Bacharach/Bruce Roberts

"Truth and Honesty"
Aretha Franklin
Carole Bayer Sager/Burt Bacharach/Peter Allen

"You Don't Know Me"
Carole Bayer Sager
Carole Bayer Sager/Burt Bacharach

1980

"Blueberry Pie"
Bette Midler
Carole Bayer Sager/Bruce Roberts/Bette Midler

"Don't You Love Me Anymore?"
Ray Charles
Carole Bayer Sager/Bruce Roberts

"Fool That I Am"
Rita Coolidge
Carole Bayer Sager/Bruce Roberts

"It's My Turn" (MOVIE SONG)
Diana Ross
Aretha Franklin
Carole Bayer Sager/Michael Masser

"Fly Away"
Peter Allen
Carole Bayer Sager/David Foster/Peter Allen

"Pass This Time"
Peter Allen
Carole Bayer Sager/David Foster/Peter Allen

"Take It from the Boys"
Cher
Carole Bayer Sager/Bruce Roberts

"Where Did the Time Go?"
The Pointer Sisters
Carole Bayer Sager/Burt Bacharach

1979
"Don't Call It Love" (MOVIE SONG)
Henry Mancini
Carole Bayer Sager/Henry Mancini

"Easy for You" (MOVIE SONG)
Candice Bergen
Carole Bayer Sager/Marvin Hamlisch

"Fallin' "
They're Playing Our Song
Carole Bayer Sager/Marvin Hamlisch

"Fill in the Words"
They're Playing Our Song
Carole Bayer Sager/Marvin Hamlisch

"I Still Believe in Love"
They're Playing Our Song
Carole Bayer Sager/Marvin Hamlisch

"I'm On Your Side" (MOVIE SONG)
Marilyn McCoo
Carole Bayer Sager/Marvin Hamlisch

"If He Really Knew Me"
They're Playing Our Song
Carole Bayer Sager/Marvin Hamlisch

"If You Remember Me" (MOVIE SONG)
Chris Thompson
Carole Bayer Sager/Marvin Hamlisch

"It's The Falling in Love"
Michael Jackson
Carole Bayer Sager
Carole Bayer Sager/David Foster

"Just for Tonight"
They're Playing Our Song
Carole Bayer Sager/Marvin Hamlisch

"Niagara"
Barbra Streisand
Carole Bayer Sager/Marvin Hamlisch/Bruce Roberts

"Right"
They're Playing Our Song
Carole Bayer Sager/Marvin Hamlisch

"Starting Over" (MOVIE SONG)
Candice Bergen
Carole Bayer Sager/Marvin Hamlisch

"That Kind"
Neil Diamond
Carole Bayer Sager/Neil Diamond

"They're Playing Our Song"
They're Playing Our Song
Carole Bayer Sager/Marvin Hamlisch

"Looking Through The Eyes of Love" (Grammy Nomination for Best
    Album of Original Score, 1980; Golden Globe Nomination for Best
    Original Song, 1980; Oscar Nomination for Best Original Song,
    1980)
Melissa Manchester
Carole Bayer Sager/Marvin Hamlisch

"Two Boys"
Peter Allen
Carole Bayer Sager/Marvin Hamlisch/Peter Allen

"You're The Only One"
Dolly Parton
Carole Bayer Sager/Bruce Roberts

"When You're in My Arms"
They're Playing Our Song
Carole Bayer Sager/Marvin Hamlisch

"Why Can't We Fall in Love"
Deniece Williams
Carole Bayer Sager/David Foster/Deniece Williams

"Workin' It Out"
They're Playing Our Song
Carole Bayer Sager/Marvin Hamlisch

1978
"Better Off Alone"
Shirley Bassey
Carole Bayer Sager/Bruce Roberts

"Come Light the Candles"
Sammy Davis, Jr.
Carole Bayer Sager/Marvin Hamlisch

"Don't Cry Out Loud"
Melissa Manchester
Carole Bayer Sager/Peter Allen

"Heartbreaker"
Dolly Parton
Carole Bayer Sager/David Wolfert

"How Do the Fools Survive?"
The Doobie Brothers
Carole Bayer Sager/Michael McDonald

"I Don't Wanna Dance No More"
Carole Bayer Sager
Carole Bayer Sager/David Foster

"I'm Coming Home Again"
Carole Bayer Sager
Carole Bayer Sager/Bruce Roberts

"It's The Falling in Love"
Carole Bayer Sager
Carole Bayer Sager/David Foster

"Nobody Does It Better" (Academy Award and Golden Globe Nomination
   for Best Original Song; ASCAP Award for Most Performed Feature
   Film Standard, 1989)
Carly Simon
Carole Bayer Sager/Marvin Hamlisch

"You and Me (We Wanted It All)"
Frank Sinatra
Carole Bayer Sager/Peter Allen

1977
"Break It to Me Gently"
Aretha Franklin
Carole Bayer Sager/Marvin Hamlisch

"Come in from the Rain"
Carole Bayer Sager
Carole Bayer Sager/Melissa Manchester

"Don't Wish Too Hard"
Carole Bayer Sager
Carole Bayer Sager/Peter Allen

"Home to Myself"
Carole Bayer Sager
Carole Bayer Sager/Melissa Manchester

"I Don't Wanna Go"
Bruce Roberts
Carole Bayer Sager/Bruce Roberts

"I'd Rather Leave While I'm in Love"
Carole Bayer Sager
Carole Bayer Sager/Peter Allen

"Quiet Please, There's a Lady On Stage"
Peter Allen
Carole Bayer Sager/Peter Allen

"Shy as a Violet"
Carole Bayer Sager
Carole Bayer Sager/Peter Allen

"Steal Away Again"
Carole Bayer Sager
Carole Bayer Sager/Bruce Roberts/ Bette Midler

"Sweet Alibis"
Carole Bayer Sager
Carole Bayer Sager/Marvin Hamlisch

"When I Need You"
Leo Sayer
Carole Bayer Sager/Albert Hammond

"You and I"
Albert Hammond
Carole Bayer Sager/Albert Hammond

"You're Moving Out Today"
Carole Bayer Sager
Carole Bayer Sager/Bruce Roberts/Bette Midler

1976
"Can't Go Back Anymore"
Barry Manilow
Carole Bayer Sager/Barry Manilow

"Help Is On the Way"
Melissa Manchester
Carole Bayer Sager/Melissa Manchester

"I Could Have Loved You"
The Moments
Carole Bayer Sager/Bette Midler/Bruce Roberts

"Just You and I"
Melissa Manchester
Carole Bayer Sager/Melissa Manchester

"Planes"
Peter Allen
Carole Bayer Sager/Peter Allen

"She Loves to Hear the Music"
Peter Allen
Carole Bayer Sager/Peter Allen

"With You"
The Moments
Carole Bayer Sager/Kenny Ascher

1975

"Midnight Blue"
Melissa Manchester
Carole Bayer Sager/Melissa Manchester

"Skybird"
Tony Orlando and Dawn
Carole Bayer Sager/Bruce Roberts

"This Lady's Not Home Today"
Melissa Manchester
Carole Bayer Sager/Melissa Manchester

"We've Got Time"
Melissa Manchester
Carole Bayer Sager/Melissa Manchester

1974

"Ah, My Sister"
Helen Reddy
Carole Bayer Sager/Peter Allen

"Continental American"
Peter Allen
Carole Bayer Sager/Peter Allen

"Everything Old Is New Again"
Peter Allen
Carole Bayer Sager/Peter Allen

"More Than I Like You"
Liza Minnelli
Carole Bayer Sager/Peter Allen

"The Natural Thing to Do"
Peter Allen
Carole Bayer Sager/Peter Allen

"Ruby and The Dancer"
Melissa Manchester
Carole Bayer Sager/Melissa Manchester

"Easy"
Melissa Manchester
Carole Bayer Sager/Melissa Manchester

"Home to Myself"
Melissa Manchester
Carole Bayer Sager/Melissa Manchester

1972
"The Same Way I Came In"
Peter Allen
Carole Bayer Sager/Peter Allen

1971
"The Girl I Left Behind Me"
The Monkees
Carole Bayer Sager/Neil Sedaka

"Jennifer"
Bobby Sherman
Carole Bayer Sager/Peter Allen

1968
"Cellophane Disguise"
Steve Lawrence
Carole Bayer Sager/Neil Sedaka

"Make the Music Play"
Frankie Valli
Carole Bayer Sager/Neil Sedaka

"Nobody's Home to Go Home To"
Jackie DeShannon
Carole Bayer Sager/Toni Wine

"Teach Me How"
Eydie Gorme
Carole Bayer Sager/Neil Sedaka

"We Were Made for Each Other"
The Monkees
Carole Bayer Sager/George Fischoff

1967
"Cold Girl"
Bobby Sherman
Carole Bayer Sager/Neil Sedaka

"Don't Look Over Your Shoulder"
Nancy Wilson
Carole Bayer Sager/Neil Sedaka

"Off and Running" (MOVIE SONG)
The Mindbenders
Carole Bayer Sager/Toni Wine

"When Love Comes Knockin' (At Your Door)"
The Monkees
Carole Bayer Sager/Neil Sedaka

1966
"A Groovy Kind of Love"
The Mindbenders
Carole Bayer Sager/Toni Wine

"Ashes to Ashes"
The Mindbenders
Carole Bayer Sager/Toni Wine

About the Author

CAROLE BAYER SAGER has written more than four hundred songs. Nominated for over fifteen awards, she has won an Oscar, two Golden Globes, and a Grammy for Song of the Year. She recorded three solo albums and with Marvin Hamlisch wrote the hit Broadway musical _They're Playing Our Song_. With Peter Allen she cowrote half of the songs featured in the Broadway musical _The Boy from Oz_, which starred Hugh Jackman and told the story of Peter's life. She is a member of the Songwriters Hall of Fame and was awarded a star on the Hollywood Walk of Fame. She lives in Los Angeles with her husband, Robert Daly, and the two share their bed with three unruly dogs who are unimpressed with their accomplishments.